ISABEL ALLENDE

Isabel Allende. Photo by William Gordon.

ISABEL ALLENDE

A Critical Companion

Karen Castellucci Cox

CRITICAL COMPANIONS TO POPULAR CONTEMPORARY
WRITERS
Kathleen Gregory Klein, Series Editor

GREENWOOD PRESS
Westport, Connecticut • London

For Jeffery

Library of Congress Cataloging-in-Publication Data

Cox, Karen Castellucci.
    Isabel Allende : a critical companion / Karen Castellucci Cox.
        p.   cm.—(Critical companions to popular contemporary writers, ISSN 1082–4979)
    Includes bibliographical references and index.
    ISBN 0–313–31695–3 (alk. paper)
        1. Allende, Isabel—Criticism and interpretation.   I. Title.   II. Series.
    PQ8098.1.L54Z66   2003
    863'.64—dc21   2002192778

British Library Cataloguing in Publication Data is available.

Library of Congress Catalog Card Number: 2002192778
ISBN: 0–313–31695–3
ISSN: 1082–4979

First published in 2003

Greenwood Press, 88 Post Road West, Westport, CT 06881
An imprint of Greenwood Publishing Group, Inc.
www.greenwood.com

Printed in the United States of America

The paper used in this book complies with the
Permanent Paper Standard issued by the National
Information Standards Organization (Z39.48–1984).

10 9 8 7 6 5 4 3 2 1

Contents

Series Foreword

The authors who appear in the series Critical Companions to Popular Contemporary Writers are all best-selling writers. They do not simply have one successful novel, but a string of them. Fans, critics, and specialist readers eagerly anticipate their next book. For some, high cash advances and breakthrough sales figures are automatic; movie deals often follow. Some writers become household names, recognized by almost everyone.

But, their novels are read one by one. Each reader chooses to start and, more importantly, to finish a book because of what she or he finds there. The real test of a novel is in the satisfaction its readers experience. This series acknowledges the extraordinary involvement of readers and writers in creating a best-seller.

The authors included in this series were chosen by an Advisory Board composed of high school English teachers and high school and public librarians. They ranked a list of best-selling writers according to their popularity among different groups of readers. For the first series, writers in the top-ranked group who had received no book-length, academic, literary analysis (or none in at least the past ten years) were chosen. Because of this selection method, Critical Companions to Popular Contemporary Writers meets a need that is being addressed nowhere else. The success of these volumes as reported by reviewers, librarians, and teachers led to an expansion of the series mandate to include some writers with wide critical attention—Toni Morrison, John Irving, and Maya Angelou, for example—to extend the usefulness of the series.

The volumes in the series are written by scholars with particular expertise in analyzing popular fiction. These specialists add an academic focus to the popular success that these writers already enjoy.

The series is designed to appeal to a wide range of readers. The general reading public will find explanations for the appeal of these well-known writers. Fans will find biographical and fictional questions answered. Students will find literary analysis, discussions of fictional genres, carefully organized introductions to new ways of reading the novels, and bibliographies for additional research. Whether browsing through the book for pleasure or using it for an assignment, readers will find that the most recent novels of the authors are included.

Each volume begins with a biographical chapter drawing on published information, autobiographies or memoirs, prior interviews, and, in some cases, interviews given especially for this series. A chapter on literary history and genres describes how the author's work fits into a larger literary context. The following chapters analyze the writer's most important, most popular, and most recent novels in detail. Each chapter focuses on one or more novels. This approach, suggested by the Advisory Board as the most useful to student research, allows for an in-depth analysis of the writer's fiction. Close and careful readings with numerous examples show readers exactly how the novels work. These chapters are organized around three central elements: plot development (how the story line moves forward), character development (what the reader knows of the important figures), and theme (the significant ideas of the novel). Chapters may also include sections on generic conventions (how the novel is similar or different from others in its same category of science fiction, fantasy, thriller, etc.), narrative point of view (who tells the story and how), symbols and literary language, and historical or social context. Each chapter ends with an "alternative reading" of the novel. The volume concludes with a primary and secondary bibliography, including reviews.

The alternative readings are a unique feature of this series. By demonstrating a particular way of reading each novel, they provide a clear example of how a specific perspective can reveal important aspects of the book. In the alternative reading sections, one contemporary literary theory—way of reading, such as feminist criticism, Marxism, new historicism, deconstruction, or Jungian psychological critique—is defined in brief, easily comprehensible language. That definition is then applied to the novel to highlight specific features that might go unnoticed or be understood differently in a more general reading. Each volume defines two or three specific theories, making them part of the reader's understanding of how diverse meanings may be constructed from a single novel.

Taken collectively, the volumes in the Critical Companions to Popular Contemporary Writers series provide a wide-ranging investigation of the complexities of current best-selling fiction. By treating these novels seriously as both literary works and publishing successes, the series demonstrates the potential of popular literature in contemporary culture.

Kathleen Gregory Klein
Southern Connecticut State University

Abbreviations

H	*The House of the Spirits*
LS	*Of Love and Shadows*
EL	*Eva Luna*
P	*Paula*
DF	*Daughter of Fortune*
PS	*Portrait in Sepia*

1

The Life of Isabel Allende

Isabel Allende's journey from wife, mother, and journalist in Chile to internationally acclaimed author/expatriate, first in Venezuela and then in California, is by no means a conventional one. In fact, her life story reads more like a plot line from one of her novels than the typical trajectory of most writers, and Allende has certainly thrived by mining her life and the lives of her eccentric relations for such exotic stories. Her survival of "one coup, a military regime, three revolutions, and the death of a child" has proved not a hindrance but instead "[has] contributed positively to [her] creative capacity" (Rodden 437). Originally interested in television and theater, Allende was forty years old when her first novel, *The House of the Spirits,* was published in 1982. Since that time, the prolific writer has authored five subsequent novels, a collection of short stories, and a memoir, as well as several other works for adults and children. Although her fame has come relatively late according to literary-world standards, in the last two decades Allende has produced a legacy of wonderful books that are sure to endure and delight for years to come.

Isabel Allende was born on August 2, 1942, in Lima, Peru, where her father, Tomás Allende, had a diplomatic post. Francisca (Panchita) Llona Barros, Allende's mother, had married Tomás against her parents' advice and the union proved disastrous. Allende knows few details about her parents' marriage and its dissolution four years and three children later.

She calls her father a "great lacuna in [her] life" (*P* 15) and understands only what little she has pieced together over the years. Her father apparently enjoyed the finer luxuries of life and began to live far beyond his means in Lima. When scandal and debt threatened his reputation, he simply disappeared. Ramón Huidobro, a consul sent by the Chilean embassy to arrange for Panchita and her children's safe return to Chile, immediately fell in love with the young, vulnerable woman. Married himself with four children, Ramón nevertheless made a promise to Panchita that he would look after her "forever" (*P* 19) and began arrangements to separate from his wife. Meanwhile, the three-year-old Allende returned with her mother and two younger brothers to her grandparents' home in Santiago where she spent the better part of her childhood. After her parents' separation, Allende had limited contact with her paternal relatives, except for future Chilean President Salvador Allende, her father's cousin and her godfather. Allende had a special relationship with Salvador Allende. Not only was he her godfather, but he also acted as Allende's witness and representative of her father's family at her wedding in 1962. Though Salvador Allende was actually Tomás Allende's first cousin, and thus Isabel Allende's second cousin, she has always thought of him and referred to him as "uncle" in her private life and public interviews (Rodden 29, n.15).

Allende's girlhood in her grandparents' large home has been fictionalized in *The House of the Spirits*. The two main characters in the novel, Clara the Clairvoyant and her volatile husband Esteban, grew out of Allende's memories of her maternal grandmother and grandfather. Like the fictional Clara, Allende's Memé was a charming, eccentric woman who dabbled in the supernatural arts and loomed large in Allende's life even though she died while her granddaughter was still a small child. Allende's Tata was a practical man who withdrew from his family after his wife's death and whose austerity and thrift made the big house a somber place. Although as a little girl Allende felt somewhat intimidated by the imposing patriarch, as a young woman she developed a special relationship with her grandfather that helped motivate her to become a novelist. For six years, Allende lived in the family home surrounded by books that enthralled her and bachelor uncles who tormented her. Meanwhile, her mother struggled to survive the cash-strapped existence and ruthless gossip that accompanied single motherhood in mid-century middle-class Chilean society.

Allende's unique relationship with her mother has played an immeasurable role in her development as a writer. Allende explains that during her mother's first pregnancy, the lonely and disappointed newlywed spoke to the daughter in her womb and "established a dialogue that continues to the present day" (P 12). When Allende's parents annulled their marriage (divorce was not allowed in Chile), her mother became a single woman with a job as a bank clerk. Panchita never earned enough money to live independently from her father and even shared a bedroom with her three children. Nevertheless, she spent evenings telling the children fantastic tales and real-life stories about their colorful ancestors. Allende explains that during those long evenings listening to her mother weave an imaginary world, "my passion for stories was born, and I call upon those memories when I sit down to write" (P 33). Allende's mother continues to play a special role in the author's work to the present day. She is the first reader and only editor Allende uses for each of her manuscripts. The novelist describes her mother as both her harshest critic and her best friend.

Two years after the family's return to Santiago, Allende's mother joined Ramón for a secret tryst, after which he abandoned his post in Bolivia to come live with the family amid an uproar from relatives on both sides. Living with a new stepfather was not an easy adjustment, and Allende admits that it took her many rebellious years to accept her steadfast "Tío Ramón" for the man he is. Though she calls him "uncle," Allende recognizes Tío Ramón as the only father she has ever known (P 49). In 1953, Allende's mother legally married Tío Ramón and the family moved with him back to Bolivia where he had been reassigned. Two years later, the family moved to Lebanon where Allende attended an English school for girls and lived a cloistered existence, passing back and forth between her subdued classes and her family's small apartment. During that period, she also first read *A Thousand and One Nights* found under lock and key in her stepfather's wardrobe. The forbidden book of exotic tales opened up a new world in Allende's imagination, one whose fantastic characters and wild adventures called up exciting visions for the young girl just venturing into womanhood.

When the Suez Canal crisis caused political conflict in Beirut in July 1958, Allende and her brothers were sent back to Santiago where they lived in their grandfather's home and completed their schooling. Because Allende's grandfather did not believe girls needed a college education and she herself assumed she would be marrying soon, Allende took a secretarial post with the Food and Agricultural Organization (FAO) of the United Nations immediately after high school when she was just seventeen. A young engineer at the university, Miguel Frías (whom she calls Michael), began courting her, and they were married in 1962. During this time, Allende continued her secretarial work and translated romance novels to earn extra money. She also was offered a television opportunity narrating a brief program sponsored by the FAO and became a well-known face in Santiago. After the birth of her daughter Paula in 1963, Allende and Michael were awarded fellowships to study in Belgium where they had the opportunity to tour Europe.

In 1966, the family returned to Chile where Allende's second child Nicolás was born. At the same time, she began to write a humorous column for the Chilean feminist magazine *Paula*. She also returned to writing for television, contributed to a children's magazine, and began to author plays. For several years, Allende kept busy raising her family and working in the media. Then, in 1970, Salvador Allende was elected president after three unsuccessful campaigns. With the first Marxist leader in Chile came a period of political unrest, food shortages, and general unease. Allende continued with her journalism, including a special invitation in 1972 to visit Pablo Neruda. During that momentous luncheon, Neruda questioned Allende's aptitude for journalism, admonishing her for positioning herself at the center of her writing, for not maintaining objectivity, and for inventing news when it was convenient. He suggested that she begin writing novels, commenting that "[i]n literature, those defects are virtues" (*P* 182). Unbeknownst to Allende, she would follow his advice only a few years later.

On September 11, 1973, a military coup led by General Augusto Pinochet Ugarte overthrew the government, leaving President Allende dead and beginning a reign of terror that would last for nearly two decades. Allende continued writing for *Paula* and followed the strict censorship of the regime, but eventually the women's magazine was shut down as "feminism was [considered] as subversive as Marxism" (*P* 201). Within two days of the military coup, Allende began to participate in the underground network that funneled money and food to the poor and helped hide subversives and political refugees as they fled the country. Gradually, she became overcome by fear that she might be found out and that her husband and children might be harmed because of her clandestine activities. In 1974, the former chief of the Chilean armed forces was assassinated in Argentina where he had fled, and Allende's parents went into hiding. They eventually sought asylum in Venezuela, a prosperous democracy that was still offering visas to Chileans. The following year Allende began to receive death threats, so she and Michael took the children and followed her parents to Caracas to live in exile.

Allende lived for the next thirteen years in Venezuela. She learned to admire the nation's "[l]ove of revelry, the sense of living in the present, and the optimistic vision of the Venezuelans" (*P* 239). Nevertheless, the adjustment was difficult for the whole family, and Allende's marriage gradually deteriorated under the strain. In 1978, she briefly separated from Michael to follow a lover to Spain. In less than three months, a depressed and disillusioned Allende returned to her husband and children. In addition to her marital problems, Allende also suffered from an inability to find work in journalism, the field that she loved. Allende spent those years working at a school and feeling paralyzed by the ambiguity of her life as an expatriate.

At the beginning of 1981, Allende was still feeling restless for a different kind of life. On January 8, she received the phone call that changed her destiny. A relative called to tell the family that Allende's grandfather was dying. Allende began writing a long letter in order to convince her Tata that "he could go in peace because [she] would never forget him and planned to bequeath his memory to [her] children" (*P* 275). The letter started with an anecdote Allende recalled about her grandfather's first fiancé, her beautiful Aunt Rosa, who died before he could marry her. Caught up in the marvelous characters of her family, Allende continued writing the stories she had heard all her life, adding new characters and fictionalized plot events as she went. Working primarily at night after her full-time school job ended each day, Allende did not stop typing until a year had passed and she had 500 pages—no longer a letter but a novel that marked the end of a "long period of paralysis and muteness" (*P* 277). Allende gave the stack of stained, corrected pages to her mother to read. It was Allende's mother who urged her to publish the book, sending inquiries to many publishing houses with no response until finally a contact in Spain saw the merit in the novice book. It was literary agent Carmen Balcells of Barcelona who read the manuscript and recognized Allende's potential. Published in Spain in 1982, *The House of the Spirits* became a worldwide phenomenon and established Isabel Allende's name in the literary world. Though banned in Chile, the book was photocopied and surreptitiously distributed there to readers deeply moved by the beautiful and revealing portrayal of their homeland.

On January 8, 1983, Allende began her second book, *Of Love and Shadows,* and established a permanent tradition of beginning each new novel on that providential date. For a time after her initial success, Allende continued her steady work at the school in Caracas, spending all her free hours writing. After the positive reception of the second novel, however,

Allende began to receive enough professional recognition from the literary circles in Venezuela and sufficient encouragement from her agent to decide to take up writing full time. By the time *Eva Luna* was published in 1987, Allende had left her school employment, bought a home in Venezuela, and begun her literary career in earnest. At this same time, Allende concluded that her marriage had moved to an irreparable stage, and she and Michael decided to end their twenty-five-year union amicably. Shortly after, Allende embarked on a two-month book tour that ended in San Francisco, where she was introduced to the lawyer Willie Gordon. He had read *Of Love and Shadows* and felt drawn to its author. Likewise, Allende felt attracted to both the man and the coastal terrain that reminded her of Chile. The day she returned to Caracas, Allende penned a contract to Willie describing what she expected in a relationship. He good-humoredly signed the document, she got on a plane, and they married on July 17, 1988.

In the beginning of Allende's new life in California, she had little time for writing. Willie was living in a chaotic household with itinerant guests, a drugged-out older son, a stepson from a previous marriage, and a hyperactive ten-year-old son for whom he had sole custody. He also had a heroin-addicted daughter who lived on the streets and only surfaced occasionally in hospitals or jails. In an attempt to create order, Allende spent much of her energy cleaning the house and providing some sort of structure for the boys' lives. From this tumultuous period came *The Stories of Eva Luna* (1989), a collection of short fiction that allowed its author to write in brief spurts of salvaged time rather than in the drawn out and disciplined hours required for a novel. Soon after its publication, Allende turned to the project that had first attracted her to her new husband; as luck would have it, his "life was a novel" (*P* 299). So Allende set about embellishing the story that would become her next full-length fiction—*The Infinite Plan,* a book set in California and focused on the coming-of-age of a native lawyer. It was while on a 1991 book tour in Spain to promote that novel that Allende's life took another unforeseen turn.

On December 6, 1991, Allende was in Madrid at a book party celebrating publication of *The Infinite Plan* when she received word that her daughter had been hospitalized in very serious condition. Paula suffered from a rare metabolic disorder called porphyria, an inherited condition she shared with her father and brother. Allende rushed to her daughter's side and arrived in time to hear Paula's last coherent words, in answer to her mother: "I love you, too, Mama" (*P* 20). On December 8, Paula fell into a coma from which she never awoke. For months, Allende lived in a tiny apartment in Madrid and visited her daughter daily, accompanied by her faithful mother. When it became clear that Paula would not recover, Allende arranged to have her daughter flown to San Rafael where she spent the remainder of her brief life in Allende's home. Paula died on December 8, 1992, exactly one year after she fell into a coma. Losing her daughter at the prime of the young woman's life left Allende devastated and suffering from depression and grief. She describes her feelings after scattering her daughter's ashes: "Then I realized that I had something inside me that was like a cavern, something empty and cold and dark that I couldn't live with" (*Giving Birth, Finding Form*). Although Allende sought therapy for the pain and loss, she wondered if she would ever write again. Months before, while visiting Paula in the hospital, her agent Carmen had urged her to begin writing down her feelings and experiences. Allende had amassed many pages from those days of waiting. Thus, even though she felt she might never write literature again, Allende sat down on January 8, 1992 to pen *Paula*, a memoir of her own life and Paula's life, written to her daughter so that "when you wake up you will not feel so lost" (*P* 3). Louise De Salvo, in *Writing as a Way of Healing: How Telling Our Stories Transforms Our Lives*, describes Allende as a practitioner of therapeutic writing in that her decision to recreate her life and her daughter's was the very invention that healed her. Immediately after its publication in 1994, *Paula* landed on bestseller lists in Europe and the United States. To this day, it remains the most popular of Allende's books worldwide.

Writing *Paula* gave Allende an outlet for her grief, but she still had not recovered her joy for writing and life. For a time, Allende was occupied with book-related projects, including theater and screen adaptations of her novels. On October 22, 1993, the film version of *The House of the Spirits* premiered with Meryl Streep and Jeremy Irons in the starring roles. In 1995, the British Broadcasting Corporation (BBC) produced the exceptional documentary called *Listen Paula* based on Allende's book and life. The screen version of Allende's second novel, *Of Love and Shadows*, appeared the following year with Antonio Banderas as the leading man. Despite all the excitement surrounding her literary accomplishments, Allende found herself "blocked and depressed" and began to wonder if she would ever write fiction again (Butler 4–6). Empty of characters and still raw with emotion, Allende turned to a new project, a nonfiction collection of recipes and anecdotes linking sex and food. Entitled *Aphrodite: A Memoir of the Senses*, this unusual "cookbook" helped

Allende "rediscover a capacity to live in the present" (Rodden 25). Even her mother got involved in the book's production, providing some Chilean recipes purported to have aphrodisiac qualities. Allende has commented with some amusement on the seriousness with which readers have believed in the powers of her recipes, confessing during a lecture in San Francisco that many were made up on the spot (City Arts and Lectures, Herbst Theatre, November 28, 2001).

After three years of grief, Allende finally found herself laughing again (Rodden 25). Through the pleasure of creating *Aphrodite,* Allende felt her muse had returned along with her invaluable sense of humor, and she turned again to writing literature. The close of this sad period was marked with an exciting event when Allende was awarded the 1998 Dorothy and Lillian Gish Prize for excellence in the arts, one of many prestigious honors she has received in her twenty-year career.

When at last the voices of her fictional characters began to speak to Allende again, the author found herself immersed in an all-encompassing project that took her only seven months to complete. The resulting novel, *Daughter of Fortune,* was published in Spanish in 1999 and then appeared in translation for American readers later that year. While the novel represents something of a return to earlier material, it also marks a departure from previous works. The story begins in Chile, like Allende's first two books, and then moves to California at the height of the Gold Rush in 1849. Similar to her preparation for *The Infinite Plan,* Allende spent much time doing research and accumulating historical material to help familiarize herself with life in mid-nineteenth-century California in order to contribute authenticity to the narrative. She ended up creating an extremely successful story that would spend eleven weeks on the *New York Times* bestseller list. When the novel was selected for Oprah's Book Club on February 17, 2000, Allende gained a new audience in the United States represented by millions of Oprah devotees who helped the novel become a bestseller. With *Daughter of Fortune,* Allende became one of the most well-known Latin American women writers in the United States and certainly the most widely read author in translation.

Following the success of *Daughter of Fortune,* Allende wrote *Portrait in Sepia,* a story that is both a sequel to the previous novel and a narrative that can be enjoyed independently. Appearing in 2000 and then in translation a year later, *Portrait in Sepia* follows the *Daughter of Fortune* characters and their offspring of three generations for another fifty years, linking these immigrants in an intricate narrative that moves from 1862 to 1910. *Portrait in Sepia* is also something of a "prequel" to *The House of the Spirits,* as the characters in the newest novel are also the grandparents of the protagonists in Allende's first book. In this way, the three novels form a non-sequential trilogy of Chilean-American immigrants. Each subsequent novel demonstrates Allende's growth as a writer with its progressively more controlled narrative and more complex plot development. In addition to a book tour in 2001 to promote *Portrait in Sepia,* Allende prepared to publish her first novel for young adults. *City of Beasts,* a story set in the Amazon rainforest, is the first book of a trilogy that will move location in each installment. If the past is any example, Allende will surely prove as popular with a younger audience as she has with her adult readers worldwide.

ALLENDE'S BACKGROUND AS REFLECTED IN HER WORK

One of the key elements that distinguishes Allende's fiction is the remarkable breadth of people and places covered in her novels. The readers of her work are transported from the big cities, rural countrysides, and stark mountains of Chile to the untamed jungles of Venezuela and to the crowded streets of San Francisco's Chinatown. Memorable characters hearken from all over the globe, with narrators both male and female, contemporary and historical. Notably, Allende weaves these fantastic worlds without moving far from what she knows. When asked by an interviewer how much her own experiences have influenced her work, Allende answered:

> I can only write about the things that I have experienced, not exactly as I write in my books, but the feelings and the emotions of my characters are echoes of me. Some of my readers send me their lives and their stories, saying "You write this down as I am not a writer," but I cannot do this as it has nothing to do with me. So everything I write, even if it seems very remote to my own life is based on my experiences. ("Photographic Memory")

Allende goes on to explain how each of her protagonists reflects a part of herself, whether it be her rootlessness as a political exile, her isolation as a feminist, her energy as a lover, or her creativity as a storyteller. Readers of Allende's body of work notice a pattern of development in her female protagonists as well as a physical movement in her settings as the novels follow their author in her real-life migrations.

Even though many of her novels deal with historical events with which Allende has limited direct experience, or in some cases none, the author relies on her emotional experiences and personal relationships to offer depth to her narrative and realism to her characters. In nearly all of her novels, Allende features women as storytellers; these character-narrators give a sense of intimacy and immediacy to their tales even as they reflect their creator's voice. In *The House of the Spirits,* the grand-daughter Alba shares many similarities with Allende in her girlhood, including her special relationship with her grandfather and her unconventional response to bourgeois life. Just as Alba ostensibly writes the novel to inscribe her family history, so did Allende begin *The House of the Spirits* to convince her grandfather that he would never be forgotten. Allende's subsequent novel, *Of Love and Shadows,* relies in part on her experiences as a journalist, while the heroine of *Eva Luna* reveals Allende's gradual embrace of a more sensual life that she learned from her years in Venezuela. The strong-willed Eliza in *Daughter of Fortune* reveals Allende's strength as a woman independent from a male-dominated society, just as the rootless Aurora reflects her author's nomadic adult life. In truth, Allende has garnered in each phase of her life new material to bring to her craft.

In the settings she selects for her novels, Allende shows a similar propensity to write what she knows. Although she had spent over a decade in Venezuela before trying her hand at a book, Allende found herself turning to the Chile of her memories when she developed the landscape for her first two novels. Her complex feelings toward her troubled homeland are reflected in the beautiful descriptions of the country that counter the brutal honesty with which Allende treats troubling historical events. After completing *The House of the Spirits* and *Of Love and Shadows,* Allende seemed better prepared to move her work to the exotic setting of her new Caribbean country which serves as the backdrop for *Eva Luna* and some of the short fiction in *The Stories of Eva Luna.* After Allende married and moved permanently to the United States, her interest in North American history surfaced in subsequent novels. Her last three novels have focused at least in part on California, with special attention given to the San Francisco Bay Area where Allende makes her home.

Though Allende draws heavily on the environment surrounding her to develop her characters and landscape, the author's years as a journalist also have left their stamp on her writing style. Notwithstanding

Neruda's unflattering observations about Allende's inexact reporting, the skills she learned during her years working on a magazine and in television have translated into effective fiction-writing habits. Certainly, the last hundred pages of *The House of the Spirits* read more like a nonfiction account of a political era than do the fanciful first sections. Likewise, Allende has described *Of Love and Shadows* as a "police story that could have been written by a journalist" (Mujica 39). Certainly, when Allende turned to California history, first in *The Infinite Plan* and then in *Daughter of Fortune* and *Portrait in Sepia*, she depended on a variety of research techniques to authenticate her novels. For the first book, she needed to get a realistic picture of key historical events and places, including the Vietnam War and Berkeley in the radical 1960s. To learn more about these moments, Allende went out on the street interviewing participants and eyewitnesses whose experiences she could incorporate. She also depended heavily on the stories her husband had shared of his upbringing in a barrio of Los Angeles and his early years in the San Francisco area. To develop a faithful account of California in the nineteenth century for her next two novels, Allende spent months in libraries, reading books, watching documentaries, and reviewing firsthand artifacts, including letters and photographs. This fact-gathering gave her the backdrop for her fiction, though she claims that the characters themselves "just walked into [her] house" (Butler 1).

A final element of Allende's fiction that is derived from her life is the author's forthright treatment of romantic relationships and sexuality. Allende attributes her comfort level in portraying the sensual side of life to her years spent in Venezuela. Brought up in a strict family environment ruled by Catholicism and middle-class values in Chile, Allende was trained to suppress sexual desire and live as a proper daughter, wife, and mother. In the years that her marriage was deteriorating, Allende was also in a foreign country, a nation that embraced the joy of life and all its pleasures. It was during that time, the same years that she was writing *Eva Luna*, that Allende learned to accept herself as a woman (Cruz et al. 217). She explains, "In *Eva Luna* I embraced my own femininity and the feminist struggle" (Piña 194). She became bolder in her writing, allowing the female characters to engage in satisfactory relationships and revel in their own sexuality. While Allende often excises these sex scenes from drafts she sends to her mother, the author feels at ease with her renditions of love despite the opinions of some critics who view these treatments as sentimental or unrealistic. In *Aphrodite* more than any other book, Allende shows the joy with which she embraces the most sensual aspects of life—food and sex—and shows how these elements spill into her fiction.

As far-reaching as Allende's novels may be, the body of fiction always circles back to its source—an imaginative woman living in exile and giving voice to her imaginings. Above all else, Allende defines her homelessness as the core of her need to write. She explains, "I suppose that it is from that feeling of loneliness the questions arise that lead one to write, and that books are conceived in the search for answers" (P 50). Examining Allende's life story against her fictional stories, readers can see the series of questions with which the author has wrestled and the books that have served as her response to the mysteries of life.

2

Isabel Allende's Fiction:
A Study in Contrasts

"Every book has a way of being written. Every story has a way of being told."

—Isabel Allende, "Questions and Answers"

As the above observation about her own novels indicates, Isabel Allende is not a writer who lends herself to easy classification. To suggest, as she herself does, that each of her stories unfolds in a unique way is to describe the diversity of content and style that characterizes this author's remarkable oeuvre. Since the publication of *The House of the Spirits* in 1985, Allende has become the most widely read Latin American woman writer in the world. In each of her books, from the classic *The House of the Spirits* to the most recent *Portrait in Sepia,* Allende employs a different tone, structure, and style to convey most vividly the fictional world of each narrative. Within this elasticity, however, common threads emerge that link the themes and characters of the books to each other and to the histories they reflect. Certainly, Allende's writing style reflects the influences of her Latin American predecessors, particularly in her treatment of magic and mysticism. At the same time, however, she relies on her training as a journalist to confront even the most atrocious political realities, including terrorism, torture, and murder. Linking the bloodshed in Latin America to a dangerously male-dominated culture, Allende counters that culture in her novels with a stalwart feminism that resists stereotypical roles. Likewise, she offsets what could become dispassionate reportage with fanciful descriptions of romance, a reverential treatment of memory, and characters who, in one critic's words, "refuse a fate of reduced expectations" (Graham 39).

When the exiled and restless Allende decided in the early 1980s to try her hand at fiction writing, she entered a literary world that was prepared for fresh voices from Latin America. Allende's rapid acceptance by a worldwide readership was facilitated by a Latin American literary renaissance that had been blossoming for over a decade. Until the 1960s, Hispanic writers were not widely read in translation. Then, two important novelists, Carlos Fuentes from Mexico and Mario Vargas Llosa from Peru, began to publish novels that received awards and recognition beyond the borders of their countries. Through English translations of their early works, these Latin American writers gained their first wide audience in the United States and Europe. Then, the emergence of a unique novelist in the figure of the Colombian Gabriel García Márquez brought Latin writers to the forefront of the English-speaking world. In 1967, Márquez published *One Hundred Years of Solitude,* his saga of a century in the life of the Buendía family. With its sweeping historical narrative, its matter-of-fact treatment of the supernatural, and its liberal use of humor, the novel ushered in a resurgence of Latin American writing that came to be called "el Boom." Included in the Boom were such important writers as Jorge Luis Borges, Alejo Carpentier, Julio Cortázar, and José Donoso. Alhough critics debate which authors should be dubbed pre-Boom, Boom, and post-Boom, they agree that this important movement changed the face of Latin fiction forever (see Nunn). Conspicuously absent from this innovative group, however, were the voices of Latin American women writers. These would come in the next decade, with Isabel Allende forging the path.

Living in exile, like many writers who make up the Boom, Allende found a publisher for *The House of the Spirits,* never imagining that it would become a best-selling novel. As an avid reader and active journalist, Allende naturally had read the great Latin American writers prominent on the international literary scene. The influences of Fuentes, Llosa, and especially Márquez are apparent in Allende's first novel. In fact, the book shares some striking parallels with *One Hundred Years of Solitude,* and this exposed *The House of the Spirits* almost immediately to unfair criticism. Negative book reviews at the time derided Allende's "shameless cloning" of Márquez, suggesting that her use of magical realism (discussed below) was a mere imitation of his masterpiece (Fernández 51). Since then, critics such as Patricia Hart (see especially her *Narrative Magic*) have shown how Allende's attention to feminist matters sets her apart from the male Boom writers. Describing Allende's short story collection, *The Stories of Eva Luna*, Hart argues for a broader understanding of Allende's literary inspiration:

> Ironic references in fact, are the only real similarity to the Boom authors that I see in these stories. . . . Otherwise, a host of different and more appropriate comparisons suggest themselves. Like the James Joyce of *Dubliners*, Allende builds each of these stories to a moment of epiphany; like the Edith Wharton of "Roman Fever," she poises her characters on the brink of a moment of social change, so that they often seem to be struggling with one foot in the nineteenth century and one in the twentieth. Like Jorge Amado, Allende can spin a funny, sensual yarn, but like Clarice Lispector or Luisa Valenzuela, she can use her narrative skills to remind us that parallel to our placid and comfortable existence is another, invisible universe, one where poverty, misery and torture are all too real. ("Review of *The Stories of Eva Luna*," 316)

Allende's association with the major Latin American writers who preceded her, then, is an appropriate linkage but one that must be balanced with the wide range of authors who influenced her style. Her subsequent publications are a testament to her ability to invent a fresh narrative voice and literary style for each story, its own "way of being told." Whether the story is a journalistic account, a captivating romance, or a historical fiction, Allende has proven for over fifteen years that she is no mere imitator. Her earliest readers seemed already to understand Allende's originality as they bought her first novel in unexpected numbers, boosting her rapidly to a prominent position from which she could become a key figure in opening the Boom to women writers.

MAGICAL REALISM AND POLITICAL REALITIES

The primary distinguishing characteristic of the Latin Boom writers was a narrative technique termed *magical realism*. Coined by German art critic Franz Roh in the 1920s to describe painters experimenting with reality on their canvases, the term came to represent a particular literary mode that proliferated in the works of Latin American novelists who, like Márquez in *One Hundred Years of Solitude*, adapted conventional realism to make it distinctly their own. Broadly defined, realism is a literary term applied to fictional narratives that remain faithful to the actual rules of the modern physical world. In other words, the plot events that unfold in a realistic novel are presented in an authentic way; though fictional, the story could also happen in real life. Even an unlikely occurrence, such as a character winning the lottery, can take place in a realistic novel as long as the event is possible in the real world. The term *realism*, however, is more often attached to novels that replicate everyday life. In other words, a wish fulfillment novel (like the one described about winning the lottery) is not as common as a novel that mirrors more universal experiences. Many realistic novels, then, focus on the harder experiences of life, such as unrequited love, disappointed dreams, or death. The most common American realist novels, from the Civil War period to the end of the nineteenth century, were interested primarily in the rise and fall of individuals in the various social classes.

Rules of verisimilitude need not be adhered to in other genres where what is expected is the unexpected, such as in science fiction, where a spacecraft full of aliens might land on Earth, or in ghost stories, where a thousand-year-old mummy might come back to life. Unlike the characters in genres of the fantastic, characters in the world of realistic fiction think and behave in ways that parallel real people. Realistic narratives do not disappoint their readers by allowing one set of laws to seem to govern the fictional universe, only to violate those laws without warning by inserting unexplained or supernatural occurrences into the story. Latin American writers, however, became notorious for their tendency to bend these conventions with a new brand of realism that allowed competing visions of reality, however unusual, to merge in the same narrative. For example, in *One Hundred Years of Solitude*, the gypsy Melquíades can predict the future, the entire village is struck with a plague of insomnia, and Remedíos the Beauty floats to heaven one day without warning. Strange as these events may be, the story is narrated in a matter-of-fact manner that presents such magical plot elements as perfectly plausible, even expected occurrences. The blending of the normal, rational world with the unexplained—the magical with the real—creates an alternate worldview that allows the two seemingly irreconcilable perspectives to coexist. For many years, magical realism came to be the most widely recognized trademark of Latin American writers.

When newcomer Isabel Allende published *The House of the Spirits*, her inclusion of magical elements received more attention than any other feature of the novel. In the book, Clara the Clairvoyant can predict deaths and earthquakes, decipher the meaning of dreams, and move the salt-cellar across the table with her mind. Like Márquez, Jorge Luis Borges, and other Latin writers before her, Allende narrates these mystical plot events as factual, unsurprising occurrences. Describing Clara's telekinetic abilities, the narrator notes that Clara "was so accomplished that she could move the keys on the piano with the cover down, even though she never learned to move the instrument itself around the drawing room" (*HS* 67). True to the hallmark of magical realism, Allende fuses the real and the fantastic seamlessly, offering the account of Clara's special gifts in the same straightforward tone that she narrates the novel's more commonplace events. As the story turns darker with the advent of a tyrannical dictator, such supernatural elements diminish but they do not disappear. Toward the novel's close, Clara's granddaughter Alba has been tortured in prison and lies near death. The long-dead grandmother visits the girl in her cell and insists that she survive to write her country's story. Nothing about this ghost seems fearful or strange; rather, she arrives like a long-awaited guest and leaves just as discreetly. In Allende's narrative, the line between life and death is not a barrier, as it might be in a strictly realistic novel. She explains that she is "marked by the fact that I live on this continent. Here, strange and bewildering things happen, and you, the outsiders, call that 'Magical Realism.' But for us that is everyday life" (Moody, "On Shadows and Love" 61). The rational and the supernatural, particularly in Allende's childhood, played equal parts in shaping her imagination.

The frustration Allende has expressed at being so closely aligned to the magical realists of the Boom grows, in part, out of a presumed assumption that she is imitating a style rather than expressing life as she personally experienced it. As she has explained in countless interviews, the fantastic tales in *The House of the Spirits* were drawn from her family stories, as accepted in the Allende/Llona household as any natural laws of the universe. While she admits to exaggeration in her novel, Allende also insists that her grandmother was clairvoyant and did move salt-shakers on the table. Growing up in an unconventional family, Allende did not draw a line between the rational world and the supernatural in a childhood "full of magical things" (Agosín 40). Suggesting that Hispanic cultures are more open to psychic possibility than other groups of the industrialized world, Allende also points to a unique characteristic of the women in her family that opened her to the supernatural: "My great-grandmother, my grandmother, my mother, my daughter, and I all communicate with each other telepathically, even after death" (Gautier 136). Much of the magic in her novels, then, grows out of Allende's own remarkable family life and upbringing. At the same time, the novelist does not deny the influence of her literary predecessors. She says, "I am of the first generation of Latin American writers to grow up reading Latin American authors: Borges, García Márquez, Carlos Fuentes. What we have in common, among greatly varying styles, is the inclusion of the invisible world, not ghosts and spirits, but emotions and passions. When I write about spirits, they stand for things" ("A Mule," 57). Often, these spirits stand for the qualities of hope, courage, and resistance that help Allende's female characters survive. Likewise, she feels that the magic in her novels stands for the "invisible forces that move the world: dreams, legends, myths, emotion, passion, history" (Snell 238).

In the novels that follow *The House of the Spirits,* Allende's application of magical elements changes as she explores other techniques for expressing those "invisible forces." For instance, *Of Love and Shadows* exhibits far fewer characteristics of magical realism than its predecessor, reading more like the highly journalistic final section of *The House of the Spirits.* In fact, the only unexplained occurrences in the second novel surround the adolescent peasant girl, Evangelina Ranquileo. Her noonday convulsive episodes that follow the "convention of frogs" (*LS* 33) seem to have limited miraculous power, achieving what the narrator terms a "carnival of insignificant wonders" (*LS* 60). These events culminate in Evangelina tossing a lieutenant like a child across her patio, with the townspeople watching in wonder. The main characters Francisco and Irene, a photographer and journalist respectively, provide the objective outside view, one that might throw into question the veracity of the bizarre spectacle. Yet, they respond to Evangelina's feats with astonishment rather than disbelief, accepting without question the impossible scene they have witnessed. After this episode, Evangelina becomes one of the many victims of the dictatorship, and the narrative turns toward solving the chilling mystery of the massacre and uncovering the perpetrators, thus exchanging magical realism for a grim view of the country's political realities.

Readers notice a recurring pattern in Allende's novels that move from an elemental world dominated by the spiritual realm into a rational world ruled by social and political concerns. Critic Ruth Jenkins calls Allende's brand of magical realism mixed with political hardship "fantastic realities" (61), the realities made bleaker by their juxtaposition to the ethereal spirit world. For most of Allende's female characters, this move into the cruel world of experience marks the loss of innocent mysticism. Chapter headings in *The House of the Spirits* demonstrate this pattern as Clara inhabits a pre-junta world called "The Time of the Spirits," during which she devotes herself to celestial activities, while Alba's adolescence, entitled "The Awakening," coincides with the rise of the dictator. With her eyes open, Alba experiences firsthand "The Terror" and then faces "The Hour of Truth," as the young woman moves from the supernatural world of her childhood to the grim reality of life under a cruel totalitarian government. Likewise, in *Of Love and Shadows* Francisco is frustrated by Irene's ability to float above the anguish of her country, "buoyed up by her good intentions," and he imagines shaking her "until her feet touched the ground and she opened her eyes to the truth" (*LS* 73). The heinous crime at the center of the book serves to awaken Irene, revealing her at the novel's close fleeing into exile as she looks one last time at her homeland and sobs, "My country . . . oh, my country" (*LS* 273). Even in *Eva Luna*, a novel suffused with exuberant vitality, evidence of magical realism is slight and limited to sexual experiences—a coupling between Eva Luna's mother and Indian father that cures the man's mortal snakebite, and sensual romps between Rolf Carlé and his cousins that fulfill the "basic requirements of levitation" (*EL* 88). Despite marvelous coincidences and felicitous meetings between eventual lovers, the narrative remains rooted in a heroic story of revolutionaries and their oppressors. As in the two previous novels, the timeless flavor of magical realism gives way to a more journalistic style with an urgent imperative to expose evil in modern life.

When Allende turns to a North American landscape in *The Infinite Plan*, she leaves magical realism almost entirely behind, opting instead for a style that replicates historical fiction in its rendering of real times and places. While Gregory Reeves may encounter good luck in chasing trains and dodging bullets, his story is largely a plausible one focused almost exclusively, and quite literally, on the material world. His mother's tenacious belief that her dead husband visits her regularly, a distinct possibility in earlier novels, is treated by the characters here with patient condescension. The case is somewhat different in *Daughter of Fortune*, where Tao Chi'en's conversations with his wife's ghost are rendered sincerely, but even magical elements in that novel are limited to those interchanges and to Eliza's occasional mystical dream about her vanished lover. Central to that tale is not what is magical about the Gold Rush in California but what is only too real in a frontier territory where immigrants are mistreated and innocent girls are tricked into prostitution. While these later novels may leave distinct features of magical realism behind, they continue to treat life as fateful and awe-inspiring; as one critic notes, "there are always intimations of the transcendent" (Donaldson 57). If nowhere else but in the inspiration of history, the characters of these novels believe that the past is with them and urges them forward.

FEMINISM IN A MAN'S WORLD

Allende's inclination to have magical events give way to political ones in the course of her narratives is not the only trait that sets her apart from the Latin Boom writers. When asked in an interview whether she was influenced by fellow Chilean writer José Donoso, Allende responds that "our ghosts and obsessions are different, we belong to different generations, and our sexes have affected both our works" (Gautier 132). As a woman and a feminist, Allende makes the concerns of the female central to nearly every book she writes. (The only exception is *The Infinite Plan*, a book with a male protagonist who is shaped, nonetheless, by his relationship to a powerful woman.) In each of her other novels, Allende departs from her literary predecessors to challenge a Latin culture that reveres maleness and circumscribes its women into narrow, non-threatening roles. Coming of age in the mid-twentieth century, Allende witnessed the rise of the feminist movement both in her country and abroad. As a young wife and mother in the 1960s, Allende played the part of the proper bourgeois woman at the same time that she was writing for a liberal women's magazine and appearing on television in Chile. Yet, feminism as a political position did not become real for her until the coup in Chile that ultimately forced her to flee the country with her husband and children. Living in exile in Venezuela, Allende found herself alienated from her past and the male-dominated culture that had given rise to an oppressive military regime and left so many dead and homeless. Only by giving voice to the women characters who peopled her imagination could Allende begin to articulate the rage that characterized her own awakening.

The House of the Spirits is a groundbreaking work of Latin American fiction in that women make up the central characters of the story and have the most prominent voices of the narrative. Certainly, some of the characters are more overtly political than others. For example, Clara's mother Nívea participates in the women's suffrage movement, chaining herself to the gates of Congress and marching in the streets (*HS* 58). Even the unearthly Clara shows a certain degree of independence in her spiritual activities and her refusal to obey her husband's every command. When Esteban strikes Clara after twenty years of marriage, she resolves never to speak to him again (*HS* 172). Though her revolt is a small one, it symbolizes a move to reject the male violence that menaces these women. Practical Blanca, while she remains largely outside the political realm, takes a guerrilla revolutionary for a lover in defiance of her father's commands. Alba mimics her lover Miguel at political rallies and demonstrations until she begins to experience firsthand the terror of the dictatorship and her feminist beliefs become more authentic. Allende argues, "All the women in [*The House of the Spirits*] are feminists in their fashion; that is, they ask to be free and complete human beings, to be able to fulfill themselves, not to be dependent on men" (Agosín 41). In order to achieve such wholeness, Latin American women must first address the cultural mores that define the gender roles for both sexes.

The system that has made women dependent, that requires of them saintly conduct as wives and lifelong devotion as mothers, is one largely dominated by a cultural code of male behavior called *machismo*. The term machismo can carry many meanings within Latin culture, not all of them destructive. While in the United States the term has come to mean a highly chauvinistic, aggressive brute, this is not a full picture of the macho male. Machismo is not necessarily a negative attribute in Latin American cultures. In fact, the label "macho" can be a compliment to a man who provides for his family, raises his children well, and earns respect in the community. The cult of machismo essentially argues that men prove their virility through their sexual prowess, their ability to fend for themselves, and their unquestioned leadership of their families. Rudolfo Anaya, in his essay "'I'm the King': The Macho Image," describes the song the Hispanic boy sings as he becomes a man: "*Sigo siendo el Rey*. . . . I'm the king. I rule the family, like my father before me, and what I say goes" (62). As the ruler of his family "kingdom," the macho male enjoys broad authority over matters involving family conduct, financial concerns, and public life. In this system, the woman shares no equal partnership, instead serving through the work of child-rearing and housekeeping.

The House of the Spirits provides a picture of two types of machismo in the characters of Esteban Trueba and his illegitimate grandson Esteban García. The former is the patriarch of the Trueba family, a hard worker who turns his meager inheritance into an extremely profitable hacienda. True to the macho image, Esteban suffers from a sexual drive that cannot be contained. He follows the dictates of society, however, in desecrating only the peasant girls on his property and the adjoining haciendas. When he decides to marry, he looks past the women whose bastard children he has fathered and chooses instead a "woman of his own class, with the blessings of the Church" (*HS* 58). Esteban treats sex with Clara like a sacrament, retreating to a prostitute when he requires something more lively. He is an invulnerable leader, expressing none of his hidden dreams or fears and only reacting in crazed outbursts when his family pushes him too far. Yet, despite his rages and stubborn views, Esteban earns the respect of the community, eventually becoming elected to public office and serving the Conservative party for many years. He dies a man misunderstood by most of the women in his life, except his granddaughter Alba with whom he shares his final days. The picture of Esteban by the novel's close is that of a deeply flawed man who has tried valiantly to live according to a social code that has become a thing of the past.

The grandson Esteban García presents a more sinister picture of the macho male. Like many of Allende's most memorable villains, García is a military man who has absorbed the masculine code that drives armed conflict. Allende asks with wonderment in an interview, "Have you ever seen anything more *machista* than the military mentality? It is the synthesis, the exaltation, the ultimate exaggeration of machismo" (Levine and Engelbert 46). In *The House of the Spirits,* García is presented as just such an exaggerated representation of male aggression and arrogance. The narrator introduces him as an "evil, dark-skinned creature" who amuses himself by poking nails in the eyes of chickens (*HS* 161–162). As a boy, García craftily reveals Pedro Tercero's hiding place to the raging Esteban, and seems in that episode to mirror the older man. Like his namesake, García harbors revenge for years, channeling his fury over his illegitimate status into sexual violence toward Alba. On three occasions, García violates the girl who represents the social class barred to him—first, when he molests her as a little girl, then when he forces her as an adolescent to kiss him, and finally when he has her imprisoned as a traitor and repeatedly rapes her. Esteban García is a man tormented by his own social impotence, a pain he seems unable to assuage through any route except to exert power over women.

This pattern repeats itself in Allende's subsequent novels. In *Of Love and Shadows,* Lieutenant Ramírez acts with impunity, killing Evangelina as revenge for her embarrassing him in front of his troops. When Faustino Rivero imagines the scene, he assumes that Ramírez has raped the girl before shooting her, "recovering the macho pride she snatched from him that day in the patio of her house" (*LS* 229). The heroine of *Eva Luna* nearly meets the same fate when she encounters the machismo of a lieutenant determined to torture her until she confesses to murder. A "cheerful, handsome, dark-haired man who cut a wide swath among the girls" (*EL* 172), the suave lieutenant becomes a swaggering bully in the private interrogation room, beating the girl and blackmailing her guardian. Yet, Allende does not limit such abhorrent exhibitions of machismo to Latin America. In that same novel, she creates the repugnant character Lukas Carlé, an Austrian tyrant who marries his wife because "he liked the sudden gleam of terror he saw in her eyes" (*EL* 26). Lukas is a genuine masochist, a cruel parent and violent soldier who harbors the "conviction that only gunpowder and blood can produce men capable of steering the foundering ship of humanity to port" (*EL* 33). Allende links these attitudes to a universal cycle of war and terror that can only be broken through a new vision of the masculine and feminine.

Allende reveals her alternative vision not only in the many feminist women she creates but also in the marginal characters, both male and female, who exhibit a wisdom their more gender-bound peers lack. These characters operate outside the proscribed roles of saintly woman or macho man, often taking the part of prostitutes or homosexuals who act as saviors in the novels. One example is Tránsito Soto, the prostitute and longtime friend of Esteban. Though she is certainly not Esteban's social equal, Tránsito pleases him with her ambition and business sense (*HS* 101). More modern than the *patrón,* Tránsito is one of the first in the book to acknowledge the wisdom of cooperatives, a novel idea in her profession that proves both profitable and just. When the recently widowed Esteban comes to her broken with grief, the motherly Tránsito bathes and cares for him until he feels "practically cured" (269). In the final chapter, she is also the only woman who can free Esteban's granddaughter, saving the girl's life and the grandfather's sanity. In *Of Love and Shadows,* the beauty stylist Mario saves the lives of Francisco and Irene, first by disguising them to sneak out of the hospital and then by harboring them in his apartment until they can flee the country. Likewise, in *Eva Luna,* the transsexual Melesio/Mimí urges Eva Luna to begin to write, the single activity that finally gives Eva Luna the independence she has craved. *Daughter of Fortune*'s Chinese immigrant Tao Chi'en succeeds in smuggling Eliza onto a ship bound for California because his ethnicity makes him invisible. In the same novel, Joe Bonecrusher, the madam with a "motherly heart" (*DF* 301), nurses the entire town through an epidemic of dysentery, demonstrating a goodwill that belies her objectionable lifestyle. In each of these cases, it is the men and women on the edges of society—those who reject the extreme gender stereotypes—who end up having the keenest intellects and the kindest hearts.

HISTORY, MEMORY, AND IMAGINATION

In addition to developing memorable characters who embrace life and resist stereotypes, Allende adopts several broader themes that recur in her fiction. In particular, she is interested in the confluence of three otherwise contrasting elements—the historical record, personal and collective memory, and the private imagination. Each theme has developed from different influences upon the author. The child of diplomats, Allende lived in a number of countries and had her worldview shaped by significant international events, as well as by her native Chile's tumultuous political history. As a young reader, Allende was likewise deeply influenced by nineteenth-century fiction and, in particular, by historical novels (Gautier 125). The impact of these experiences can be seen in Allende's close attention to historical detail, though the author has no reservations about manipulating the facts if her narrative warrants the change. Standing in counterpoint to such historical accounts is Allende's interest in personal memory. Many of her characters live, like she does, in exile or estrangement from their homelands and their families. In these cases, the ability to piece together the past from deeply cherished recollections often becomes for Allende's characters an impulse more urgent than any factual account of history. The memories become as valuable an inheritance as the historical truths, regardless of their manipulation by the imagination. This final theme is central to Allende's interest in magical realism discussed above, as well as to her treatment of fateful love relationships and her attention to the factors that enable human survival. While these subjects receive different treatment in each novel, their interrelationship can best be seen in the trilogy made up of *The House of the Spirits, Daughter of Fortune,* and *Portrait in Sepia.*

The correlations between the three novels are both thematic and literal, in that the books focus on parallel issues while they follow the same extended family from the mid-nineteenth century to contemporary times. Allende admits that the literal connections are largely spontaneous, in that she had not intended to write a sequel to *Daughter of Fortune* when she turned to *Portrait in Sepia*. Rather, she explains that after writing the first chapter of *Portrait*, "I realized that I could connect both novels without really writing a sequel as they could be read independently. Then by the time I was writing the third chapter I realized that these characters could be the grandparents of the characters in my novel *The House of the Spirits* and therefore I would have a trilogy—I would have 120 years of a story of the same family" ("Photographic Memory"). Separated by generations, the characters' stories in the second two novels are only loosely intertwined with those in *The House of the Spirits*. However, *Portrait in Sepia* answers numerous questions about the fate of the central characters in *Daughter of Fortune*, though they play a minor role in the second novel. All three books draw on Allende's major themes of history, memory, and imagination to weave a family story that bears witness to them all.

In Allende's first novel, *The House of the Spirits*, the narrative moves to the rhythm of the generations, as interpreted by the ostensible narrator and youngest family member Alba. Her age and perspective play a major role in foregrounding one theme over another. As explained above, the greater part of the novel is taken up with a mysterious, even ageless world that seems almost untouched by history. It is a setting where anything can happen, a perspective on the world as a child might view it from the vantage point of innocent youth. Alba's eccentric family stories and magical childhood, described in imaginative terms, give way to history with the arrival of political tyranny. At the book's close, however, Alba is surrounded by her grandmother's notebooks and letters, her grandfather's brief memoirs, the family photographs, and her own writings from jail. As she pieces together the many decades of family history, she feels as if "I had lived all this before and that I have already written these words" (*HS* 367). The history of the Trueba women melds into a collective memory for Alba to record, one that will document the history of her native country even as it authenticates her magical past.

In contrast to the first novel, *Daughter of Fortune* places fact and fiction, the historical and the imaginary, in counterpoint. In many ways, the narrative reflects Allende's early interest in historical fiction, taking place as it does during an important period in the development of California and offering accurate details of the Gold Rush and the countless miners who met with disappointment. However, the most compelling story line in the novel centers on Eliza's quest for an elusive lover that leads her both to true love and to genuine freedom. The "fiction" that has propelled her thousands of miles proves no less elusive than the tales of gold-paved streets that brought so many to San Francisco. For Allende, this shift to stories on the margins of society demonstrates the unique way that fiction can make history accessible. She explains that "[w]hen we read a history we read the dates, the battles, the generals, the political events, but this is not the narrative of what really happens to people, especially to women and children, as it is always about men" ("Photographic Memory"). In writing *Daughter of Fortune* explicitly about one such woman, Allende has the opportunity to shift the historical perspective so that it focuses on the edges of the story, at the margin where women, immigrants, and supplanted natives can have their stories told.

Portrait in Sepia links the worlds of *The House of the Spirits* and *Daughter of Fortune* by connecting characters in the latter novel to their successors in the twentieth century. Just as *Daughter of Fortune* takes the Gold Rush as its anchoring device, *Portrait in Sepia* focuses on the political turmoil and military skirmishes in Chile during the second half of the nineteenth century. Allende explains that primarily the "book is about memory, it's about the importance of revealing the secrets or finding out what has happened" ("Photographic Memory"). In the novel, the main character Aurora lives in an environment dominated by hidden secrets. She is haunted by her memories, especially the ones that come to her in nightmares. Uncovering these secrets requires Aurora to face that her marriage is a sham and that her parentage is no less murky. Not only that, she discovers that her terrifying dreams are actually suppressed memories of watching her grandfather's violent death. Identifying the source of her anxieties and the truth about her husband, Aurora faces adulthood independent and whole. Embracing memory rather than erasing it proves the most important step to genuine healing for her, as it does for the majority of Allende's fully realized characters.

Isabel Allende's literature resonates with her contemporary readership because she addresses universal themes while inventing unique and memorable characters. A principal aim for her is to share the stories on the margin and, in that way, validate and retain them. As she reveals, "Storytelling is a way of preserving the memory of the past and keeping alive legends, myths, superstitions and history that are not in the textbooks—the real stories of people and countries. I have tried desperately to do that in all my novels" (Sanoff 67). Allende draws attention to the untold stories by featuring silenced characters in each narrative, just as she presents emerging feminists in every book. She gives a historical rationale for both the silenced and the liberated women in her novels: "[I]n my continent, women have been condemned to silence, and speaking up, having a voice, is a very subversive thing for a woman" (Ross 100). Allende was nearly forty years old and living in exile before she determined to give voice to the women characters clamoring inside her imagination for their chance to speak. Prompted by her desire to preserve personal and national history, Allende was likewise impelled by a need to give a shape to her private memories. She explains, "I am always looking for something, looking for my identity, trying to unveil the secrets and the mysteries and this is what I do in my writing" ("Photographic Memory"). Through the engaging stories of subversive women that she has brought to life for almost two decades, Allende reveals a fiction marked by contrasts—a mélange of magic, feminism, history, and memory that is her unique trademark.

3

The House of the Spirits
(1985)

With the publication of her first novel, *The House of the Spirits*, in 1982, Isabel Allende garnered immediate attention and praise from much of the international writing community. A bestseller translated into more than fifteen languages, the novel was embraced both for its political importance in documenting contemporary Chilean history and for its artistic merit as an engaging epic by a Latin American woman writer in a previously male-dominated tradition. Some critics charged, however, that Allende was merely duplicating the formula that had earned Gabriel García Márquez acclaim for his *One Hundred Years of Solitude* fifteen years earlier. Like that novel, Allende focuses her saga on a multi-generational family living in an unnamed South American country. Echoes of Márquez can also be seen in her attention to political themes and her use of magical realism, which blends fantastic occurrences with everyday life. (For further discussion of magical realism see chapter 2.) It is there that the similarities end, however, as Allende proves unique in her ability to fashion an imaginative, thought-provoking tale that includes memorable characters and arresting images all her own. The novel received due admiration both in Chile, where it was named Best Novel of the Year in 1983, and overseas, earning Allende Author of the Year and Book of the Year honors in Germany in 1984 and a Book Club New Voice award in the United States in 1986. In 1994, *The House of the Spirits* was made into a feature film with an all-star cast, including Meryl Streep, Jeremy Irons,

Glenn Close, and Winona Ryder. Balancing sweeping historical events with sensitive individual portraits, Allende's debut novel reveals her extraordinary facility to meld fact with fiction as she imparts a discerning vision of her homeland.

The events in *The House of the Spirits* span three generations of the Trueba family, beginning in the early twentieth century and ending with a military coup in the 1970s that splinters the clan. While the narration occasionally shifts to the first person, particularly when allowing Esteban Trueba, the patriarch of the family, to speak his mind, most of the book is presented in the limited third person. This third-person perspective is attributed to Esteban's granddaughter Alba, the purported writer of this "true" story. A third-generation Trueba, Alba preserves the family history as she has compiled it from her grandmother's notebooks, her grandfather's stories, and her own experiences. In part because Isabel Allende has indicated as much, critics generally see Alba as the author's literary self-portrait and the saga of the Truebas as a fictionalized rendition of the rise and fall of the Allende clan in Chile. The novel began, according to interviews with Allende, as a letter to her dying grandfather, a promise that his life would not disappear into oblivion. "My grandfather thought people died only when you forgot them," the author has explained. "I wanted to prove to him that I had forgotten nothing, that his spirit was going to live with us forever" (Shapiro 145). Allende's grandfather died before her letter could be finished; nevertheless, the end result was the novel that preserves the historical record of a country in turmoil and a family ravaged by external forces and internal passions.

PLOT

Allende has confessed in an interview that she finds herself, as both reader and writer, attracted to thick plots full of vivid characters in dynamic situations (Piña 195). Certainly her first novel illustrates this bent with its over 400 pages of fictionalized family drama interwoven with harsh historical and political realities. The novel spans approximately seventy-five years, beginning at the turn of the twentieth century and ending after the military coup and installation of a dictatorship in 1973. Ostensibly narrated by Alba, the granddaughter of the Trueba clan, the novel imparts her family history and mirrors her perspective as it is limited by time and understanding. In the first half of the book, Alba is not yet born and dictates the fantastic family tales that have been passed on orally or transcribed in her grandmother's meticulous notebooks that bear "witness to life" (*HS* 368). Here spiritualism and magical episodes have a central place, as they do in folklore and other kinds of oral traditions. With Alba's birth midway through the novel, family lore gives way to the eyewitness account of a young child. As the granddaughter matures, the mystical tone of early sections shifts into a journalistic realism that dominates the last hundred pages of the novel. In these final chapters, Alba experiences an "awakening" into adulthood with the arrival of political forces that threaten to crush her family.

The House of the Spirits opens with the words "Barrabás came to us by sea," introducing young Clara del Valle—the matriarch of the Trueba family—and the dog who is often seen as a symbol of her innocent childhood. The youngest daughter of Nívea and Severo del Valle, little Clara is already showing signs of unusual psychic powers and prophetic abilities. Her eldest sister, dubbed Rosa the Beautiful for her astonishing green hair and yellow eyes, is engaged to Esteban Trueba who has gone North to the mines to seek his fortune. Severo decides to run for Congress and a bottle of poisoned brandy meant for him ends up killing Rosa, as prophesied by Clara. Clara falls silent for the next nine years and wanders wordlessly through her family home, always accompanied by the faithful Barrabás, a dog of gargantuan proportions. The next time Clara speaks, it is as a young woman announcing her impending marriage to her sister's former fiancé; within two months Esteban arrives to ask Clara's father for her hand. Esteban has been living on his hacienda, Tres Marías, and making steady improvements to the property even as he tyrannizes the peasants and rapes their daughters. The night of his engagement party to Clara, her beloved Barrabás is stabbed mysteriously and dies in a pool of blood at her feet. Clara's girlhood is over.

The marriage of Esteban and Clara is a tragic one, as he loves her nearly to madness and she finds such human connection distracting and unnecessary. In fact, she knows before she ever agrees to the match that hers will be a marriage without love. Esteban, for his part, wants nothing less than to possess her utterly; yet, she is a woman of another dimension who eludes him throughout his life. They settle in a large home in the capital, where Clara becomes pregnant and delivers a daughter, Blanca. Mother and child are put under the jealous and obsessive attentions of Férula, Esteban's older sister, as he returns to his role as *patrón* of their countryside estate. When Blanca is a small child, the family follows Esteban out to Tres Marías for the summer. There, Clara discovers her "mission in life" as mistress of a hacienda, devoted to educating the peasantry and improving rural life (90). At the same time, little Blanca meets the foreman's peasant son, Pedro Tercero García, who will become her lifetime love, a renowned folksinger, and an influential revolutionary. The family remains in the countryside until a second difficult pregnancy forces Clara to return with her entourage to the big house in the capital. Her prognostication, that twin boys named Jaime and Nicolás will arrive shortly, drives Esteban into a fury and causes him to visit a local whorehouse where he reunites with a prostitute from his earlier days at Tres Marías. Tránsito Soto had once borrowed fifty pesos from Esteban to get ahead, and his investment in this shrewd businesswoman plays a key role in saving his family during the dictatorship.

After the twins' birth, Clara turns over the maintenance of children and household to her sister-in-law and renews her interest in the supernatural. One day three women arrive at her door as if summoned from the other world. Clara and the three Mora sisters develop a lasting bond and delve into the spirit world, speaking with disembodied souls, moving objects, and divining the future using a little three-legged table. Esteban's jealous need to command Clara's full attention and gratitude competes with his sister's own obsession to pamper and coddle the inattentive Clara. The antagonism between brother and sister comes to a head one night when Esteban finds Férula in bed with his wife during a thunderstorm and uses it as a pretext to throw her out of his house forever. His sister's curse—that he will always be alone—proves true, as each enraged act Esteban commits pushes his wife and family further from him (113–114).

The Trueba clan, safely entrenched in the privileged class, grows richer as the country drifts into a time of widespread poverty and disease. Esteban places his sons in boarding school to protect them from the occult influences of their mother while Blanca is allowed to follow Clara everywhere. The summers spent in Tres Marías fortify Blanca's love for Pedro Tercero, who has become a voice of change on the hacienda despite frequent beatings from his father and Esteban for such impertinence. The two adolescents become furtive lovers, meeting secretly at night for three years.

The summer when Blanca is eighteen, Clara prophesies a terrible earthquake. This tragedy kills thousands, leaves tens of thousands homeless, and unleashes disease across the country. Esteban is nearly killed when part of the roof collapses on him. His four months of convalescence further sour his already impatient and explosive temperament. Blanca, feigning illness at the convent school, returns to Tres Marías. Although

Pedro Tercero has been expelled from there, he often meets secretly with her, disguised and speaking of the coming revolution. As Esteban's tantrums worsen, Clara withdraws from him, even removing herself to a separate bedroom. At this time, the penniless Count Jean de Satigny—an effeminate Frenchman looking to marry a rich woman—establishes himself in the Trueba household. Blanca, now twenty-four, refuses the Count's marriage request and infuriates her father with her obstinacy. The twins arrive home from school—Jaime, an odd recluse studying for a life of medicine and servitude to the poor, and Nicolás, an intelligent but ineffectual dabbler and lady's man. The Count continues his attentions toward Blanca and, while spying on her, discovers her nightly trysts with Pedro by the river. He promptly informs her father who beats her in a rage and then strikes Clara for pointing out that Esteban had done much the same in his day. Clara, electing never to speak to her husband again, withdraws with Blanca to the capital.

Esteban is left alone at Tres Marías to vent his rage on Pedro, who has gone into hiding. A young boy, Esteban García, approaches him with information. Unbeknownst to the elder Esteban, the boy is actually his grandson, born from an illegitimate daughter the *patrón* had fathered with a peasant years before. When the boy leads Esteban to Pedro's hiding place, the infuriated father leaps at his nemesis with an axe and chops off several fingers before Pedro escapes. In a rage, Esteban refuses the boy his promised reward and thus fosters in the younger Esteban a lifelong hatred that will smolder for years before finding an outlet. In the capital, Clara renews her spiritualist circles and Blanca's growing belly reveals her pregnancy. When Esteban is told of the impending child, he forces Count Satigny to marry his daughter and the newlyweds leave for the North. At this time, Jaime is studying at the university and Nicolás is experimenting with numerous callings. Nicolás is also courting a young woman named Amanda, who cares for her orphaned younger brother Miguel. Jaime secretly loves Amanda and suffers deeply when Nicolás brings her to him for a covert abortion. During this period, Esteban runs for office and becomes a senator for the Conservative Party. The newlywed Blanca discovers that her husband has no interest in sexual love with a woman, and they settle into a companionable existence until she discovers his perverted pictures and strange erotic tastes. That same day, she flees back to her mother and delivers a baby girl, Alba, under the secret watch of little Miguel, who is hidden in the closet.

The final 200 pages of the novel chronicle Alba's girlhood and growth into a sensitive and politically active woman under a despotic regime.

Alba spends an unconventional childhood under the tutelage of a permissive mother, a psychic grandmother, two eccentric uncles, and a tyrannical grandfather whom she adores. Senator Trueba and his little grandchild develop a unique relationship that carries them through the terrors of the coming years. Blanca continues to meet secretly with Pedro Tercero for decades, often bringing little Alba with her, though the girl does not know he is her father. Pedro has become a hero of the peasant class and a famous singer whose revolutionary ballads are played frequently on the radio. When Alba is a small child, she meets up with Esteban García, who has come to ask Senator Trueba for permission to join the police academy. García, deciding he hates this little girl who represents all he might have had with a legitimate name, molests her during an unobserved moment but is never caught. Near this time, Clara finally decides to die, stops eating or drinking, and drifts into oblivion. Her death leaves Senator Trueba nearly inconsolable, but as his obsession gradually transforms into genuine love, she begins to appear to him in the old house, finally becoming his in death.

The Trueba household is set adrift by Clara's departure. Jaime, to his conservative father's dismay, becomes more politically extreme, while Nicolás continues to dabble in bizarre spiritual practices in an effort to find himself. Alba is enrolled in a British private school to prepare for a useful life, and Blanca works within the family more like a servant than a daughter. Senator Trueba expends his political influence in an effort to stamp out Marxist and Communist uprisings. Time passes, and Alba enters the university where she falls in love with Miguel, the little brother of Amanda from years before. Miguel influences Alba's awakening into an understanding of politics, oppression, and the need for revolution. With him, she participates in rallies and even a school-building takeover. At the same time, her brother Jaime begins to support "the Candidate," a left-wing favorite who has often lost against the Conservative Party but who is finally expected to win the Presidency. When the Socialists win, the rich families hide behind their heavy curtains while the lower classes take to the streets in impromptu parades. Almost immediately, the Conservative Party, aided by "gringos" from the North, sets about toppling the presidency through indirect means, primarily by engineering shortages of goods and food. Over time, these impositions create unrest among the previously supportive lower classes.

The last section of the novel chronicles the rise of the military coup that finally removes the president in a bloody battle that leaves many dead, including Alba's uncle Jaime. Many of Alba's friends are kidnapped in the night by military henchmen and never heard from again. Alba finds it hard to convince her grandfather that the torturing and killing of dissidents is going on every day, until she, too, is taken away right in front of him as punishment for her complicity in helping threatened revolutionaries gain asylum. Alba finds herself subjected to severe torture at the hands of her grandfather's unknown archenemy—his illegitimate grandchild Esteban García. When three of Alba's fingers are mailed to Senator Trueba, he uses the only influence he has left, his connection to the prostitute Tránsito Soto whose brothel services the military. The powerful madam is able to contrive Alba's release, and the battered young woman returns to her grandfather's home. At Esteban's suggestion, Alba begins to write the story that is *The House of the Spirits*, using the diaries and documents her family has saved through the years. As Alba writes, her grandfather dies quietly on the bed he shared with Clara, and Alba contemplates the baby growing in her womb, "the daughter of so many rapes or perhaps of Miguel," a child who promises, above all else, "better times to come" (368).

CHARACTER DEVELOPMENT

In a move that clearly separates her from other Latin American Boom writers, Allende constructs the narrative of the Trueba clan around its women. (See chapter 2 for more information about the Latin American literary Boom.) These female characters, exhibiting different strengths in each generation, bring peace and clarity to the turbulent family saga. The importance of their role in cleansing a history tainted by the selfish acts of Trueba men is evidenced by their associated names, all Spanish variations of the color "white." In choosing this color, Allende hoped to assign a kind of integrity to her female characters, "the purity of facing the world with new eyes, free from contamination, without prejudice, open and tolerant" (Pinto 79). The women should not be seen merely as indistinguishable types, however. Allende suggests that together they "symbolize [her] vision of what is meant by *feminine*, characters that could illustrate the destinies of women in Latin America" (Agosín, "Pirate" 40). Though a minor character, the great-grandmother Nívea plays a key role in establishing such a legacy. A vocal suffragette during the infancy of the women's movement, Nívea is viewed by her peers as "the first feminist in the country" (104). An eccentric, headstrong woman, she becomes an inspiration to her female descendants and sets the stage for a series of powerful Trueba women whose unconventional life choices will match her own.

The youngest and most unusual of Nívea's children, Clara, "The Clair-voyant," is positioned as the true matriarch of the book, "the soul of the big house on the corner" (240), who gives her family stability, direction, and protection from her violent, impulsive husband. Clara's character is made up of contradictions. On the one hand, she is a fragile, asthmatic child who spends nine years of her girlhood in silence because "speaking was pointless" (64). On the other hand, she is uniquely attuned to the spirit world, able to interpret dreams, predict the future, and engage in telekinesis at will. As a young woman, Clara gives herself to Esteban, having "summoned him with the power of her thought" (78) knowing that she will never love him. In an unhappy marriage to a dominant husband, Clara moves between periods of "absence," in which she falls into silence and raises herself to a state of consciousness above the harsh realities of daily life, and periods of intense industry during which she fights for the rights of the poor and disenfranchised. The narrator de-scribes her as one who lives in a fantastic world she has created for herself that follows its own mystical laws. During her spiritual forays, Clara links up with the "three Mora sisters" who help her conduct séances and commune with the dead. Like the three Muses, the Mora sisters nurture Clara's supernatural creativity. Lacking skills in house-keeping and basic child care, Clara instead offers her offspring intermit-tent affection, spiritual training, and a love of stories. She opens her home to the needy against Esteban's firm admonitions, and yet she ap-pears regularly at government functions to support her husband's polit-ical aspirations. Throughout the novel, Clara is explicitly likened to the bed on which she conceives and births her children—"the sailboat of the gentle blue silk sea" (248)—as if she is the helm that steers her family through rough waters, her death the shipwreck that sets all the Trueba clan adrift.

Clara's only daughter Blanca is the most practical of all the female characters, considered by her family to be "the only normal person for many generations . . . a miracle of equilibrium and serenity" (123). Yet, even Blanca's stable life is marked by the tragedy of her forbidden love for the peasant Pedro Tercero. From their first meeting, Blanca and Pedro form an inseparable bond, forging their illicit love across class lines in an act that will have long-term ramifications. In early adolescence, they share a magical moment in the pasture of Tres Marías watching a mare give birth at dawn and, inspired by this vision, Blanca vows to marry

Pedro someday. The poor boy, knowing his place, denies her promise immediately. His insight proves prophetic when Esteban discovers the objectionable relationship and nearly murders Pedro for his insolence. Though the pregnant Blanca appears passive when she allows herself to be married off to the Count de Satigny, she demonstrates the iron will of her female forebears when, to protect her unborn child, she immediately abandons the comforts of his house to return in shame to her family. Blanca's decision to remain in the Trueba household, married yet restricted and without money of her own, suggests an unwillingness to subject her young daughter, or even herself, to the strictures of a penniless revolutionary's life. Even in later years when she might be free to follow her heart, Blanca chooses to live under her father's strict edicts rather than share Pedro's lower-class existence. Alba analyzes her mother's behavior, concluding that Blanca "had not gone with Pedro Tercero simply because she did not love him enough, for there was nothing in the Trueba house that he could not have given her" (237). This assessment is at least partially accurate, as Blanca lives like a poor servant in her father's home, wearing threadbare clothing and eating for pennies a day to avoid being humiliated by his charity. It finally takes a bloody revolution to drive Blanca back to the endangered Pedro's side. In an act of reconciliation toward his daughter and her lifelong love, Senator Trueba engineers their escape at the height of "the terrors" and the two live out old age as reunited expatriates.

Blanca's daughter Alba plays a central role as the narrative voice of the novel. Her character is shaped by dueling loyalties between an adoration of her psychic grandmother, an intense connection to her thwarted mother, an attraction to her unconventional uncles, and an intense devotion to her difficult grandfather. Growing up in such an eccentric household, Alba acquires a unique education due in part to her careful observation of the Trueba adults, as well as to her unlimited access to an extensive and eclectic family library. Like her female predecessors, Alba manages to circumvent the traditional Hispanic upbringing that might have prepared her for motherhood and household caretaking. Instead, she is left to herself as a small girl and later educated at a private British school to prepare for the university and a career. Maturing at a time of profound social change, Alba achieves the freedom her mother and grandmother could not. She attends the university where she is free to study philosophy and music. She engages in a torrid sexual affair with Miguel, Amanda's brother, without either realizing they have known each other in the past. Most importantly, Alba begins to join in the late-night conversations in cafés where the revolution among students is sparked. Although she joins the revolution primarily because of her devotion to Miguel rather than to any cause, Alba gradually develops a powerful political consciousness of her own, exemplified by her courage in aiding the poor and helping revolutionaries gain asylum, as well as by her stalwartness when subjected to physical and mental torture during imprisonment. These terrors prove vital to Alba's developing consciousness as an artist. As Susan de Carvalho notes, Alba only makes the transition from observer and storyteller to serious chronicler of her family's stories during this period (Carvalho 64). Visited by the ghost of her grandmother, who spurs Alba to give a voice to the crimes she has witnessed, Alba narrowly survives her torture through her devotion to writing. The final pages of the novel attest to Alba's commitment to bring her grandmother's words full circle and give the other women in her family a voice for their stories. Allende notes that when Alba picks up the pen, she defies the rules of patriarchy by returning to the collective memory of her ancestors, and "this book is the product of her writing, of her defying the rule" (Dölz-Blackburn 155).

The male characters in the novel demonstrate the narrow choice of masculine roles available in this early modern Latin culture. Esteban Trueba is characterized as a tyrannical patriarch whose impulses regularly spin out of control. Between fits of rage and sexually violent acts committed against peasant women, Esteban terrorizes both his family and his hacienda workers. Despite his many faults, Esteban is treated with some sympathy by the narrator, evidence of a loving granddaughter's attempts to understand him. Esteban himself has been a kind of victim, controlled by a sickly mother and sacrificial sister who manipulate his guilt feelings. When he escapes to Tres Marías, it is through a misguided belief that the land can protect him from downturns of fate. Even his "exaggerated love" for Clara is portrayed as obsessive and selfishly manipulative (111). Esteban's service in Congress exposes the function of the Conservative Party to nurture the divide between a wealthy upper class and the poverty-stricken masses. Only much later in the novel, after the *patrón* has mellowed from hardships, disappointments, and years of Clara's silence and then death, does Esteban show enough maturity to embrace Alba's emancipation and encourage her to write the family history.

The other male characters with parts in the Trueba drama act out the sociopolitical chaos inherent in the system. Esteban García can be viewed as his grandfather's evil double, a man driven by blind rage at life's injustices and a hunger for revenge. Fantasizing about grave misfortunes that might fell the whole clan and leave him with everything, Esteban García embodies the outrage of the peasant oppressed by the feudal existence of hacienda life and enslaved by a tyrannical *patrón*. Into adulthood, the younger Esteban curses the wealth of the legitimate Truebas and feels abused by their existence, a conviction that endures even during the dictatorship when circumstances place them all at his mercy. Believing that it is his illegitimacy alone that bars him from rightful ownership of the Trueba fortune, Esteban García finally unleashes this lifelong grudge against the family in physical and sexual violence against Alba. As the young Esteban embodies the dangerously channeled rage of the oppressed peasant, he also illustrates in microcosm the menacing side of the dictatorship and the very oppression that Pedro Tercero devotes his life to overturn.

Pedro Tercero, an example of more productively channeled outrage, represents the gradual awakening of political activism among the rural poor. A guitar-playing revolutionary modeled after the popular Chilean folksinger Victor Jara, Pedro typifies the ideals of the Socialist reform movement, working to mobilize a grassroots revolution that will free the peasantry from centuries of exploitation. Alba's lover Miguel characterizes a second force behind the revolution, the more privileged university students who demonstrate in public gatherings and march for change. Although these bourgeois resisters first seek action through methods of civil disobedience, they gradually embrace the ideology of the guerilla forces, who regard violence as a necessary result of full-fledged defiance against the regime. Ultimately, both sides prove their willingness to risk their lives for positive and permanent change.

Other minor characters serve to accentuate the disparities in this conservative, patriarchal culture between rich and poor, male and female, titled and nameless. For example, Esteban's sister Férula, once she has dutifully nursed her mother until her death, has no real place in society. As a powerless spinster in a male-dominated culture, she lives at the mercy of her brother until her personal obsession and his impossible temper drive them apart. The separation does not change Esteban's life, but it relegates his older sister to rapid aging in a disease-ridden tenement. Like Férula, the drug-addicted Amanda lives unprotected by a male provider and suffers the horror of an illegal abortion and a life of abject poverty. The hopeless situations of these women stand in contrast to the malleable opportunities of any titled male character. One example is the Count de Satigny, a dissipated pseudo-nobleman whose royal origins are highly questionable. Nevertheless, the society grants him utter freedom to marry, engage in dubious business practices, and enjoy an outlandish private life with few restrictions. He enjoys these privileges solely due to his status as a potentially wealthy male. Taken with the major characters in the novel, these figures present a society shaped by dangerous machismo and further marked by a precarious imbalance of power and wealth.

THEMES

The House of the Spirits comprises a number of sweeping themes, the most prominent being the affirmation of life even in the face of devastating political, personal, and social pressures. By the novel's close, events that have seemed inexplicable and menacing begin to reveal a fateful pattern that points to meaning within the apparent discord. At the root of this tentative harmony, Allende stresses the value of forgiveness. Alba's victory over death and hatred comes only when she absolves her enemies of their repellent crimes. That Alba, rather than her grandfather or uncles, extends this forgiveness is another important theme in a novel that foregrounds women and their integral place in an often repressive patriarchy. Linked to the subject of women is Allende's focus on family relationships as the foundation of a society that has become the victim of its own political missteps.

The importance of political power, its uses and abuses, cannot be understated in the novel. As she will in later works, Allende synthesizes fictional narrative with actual historical events to paint a picture of a country torn apart by a selfish social system and its narrow-minded leadership. By tracing the intractable politics of the conservative right through Esteban and the mounting malice of the military through Colonel García, Allende creates an interpretation of the historical drama in which public events are never divorced from personal responsibility. In fact, a key theme in the novel is the direct relationship between apparently fateful occurrences and the tangible human choices that have provoked them. Thus, it is not inconsistent for Allende to render Alba's fate as a tortured political prisoner as a direct consequence of not only her illegal harboring of revolutionaries but also her grandfather's promiscuity, her family's wealth, and her country's general mistreatment of the lower classes.

Defending herself against those critics who accuse her books of being too political, Allende explains, "The situation in our continent is so terrible—with the violence, the poverty, the inequality, the misery—that writers have necessarily assumed the voice of the people. What else can they write about?" (Brosnahan 164). Thus, Allende's saga meshes the historical and fictional to give voice to those people. In the most prominent instance, the grandmother Clara salvages the thoughts, words, and events that might have been lost to a silenced history. Writing copiously in her journals as if all daily events have equal historical importance, she never guesses that, decades later, her grandchild will use them to "reclaim the past" (3). When Alba suffers in solitary confinement at the novel's close and awaits her death, the grandmother comes to her as a ghost and urges her not to die, "since death [comes] anyway, but to survive, which would be a miracle" (351). Obeying Clara's command to write everything down and using the elder woman's massive writings as her source material, Alba begins to piece her family history together like a jigsaw puzzle and to see the harmony in each seemingly fortuitous or malevolent event.

Paired with this harmony is a theme of forgiveness that permeates the final chapters of the novel. After Clara's death, Esteban experiences spiritual visits from his wife and comes to believe that she has forgiven his violent outbursts and possessive behavior. As the political system deteriorates, Esteban and Pedro Tercero, once bitter enemies, find ways to protect each other—first, in Pedro's helping to free Esteban from captivity on his own hacienda, and then, in Esteban's act of reparation by securing safe-conduct passes for Pedro and Blanca to flee the country. It is at this point that Esteban first asks for his daughter's forgiveness and then embraces Pedro, releasing a lifetime of animosity between them. Likewise, Alba discovers that her writing gradually liberates her from a burning hatred toward Esteban García and, even though she does not forgive his wickedness, she begins to understand it. Even the baby in her womb, a probable result of García's multiple rapes, signals absolution, hope, and continuity for the Trueba family and its line of strong females.

Another central theme of *The House of the Spirits*, and one that sets it apart from novels by other Latin American writers, is its attention to the roles women play in shaping cultural and political realities. Describing Esteban as the "spinal column" of her novel, or the character at the center of the narrative action, Allende identifies the women's collective viewpoint as "the voice of emotion, . . . the voice of the soul, that is telling the underlying story" (Pinto 80). In her novel, Allende critiques the limitations that the traditional patriarchy sets on its women, and she celebrates the changes ushered in by feminist activism during the latter twentieth century. The central female character of each generation represents a different strength and a new way to overcome the confines of tradition. In Alba, Allende creates the culmination of such strengths, a young woman who stands against the conventions of her grandfather's world and gives voice to a new narrative with women's stories at its center. It is Alba who first recognizes that the women of the country harbor its promise for the future. Nurtured by her fellow prisoners in the concentration camp, Alba is struck by their uniform sense of justice balanced by infinite tenderness and charity. When she is rescued by the brave peasant woman the night she is released from prison, Alba affirms that the evil men controlling the country will never last forever with such fearless, kind-spirited women outnumbering them. While the novel closes before such a victory can be claimed, the reader is left with the distinct impression that the daughter in Alba's womb will be such a spirit, that the country will be saved by the next generation of women even stronger and more steadfast than Alba herself.

Directly related to her interest in women characters is Allende's attention to family relationships and the privileged place kinship holds in most Latin cultures. In *The House of the Spirits,* the importance of family is underscored by the complex associations among parents, siblings, and extended relations. Commitment to family is a recurring theme as characters are rewarded or punished for their treatment of their kin. Esteban's choice to distance himself from his mother and then abandon his sister to the streets results in his own isolation and rejection from nearly every other relation in his life. In a similar way, Esteban ignores the children born of his licentious bachelorhood, never realizing that his indifference will cost him inordinate pain and suffering decades later. Taken as a whole, Esteban's selfish removal from family life causes a series of tragedies to befall the Trueba clan. In contrast, Clara is so carefully attuned to her family members that she can foresee the deaths of her sister and parents and the births of all her children. Clara's expansive generosity toward her sister-in-law affords her Férula's loving friendship that lasts beyond the grave. Likewise, Alba's steadfast devotion to her elders, especially her intractable grandfather, prompts her protection by loved ones and family spirits during the trials of the dictatorship. The close of the novel, with its emphasis on forgiveness and survival, suggests that family ties are a powerful antidote to the human failings of greed, oppression, and violence—and in Allende's universe, perhaps the only remedy to such inevitable flaws.

HISTORICAL BACKGROUND

Although *The House of the Spirits* takes place in an unnamed South American nation, the setting for the story is unquestionably Allende's homeland of Chile. Just as the tribulations of the Trueba family echo those of Allende's own family, historical and political events presented in the novel closely mirror the state of Chile during the first three-quarters of the twentieth century. Like many of its neighboring countries, Chile was colonized by Spain in the sixteenth century, and a great majority of its indigenous peoples were felled by disease and war in the years that followed. Most of the surviving Amerindians resulted from interbreeding with Spanish settlers, a practice that gave rise to a mixed race called *mestizos*. Much of the peasant population in contemporary Chile is categorized as *mestizo*, while the upper class historically has considered itself a "purer" Spanish line, though in truth nearly all Chileans today can trace their roots to both Spanish and Indian ancestry (Collier and Sater 5–9).

Chile remained a Spanish colony until 1818 when it declared independence and gradually began to industrialize. At the beginning of the twentieth century, the country was run by a democratically elected government but largely controlled by a powerful oligarchy—a small group of rich families of Spanish descent who made their fortunes in mining and agriculture, just as Esteban Trueba does in the novel. It was common for these families to own huge pieces of land, some spanning thousands of acres, which were called haciendas. The South American equivalent of a plantation, haciendas employed *mestizo* peasants who lived on the land and worked the fields in a semi-feudal arrangement that promoted exploitation of the lowest classes. The landowners lived in the major cities, such as the capital of Santiago, hiring overseers to manage their property and living off the wealth generated from the land. These *patróns* supported the democratic process through the major conservative political parties and often coerced the peasants on their land to vote for a particular candidate, thus ensuring maintenance of the lucrative status quo.

As the gap between rich and poor widened in Chile, the underclass grew more impatient for change. In 1969, a left-wing alliance of socialists, communists, and radicals united to form a new political party, the *Un-*

idad Popular. They named Salvador Allende, Isabel Allende's godfather and second cousin (often respectfully referred to as her "uncle"), as their candidate for president. Allende had already run for president three times on the socialist platform and lost. This time, however, he defied conservative expectations and won, becoming the first democratically elected left-wing leader in Chile and, in fact, all of Latin America. When Allende took office, there was widespread concern in the international community over the dangers of a marxist leader in South America, and support for his ouster came from many democratic countries, including the United States. Likewise, the Conservative Party within Chile worked behind the scenes to undermine Allende's work. Though his government nationalized many public services and turned thousands of haciendas into cooperatives, the peasants were not satisfied with the arrangements, particularly as a widespread food shortage and economic depression gripped the country. In 1973, the military staged a violent coup against President Allende that cost him his life and brought the dictator Pinochet to power for a seventeen-year reign that would prove to be the bloodiest of Chile's modern history. It is with the early years of this chaotic period that Allende closes her novel.

ALTERNATIVE PERSPECTIVE: FEMINIST CRITICISM

Feminist literary scholars read fiction through the lens of gender issues and sexual politics. That is, they attempt to understand how women writers through the ages have addressed the social conventions and male-female interactions that control their art and lives. Interested not only in writings authored by women, feminist critics examine the ways women are characterized in literature written by both sexes. Such critics hope to elucidate the dominant stereotypes that circumscribe women's roles and direct attention to the cultural patterns that proliferate regarding the position of women in society. Feminist critic Sandra M. Gilbert notes that every text "can be seen as in some sense a political gesture and more specifically as a gesture determined by a complex of assumptions about male-female relations, assumptions we might call sexual poetics" (31). In order to map the dominant characteristics of gender interpretation in literature, feminist critics notice in particular the ways in which authors reflect, critique, or overturn common assumptions about gender roles or mythologies regarding either sex. In *The House of the Spirits,* Allende could be said to do all of these in her portrayal of a traditional South American family and her critique of the machismo attitudes that dominate the lives of its members, both male and female. The word machismo refers to a masculine code of behavior that is common in Latin American cultures. A male who is labeled "macho" is usually seen as the supreme authority in his household and may behave chauvinistically toward women. (See chapter 2 to learn more about how Allende's characters exhibit and act out against the machismo culture of Latin America.) Indeed, Allende has received much attention from feminist scholars who notice a departure from other major Latin American writers in her primary focus on female characters and her explicit critique of the patriarchal society that circumscribes them.

As discussed above, roles for women are revealed as narrow and constricting in this traditional Latin culture. When Esteban imagines the appropriate wife he might marry, he compares this image against the most extreme example he has witnessed—the feminist suffragette, Nívea del Valle. Remembering her marching for women's rights to vote and attend the university, Esteban exclaims that she is "sick in the head" and forgetting the woman's proper duty of "motherhood and the home" (58). When Nívea's daughter Clara begins similar educational campaigns among the women of Tres Marías, Esteban throws a tantrum, reminding her that he isn't "some ninny whose wife could go around making a fool of him" (92). Esteban speaks for an entire class and generation of Latin patriarchs whose women were to handle domestic affairs and raise the children, dabbling in spiritual matters if interested but staying out of politics and public life.

Ironically, in Allende's interpretation of this South American country's downward spiral, a central source of the disorder can be traced to the absence of women in shaping the country's destiny and to the tenacious power of machismo in directing male behavior. Allende has commented in an interview that "machismo and sexism harm both women and men" in keeping both sexes from living the fullest possible lives (Gautier 137). In *The House of the Spirits*, the ideology of a virile, aggressive masculinity so grips the central male characters that they become blind to the consequences of their contemptible behavior. Esteban never questions his right to rape the peasant women on his land. Taking a fifteen-year-old girl by force, he discovers too late that she is a virgin, but "neither Pancha's humble origin nor the pressing demands of his desire allowed him to reconsider" (50). When the result of his violation begins to show, Esteban feels repulsed by Pancha, seeing her as "an enormous container that held a formless, gelatinous mass" (54) that he cannot imagine as his own child. Esteban's conquests reach mythic proportions until he has bedded every adolescent girl on Tres Marías and the outer regions with no thought to his illegitimate children or their exploited mothers. In later years, Esteban sees no relationship between his abuses and either the failure of his marriage or the exploits of his male offspring.

Nicolás's neglected girlfriend Amanda undergoes a dangerous illegal abortion when her lover, like his father before him, is unable to take responsibility for his behavior. Alba is subjected to Esteban García's sexual predation on three occasions. First, as a six-year-old, she is tricked into his lap and fondled. Then, on her fourteenth birthday, Alba is forced to endure García's violent kiss that nearly turns to strangulation. Finally, when Alba becomes a political prisoner, García exacts his long-awaited revenge by repeatedly raping and physically abusing his helpless cousin. Like his grandfather, Esteban García demonstrates his masculinity through sexual conquest, and sex itself becomes a violent weapon in his arsenal. Even Alba's three lost fingers parallel Esteban's mutilation of Pedro Tercero's hand for the affront of sleeping with Blanca. In short, each violent act against a Trueba woman can be traced back to the machismo culture that transforms women into sex objects and upholds revenge as the ultimate masculine act. Likewise, the bloodbath of the military coup and subsequent terrorism against the country's citizens can be read as an act of male aggression against "softer" elements like the unnamed socialist president, a rape of the countryside that mirrors both the elder and younger Estebans' violations against defenseless women.

For all their eccentricities, the Trueba women live very limited existences within this machismo culture with its strict gender roles. While they are not victims, per se, they are each at different times victimized by the husbands, fathers, and military leaders that control their lives. With few outlets for frustration or outrage available to them, these women retreat most often into silence to express their disappointment or pain. Clara is the first to use this means of retreat. After seeing her eldest sister Rosa's corpse subjected to an autopsy and sexual caresses by an assistant mortician, Clara, "feeling within her the silence of the entire world" (35), decides not to speak again for nine years. During pregnancy or times of difficulty, Clara regularly reverts to periods of withdrawal and speechlessness. In these years, Esteban is patient with her reticence, commenting that he "had come to understand that silence was [his] wife's last refuge" (97). When Esteban loses his head and beats her the evening of Blanca's humiliation, however, Clara uses the withdrawal of speech as her only source of control and power. She does not speak to Esteban again for their entire life together, taking off her wedding ring and moving to another room. This emphatic withdrawal of words and affection is her only weapon in a culture that will allow her neither divorce nor legal protection.

Blanca uses a similar strategy when her tryst with Pedro Tercero is exposed. As her father beats her and threatens to kill her, Blanca sobs that she will never tell the name of her lover. Later, when her pregnancy can no longer be hidden, Blanca again refuses to reveal the name of the father. In declining to participate in these betrayals, Blanca fights the macho code of honor and revenge. Years later, her daughter Alba uses the same strategy during torture at the hands of Esteban García. Never revealing the whereabouts of Miguel, who has joined the guerrillas, Alba answers García's queries always with the same response, "I want to go to the bathroom" (346). In a culture that does not value them as whole persons, these women have learned that silence, in particular the withdrawal of words that another has demanded, can send a more formidable message.

That is not to say, however, that these women are rendered utterly speechless. Clara's hundreds of notebooks, Blanca's letters to her mother, and Alba's precise memory together tell the story of their combined fates. It is not a silenced story, but neither is it one that requires further retribution. Breaking the chain of revenge that characterizes the males in the novel, Alba frees herself from rage by accepting that García's behavior corresponds to a "fate laid down before [Alba's] birth" when the elder Esteban first forced Pancha to the ground. In embracing the child within her and picking up a pen to write the Trueba story, Alba separates herself from a masculine interpretation of the past and a need to blame, instead using the book to "reclaim the past and overcome terrors of [her] own" (368). The novel itself can be read as a victory for the Trueba women as it allows them, for the first time, a public voice with which to speak aloud the pain that male aggression has wrought.

4

Of Love and Shadows
(1987)

With her debut novel *The House of the Spirits* garnering numerous awards and worldwide critical acclaim, Isabel Allende had both an eager readership to gratify and a challenging precedent to meet with her much-anticipated second book *Of Love and Shadows*. In this novel, Allende adopts the journalistic tone that characterizes the final section of *The House of the Spirits*, beginning approximately five years after the military coup and aftermath with which the first novel ends. In illustrating the full impact of life under a totalitarian regime, Allende attempts a most difficult balance in *Of Love and Shadows*, that is, to blend the malevolence of an all-powerful dictatorship with the sublimity of true love. By some critical accounts, the book is only partially successful, periodically capitulating to a passionate sentimentality that does not ring true when juxtaposed with gruesome acts of unchecked cruelty. Nevertheless, *Of Love and Shadows* achieved bestseller status in Western Europe and Latin America, and enjoyed an exceptionally warm reception by Chilean readers. Admirers of the novel cite its compassionate documentation of historical injustices and its offer of hope in the face of desolate circumstances. In 1994, the novel was made into a movie starring Jennifer Connelly and Antonio Banderas, and the book remains in print as an important contribution to the historical and political fiction of Latin America.

The plotline of the novel is inspired from real events, primarily journalistic accounts taken from magazines, newspapers, and unpublished interviews that Allende gleaned during her pre-exile years as a journalist in Chile and then later as a writer and researcher in her new home in Venezuela. Like Allende herself, the protagonist Irene Beltrán works as a journalist in an unnamed country that bears a striking resemblance to Allende's Chilean homeland. Irene's position as writer for a women's magazine affords her opportunities to witness the true oppression and poverty gripping the country, a view hidden from most of her upper-class counterparts who prefer to cloister themselves in a well-guarded world of private clubs, swimming pools, and fancy restaurants. At the center of the story is Irene's discovery of a secret grave, the hidden burial site of a number of villagers who have been massacred by the military police. In developing this part of the narrative, Allende depends heavily on newspaper coverage of an actual disclosure involving the remains of assassinated peasants concealed in an abandoned mine in Chile. With such grim subject matter anchoring the plot, the book is often categorized as a "protest" novel, written with political intent as a means to object to officially permitted atrocities.

In truth, Allende had planned to write *Of Love and Shadows* as a testimony to those Chileans most victimized by the military coup, including the families of the disappeared, the persecuted and tortured, and the unemployed and hungry. Here, she wished to be as historically accurate as possible, with portions of the novel almost literal repetitions of court reports from the military and witnesses at the Lonquén trial that served as her model (Moody, "On Shadows" 52). However, as Allende began to interview participants she discovered that this was "not only a story of violence, but that it was mostly a story of love and solidarity" (Invernizzi and Pope 123). As a tribute to this significant paradox, Allende counters the ugly acts of the dictatorship with an ageless narrative of true love, paralleling the discovery in the mine with Irene's personal discovery of genuine companionship with a man from another class. In this way, Allende asserts what she found to be true in her research for the novel, that "in contrast to extreme violence there is also extreme love" (Moody, "On Shadows" 53). In blending the fictionalized love story with the documentary-style historical retelling, Allende's novel is a clear example of how she prefers to write: "I take something from real life, something from the papers, things I know, interviews I do, and I add fiction to it (Pinto 83). In *Of Love and Shadows*, as in Allende's other works, this proves an excellent recipe for producing an engaging tale.

PLOT

Of Love and Shadows is a compact narrative, taking place over a period of about six weeks and encompassing the lives of a small group of characters. The opening chapter of the novel introduces these central players, members of three strikingly different families in South American society. The first is Irene Beltrán, who lives with her mother, Beatriz, and their longtime servant, Rosa, on the top floor of the family mansion. Members of the upper class, the Beltráns have been reduced to impoverished circumstances aggravated both by Irene's father's mysterious disappearance four years earlier and by the military coup that has sent the country into economic turmoil. In order to maintain something like their previous lifestyle, Beatriz has transformed the bottom floor of the home into a nursing facility for the elderly. Dubbed "The Will of God Manor," the home provides a meager income to keep the Beltrán women in relative comfort. Irene adds to their income by working as a journalist for a women's magazine as she waits to be married to her fiancé, Army Captain Gustavo Morante.

Next, the narrative turns to the Ranquileo family—Digna, her husband, Hipólito, and their brood of children born over more than twenty years of marriage. Unlike the temporarily insolvent upper-class Beltráns, the Ranquileos are poor peasant farmers who own little else than the small plot of land that they till. Thus, they have survived relatively unscathed both the fall of the government and the collapse of the Agrarian Reform that followed it. Hipólito spends half the year working as a clown in a traveling circus, while Digna manages the household and farm. Along with their numerous children and their illegitimate grandson, Jacinto, whom they are raising as their own, the Ranquileos also shelter an unusual child, Evangelina. Switched, through a series of mishaps, with their real daughter at birth, the blond and fragile Evangelina grows up in their household. She is aware of her blood relatives, the neighboring Floreses, and the other Evangelina, whose place she has supplanted. At the story's opening, the fifteen-year-old Evangelina has been struck with a strange ailment that has caused her to have epileptic-like seizures, which have occurred daily at the stroke of noon for the last five weeks. Visitors have begun to gather each day to witness the trance "in hopes of being benefited by some minor miracle" (36).

The third family to be introduced is headed by a political exile from Spain, Professor Leal, who fled with his young wife, Hilda, during the Spanish Civil War almost forty years earlier and has taken permanent refuge in South America. Just as their name means "loyal" in Spanish, these middle-aged expatriates are faithful—to each other, to their family, and to their political beliefs. Within a middle-class circle of intellectuals, they have raised three boys and have continued their political activism. Professor Leal, all the while, threatens to return to Spain when democracy reigns there again. The dictatorship in his adopted country has since stripped him of his teaching duties, but he continues to print illegal pamphlets off the printing press in his kitchen until his worried sons remove it. The eldest son, Javier, is a blacklisted biologist whose associations, including his father's status as an "undesirable," make it impossible for him to support his wife and children (24). After a year of unemployment, Javier has become increasingly dejected, and has recently taken to methodically making knots in rope for hours on end. The middle son, José, to his communist father's horror, has become a priest and spends his days serving the poor and making extra money as a plumber. The last child, and Hilda's favorite, Francisco, is a psychologist who has been suspended like his father from the university and unable to find work in the poverty-stricken country. He earns money as a photojournalist, traveling with Irene on nearly all her stories and supplying the photos to accompany them. On his free days, he helps smuggle endangered political refugees out of the country and works in the free clinic organized by his older brother, attempting to assuage the misery of the working-class poor.

The first section of the novel, called "Another Spring," invites the reader into a world terrorized by a dictatorship but also filled with modest moments of everyday pleasure. On the day that opens the novel, Francisco is to accompany Irene to the Ranquileo home to view one of Evangelina's celebrated trances. In an effort to cure her daughter, Digna has already taken Evangelina to see the local folk healer *don* Simón, the medical doctor at Los Riscos Hospital, and the midwife Mamita Encarnación, all to no effect. Gradually, pilgrims from local villages have begun attending the daily spectacle, believing that Evangelina's suffering may be a sign of sainthood. The gathering witnessed by Irene and Francisco includes the usual pilgrims, as well as the local priest, Father Cirilo, and the minister of Digna's Protestant congregation. Evangelina's trance disfigures her face and body, while at the same time her bed and other furniture in the house begin to shake and move unaccountably. In the middle of the seizure, Army trucks arrive and invade the building, ostensibly at the wish of Evangelina's brother, Pradelio Ranquileo, whose superior, Lieutenant Juan de Dios Ramírez, hopes to frighten the girl out of her trance. Instead, Evangelina strikes the lieutenant and carries him out to the courtyard where she unceremoniously dumps him in front of the astounded onlookers. Though the villagers fear the worst, Lieutenant Ramírez orders the other soldiers back into their vehicles and speeds away.

In Part II, "Shadows," a week has passed since the visit to the Ranquileo farmhouse. Francisco has not seen much of Irene since then, as he has been busy shooting a fashion layout for the magazine within the capital city's military compound. Mario, the famous hairstylist overseeing the models, gradually becomes attracted to Francisco, in part because the gentle photographer takes Mario's side against Captain Morante's public sneers regarding homosexuality. During an evening in which Mario expresses his growing love for Francisco and the photographer sensitively explains his desire for deep friendship only, the two men grow closer and ultimately disclose their mutual hatred of the dictatorship. Based on this political solidarity, they develop a fast friendship and work together on subversive activities to oppose the government. The men keep their covert operations a secret from Irene, as they feel her class, upbringing, and engagement to a military captain recommend such discretion. Nonetheless, when she meets the Leal family for a meal that weekend, Irene is fascinated by Professor Leal's discourse on the virtues of anarchy and the misguided evils of nationalism, a perspective utterly foreign to her world. In like manner, the entire family is enraptured by Irene's ingenuous nature, and later Hilda urges Francisco to find a way to marry her.

The novel briefly flashes back to Captain Morante's return from the Antarctic where he has lived for twelve secluded months, guarding the country's outpost there and earning six times his regular pay. Now, with enough money to give Irene the home and luxuries in which she shows no interest, the captain joins Beatriz in preparations for a lavish wedding. Francisco burns with jealousy as Morante and Irene sneak away for amorous meetings in secluded hotels. When the Captain is restationed to Panama, Francisco and Irene resume their daily companionship. One evening, they mistakenly work past curfew and have to spend the night at the office, sleeping together on a lavatory couch. That night, while Irene lies sleeping, Francisco wrestles with the competing emotions that urge him to confess his affection for a woman from the "other side of the fence" and compel his silence since she is upper class and already engaged (102).

When Irene and Francisco return to the Ranquileo home to witness a hog butchering the following week, Irene creates a stir by fainting in the middle of the ritual, her reaction to the murderous horrors signaling the end of her innocence. At the close of the day, Irene realizes she has not seen Evangelina and urges Digna to explain the girl's absence. Digna reveals that Lieutenant Ramírez, accompanied by his underling, Sergeant Faustino Rivera, had returned to the house the night of his embarrassment and taken Evangelina by force. When the parents inquired about her the next day at headquarters, they were told she would be released shortly. That is the last they have heard of her or their son Pradelio, whom the military assures them has been transferred to another unit. After five days of fruitless searching, Digna has already gone to the Floreses to apologize for their child's misfortune. Irene and Francisco determine to discover Evangelina's whereabouts, visiting police buildings, detention centers, and hospitals. They elicit the help of Francisco's brother, José, who has access to many closed areas due to his contacts as a priest, and he gets them into the morgue. There, Irene witnesses firsthand the naked, brutalized bodies of men and women who have been tortured by the regime. When she leaves the morgue, Irene feels that she has been irreparably changed.

Frightened by the alteration in Irene, Francisco takes her to the beautiful park at the city's center, a secluded place they call the Hill. There he kisses her for the first time. When Irene answers that kiss with the words that she must marry the man who has waited all his life for her, Francisco simply tells her he does not believe it. Four days later, Francisco's brother, Javier, hangs himself in a children's park. Frustrated by his inability to find work and support his family, he finally capitulates to the rope he has been obsessively toying with for weeks. Immediately, his widowed wife takes the grandchildren and moves back to her own family in another part of the country. The elder Leals are left without son or grandchildren. For four days they sit in stunned silence, refusing food and sleeping only briefly. At last they decide to embrace life again, and the family gradually begins to heal.

Meanwhile, Irene continues the search for Evangelina alone. Learning little from a confrontation with Lieutenant Ramírez, Irene surreptitiously tapes her conversation with his subordinate, Sergeant Rivera, during a fortuitous meeting. As Sergeant Rivera gradually becomes drunk, he tells Irene all about the lieutenant, how he shook at his first execution, how he felt revulsion at his first torture sessions, and how he eventually hardened when his powerful position corrupted him. Irene gets all of it secretly on tape. At the same time, she and Francisco are visited one evening by Digna who has come for help in getting her son Pradelio out of the country. He has gone into hiding since his sister's disappearance, a desertion punishable by death. Pradelio refuses to explain the "mission" that has prompted his flight, but he has plans to hide in the mountains until the summer weather allows him to escape the country. In the meantime, Lieutenant Ramírez has combed the entire village, and Sergeant Faustino Rivera has visited Digna in secret to warn her that the mountains will be searched as well. At the same time, Sergeant Rivera reveals to Digna more about the night Evangelina disappeared, including the sight of Lieutenant Ramírez carrying her limp body to a jeep and driving away with a pick and shovel.

Irene and Francisco agree to help Pradelio all they can. Led by Jacinto into the mountains, they discover the eldest brother living a wild existence on the uppermost cliffs as he awaits his opportunity for revenge. At this point, Pradelio explains his incestuous love for his "sister," his crazed weeks spent in solitary confinement after the military debacle at the Ranquileo farm, his secret release by Sergeant Rivera, and his present need to avenge Evangelina's murder. He also reveals that he knows a military secret that he cannot divulge but that will cost him his life when he is caught. At the end of the meeting, Pradelio also blurts out that he believes his sister's body has been buried in the abandoned mine in Los Riscos, the clue that Francisco has been waiting for.

This section of the novel ends with the paradoxical image of the suntanned and beautifully coifed Beatriz returning from her biannual tropical rendezvous with her young lover Michel. The narcissistic mother reacts with uncertainty to Irene's new aura of sadness and the young woman's vague insinuations that her upcoming wedding may be off. Irene has planned a beautiful homecoming party for her mother at The Will of God Manor with gifts, cake, and a special performance by an aging actress who resides there. Even Francisco is moved by the performance and the sad realities that the diaspora has wrought in a country where children used to take care of their aged parents until death claimed them.

Part III, "Sweet Land," opens with Irene and Francisco visiting the Los Riscos mine under cover of darkness. There they make the grisly discovery of Evangelina's decomposing body. Seeking refuge from the horror in an abandoned hut nearby, the two finally relent to their growing devotion and make love until morning. After telling Digna about their discovery and attempting unsuccessfully to warn Pradelio, Francisco and Irene return to the mine to uncover more bodies and take photographs.

These Francisco develops and takes to his brother, José, who can deliver them to the Cardinal. The Cardinal gathers an envoy of protected officials and journalists to view the mass grave. Using his religious position as leverage, he then insists that the bodies be removed and the public informed. The revelation of the Los Riscos atrocity leads to a public outcry and street demonstrations, as even relatives are barred from seeing the bodies of the *desaparecidos* (the "disappeared" who have been taken into police custody and never heard from again).

In the meantime, Captain Morante returns to settle on a wedding date with Irene. She calmly explains that she can no longer marry him, as she loves someone else. Though Rosa disapproves of Irene's impetuosity in chasing after a penniless photographer, she does not respond with the same rancor as Beatriz because she sees how happy Irene is. Free of this commitment, Irene continues to pursue justice for Evangelina. She meets again with Sergeant Rivera, who recounts the night Lieutenant Ramírez abused and killed the girl. Rivera has kept all the details in a notebook that he carries tucked inside his shirt. The night after this second interview, Rivera is run over by an unidentified vehicle and the notebook that includes Irene's full name is never recovered.

Irene goes to visit the Floreses, whose men were killed or "disappeared" as punishment for participating in a farming cooperative. She finds the other Evangelina willing to talk, hoping the bodies in the mine will solve the mystery of her missing father and brothers. Evangelina Flores explains the brutality with which, five years before, her family members—men not even involved in politics but simply members of the Farmers Union—had been taken. She is able to finger Lieutenant Ramírez and his men as the culprits. The next morning, thirty hours after Rivera's murder, an attempt is made on Irene's life. Sprayed in the abdomen with bullets from an automatic weapon, Irene lies in intensive care between life and death, while Francisco and Beatriz suffer in the hallway. Beatriz does not believe her daughter could have been a political target, and Francisco prefers not to reveal the truth to the naïve Beatriz during her moment of grief. Instead, they spend the hours speaking of Irene and, with the arrival of morning, have reached a peace because they share a common love for her.

Irene is eventually removed from the respirator and begins to recover slowly. Captain Morante comes to see her and to learn why the police have ransacked her home. While she lay in a coma, the secret police searched the family mansion, killed the dog, and broke several of Rosa's ribs. Francisco tells Morante everything from finding the bodies in the mine to political abuses that include torture and murder and economic injustices that favor the rich. It is a revelation to this upright military commander that corruption is everywhere. Morante spends a while by his love's bedside, silently reproaching her for her lack of trust in him. Then he warns Francisco to get her away from the capital before the killers return to complete their mission. The only path for Francisco is to help Irene recover as quickly as possible. He stays by her side all day and sleeps next to her at night. At the same time, Mario begins working on an escape plan that will get Irene past the undercover agents who loiter at the door of the hospital.

As a result of pressure exerted by the Cardinal, Lieutenant Ramírez is ultimately brought up for trial, along with some of his men. He fabricates a story about mysterious gunfire from rebel forces that killed the Floreses and other farmers during a routine interrogation that left the lieutenant's men miraculously unharmed. Though the tale is met with incredulity, the cowardly judge transfers it to a military court to avoid entanglements. As Irene begins to lose hope that the men will be brought to justice, she sends Francisco back to The Will of God Manor to collect the tapes of her conversations with Sergeant Rivera. Acting on impulse and wishing to give purpose to an elderly friend's life, Irene had, weeks before, asked the aging actress to hide the tapes for her. Irene instructs Francisco to turn over the evidence to the Cardinal, but first they contact Mario to help them escape that very night.

Using the tricks of his trade, Mario thoroughly disguises the couple until they cannot recognize "themselves or one another beneath their masks" (253). Then they walk easily out of the clinic and past the secret police to Mario's waiting car, where he drives them to his apartment to hide out until Irene has healed enough to travel. Mario visits Beatriz to explain Irene's disappearance, but seeing that she is incapable of comprehending the truth, Mario pretends that the couple has left on a brief vacation. In contrast, when Rosa pulls him into the kitchen to get the facts, Mario sees a woman who can accept the realities of life in a dictatorship and admits that the couple is fleeing. Rosa gives him a packet of soil from the garden for Irene to carry with her into exile.

At the same time, Evangelina Flores receives José Leal's help to enter the Department of Criminal Investigation and identify the remains of her family members. Without fear, she testifies in court against Lieutenant Ramírez and his men. Then José helps her to escape the country. The narrative explains that, once safe, Evangelina becomes a voice for the *desaparecidos*, bearing witness around the world of the corruption within the dictatorship. The Cardinal agrees to hold Irene's tapes for a week, until she can also leave the country safely. Then his people distribute copies of the tapes to international journalists, and the General becomes an object of ridicule outside his country. Pressured by this turn of events, the military court declares Lieutenant Ramírez and his men guilty of murder but then releases them hours later and grants them amnesty. The public outcry, though tremendous, does nothing to sway the result, and Ramírez is promoted to captain. The only blight in his life is the rumor that Pradelio is still alive and lurking in wait to avenge his sister's murder.

Captain Morante, thoroughly disillusioned by the corruption revealed through the mine incident, gathers a group together to overthrow the General. Regrettably, his plan is discovered and he survives only seventy-two hours after his arrest. With Irene's safety in serious question, Mario organizes a small dinner party of the remaining Leals to say goodbye to Francisco and Irene. During the meal, Hilda recommends that the young people seek out the abandoned family home in Teruel, Spain. Following the tangled routes that Francisco has prepared for others before himself, Irene and Francisco finally escape the capital and head by car to a mountain hotel where a guide will meet them to escort them to the border. The guide arrives with the bad news that the manager at one of their hotel stops has reported them. Leaving immediately, they are accompanied nearly to the border. When the guide turns back, Francisco and Irene proceed to the marker he has pointed out to them, toward the border where another "friend" will be waiting, and toward their future— promising each other that someday "we will return" (274).

CHARACTER DEVELOPMENT

In developing the political critique that characterizes *Of Love and Shadows*, Allende draws clear lines between the heroes and villains who people this South American country. The protagonist, Irene, despite her bourgeois upbringing and naïve political views, is a thoroughly good person with a magnanimous nature. Her generous character is apparent from the opening pages, when she deliberately enters her home from the garden in order to greet the elderly residents of The Will of God Manor. That she is a unique and charitable person, despite her lofty birth, is best demonstrated in her treatment of all types of people. Whereas Francisco gets a chilly welcome from Beatriz, who finds the intelligentsia distaste-

ful, Irene sincerely and openly embraces the Leal family, the simple Ranquileos, and all others who cross her path. When she arrives at the
Ranquileo farmhouse to witness Evangelina's miracles, Irene immediately melts into the household, placating the animals, serving refresh-
ments, and holding herself with the "freedom and confidence of someone
born there" (64). She writes pretend letters and mails them to a lonely
occupant of her mother's nursing facility. For the aging actress, Irene
plays the part of devoted granddaughter, even promising the old woman
that should she become helpless, Irene will help her to die (133). In every
way, Irene is the faultless heroine, loving her fellow citizens and giving
of herself freely. The single characteristic about which Irene feels
ashamed is the abject terror she experiences during her flight from the
country. In interviews, Allende has described this same fear in herself:
"I know how cowardly I am. I know terror. It changes people" (Moody,
"On Shadows" 57). The character Irene is paralyzed in much the same
way, living with a sickening fear that threatens to annihilate her and
breaking out into hives like her author did in the final months before
Allende herself fled Chile. This singular flaw hardly blemishes Irene's
pure character, however, but rather humanizes her as one who, in the
end, fears death as anyone might. Allende has said that Irene is less a
self-portrait than a tribute to three journalists whom she knew in Chile,
women who fearlessly investigated the dictatorship at the risk of their
own lives (Moody, "On Shadows" 52).

Irene's counterpart, the well-educated yet penniless Francisco, is a paradoxical character made up of his mother's gentle sympathy for humanity coupled with his father's resolute political feelings. Escaping with a
young band of guerrillas at sixteen, Francisco gets his first and last taste
of military life, preferring the intellectual world his parents inhabit. He
is a quiet academic with the unassuming air of a psychologist who appears uninitiated into the darker side of life. Yet, when faced with the
atrocities perpetuated by the dictatorship, Francisco's just character urges
him to fight back. Thus, with his more fiery-tempered brother José, Francisco takes a dangerous part in the opposition, helping fugitives reach
safety, photographing secret police files, and documenting known tor-
turers. His is a generous portrait of a man barred from pursuing his
chosen career but who learns to accept his fate and serve his beliefs from
the position in which he has been placed. Like the faultless Irene, Francisco commits no blunders in this novel. When Mario makes suggestive
overtures, Francisco finds the gentlest way to reveal his true nature and
still develop a fast friendship with the lovelorn admirer. Spending the

night on a couch and embracing the sleeping Irene, Francisco controls his desire and waits for her to choose her future. Like Irene, Francisco has a naturally kind temperament that treats the elderly inmates of The Will of God Manor with as much respect as he affords to Irene's insufferable mother, Beatriz. Later, when Irene lies helpless in the hospital, Francisco nurses her back to health with the most tender and devoted care. In the end, with characteristic heroism, Francisco risks his life for his true love and gives up family and homeland to stay by her side.

Counter to the liberal-minded hero Francisco, the military figures in the book range from misguided to malevolent. Lieutenant Ramírez oftentimes seems like a caricature, the evil soldier looming wickedly at the center of the Los Riscos massacre. With an impulsive nature, acute temper, and limitless power, the lieutenant epitomizes the amorality that infects the dictatorship. His abuse of Evangelina, blatant lies at the mockery of a trial, and subsequent promotion only magnify the corruption. Irene's cousin, Captain Gustavo Morante, on the other hand, is at fault not for his vice but for his blindness to it in others. Morante is a man in ultimate control over his emotions, his sexual urges, and his personal preferences—a well-trained soldier in every sense. Strong, highly disciplined, and so handsome that he silences the typewriters when he arrives at Irene's office, Morante should be the heroine's perfect partner—except that she evolves into a revolutionary and he is tied explicitly to the other side. Yet, Morante does deeply love Irene, or at least he feels bound to her after a lifetime of childhood dreams and adult intimacies. When Irene lies near death from bullet wounds, Morante's sincerity is revealed. He silently reproaches her for not trusting him, for not believing he has remained an honorable soldier unsullied by torture and illegal acts. He stands by her motionless figure and asserts that he is not alone in his nobility, that there are many men like him ready to die for justice. While Morante's about-face so near the end of the novel does little to absolve the military of its sullied picture, Allende has made an important point in developing characters who are not easily pigeon-holed. Not only Morante, but also Pradelio and Sergeant Rivera are men of character who, while they might obey orders and even participate in sordid acts, ultimately rise above those choices to disobey their superiors.

A proud combatant like Captain Morante, Pradelio enjoys the respect he gains in his military uniform. But as if he were Morante's military foil, the eldest Ranquileo does not have the steely nerves and unwavering self-control of the perfect soldier. Instead, Pradelio is a troubled figure, haunted by an intense and forbidden love he has harbored for Evangelina throughout their childhood. His incestuous feelings drive him mad with guilt and ultimately push him to leave the family home. In the military, Pradelio excels at the dirty business of keeping civilians in line in a dictatorship. He learns to "keep his mouth shut and follow orders," preferring to place the blame on other shoulders (159). However, his ragged fingernails and nervous demeanor betray the uncertainty under his bravado. Unlike Morante, who believes wholeheartedly in the regime until the end, Pradelio reveals the same vague doubts that prompt Sergeant Rivera to keep his careful notebook and blatantly disobey orders to protect his friends. Sergeant Rivera is the most heroic of the novel's military men, risking his life—and ultimately losing it—to see Pradelio freed, Evangelina avenged, and justice done. Yet, the sergeant is a naïve character who seems to comprehend neither the full impact of Lieutenant Ramírez's crime nor the full danger he himself runs in speaking openly with Irene and carrying around the incriminating journal.

The matriarchs of the book, while they play minor roles in the plot, together embody a variety of responses to the tragedy of the *desapareci-dos*. Beatriz Alcántara de Beltrán, though born into the middle class, possesses sensibilities that are purely high society. As a social climber with limited resources, she has used her looks and charms to gain the aristocratic Eusebio's temporary infatuation and subsequent marriage proposal. Yet, her machinations have also engineered Beatriz's great irony— that now she suffers waiting for news of her *desaparecido*, just as the peasants, Señora Flores and Digna Ranquileo, wait. Yet, Beatriz demonstrates neither the long-suffering dignity nor the deep love these women share for their lost ones and prefers instead to shut her eyes to the political violence and hire secret detectives to search out her husband. In direct contrast to Beatriz, Hilda Leal demonstrates perfect devotion to her politically extreme husband. When she flees Europe with fellow Spanish refugees, Hilda is the only one standing at the bow of the ship, not weeping for her homeland but "gazing toward the future" (91). Her response to the suicide of her first child, the terrible risks taken daily by her second, and the exile of the third, is to continue to move forward, standing by her convictions that the tyrannies of life must be met with strength. She offers the old home in Spain to the fleeing children as a way of coming full circle, accepting life's changes in a way that Beatriz and the women of her class could never adapt to or even comprehend.

THEMES

The prominent theme of the novel rests in the contradiction suggested by its title—love, and the life that it engenders, juxtaposed against the shadows of darkness and death. Allende has explained that she sees these two elements, love and violence, as inseparable halves of human life. In *Of Love and Shadows*, Allende attempts to illustrate this dichotomous relationship by showing the "invisible frontier that separates the apparently orderly world where we live and whose laws we believe we understand, from . . . the world of violence whose laws we must improvise" (Moody, "On Shadows" 54). Within such a split world dwells the age-old battle between light and darkness that plays out behind Irene and Francisco's blossoming love story. Class differences, as a secondary theme, provide the scaffolding for both the political drama and the personal liaison. Like the dual themes of life versus death and light versus darkness, the rich and poor exist in counterpoint and constant tension.

The stark contrasts in the narrative serve to accentuate its double themes. Even in the Beltrán mansion, where the specter of death hangs about The Will of God Manor, the desperation of the deserted elderly inmates who wander about like ghosts is counteracted by the young love blossoming in the rooms above them. Clearly, the novel is meant as a political statement on one level, an indictment of war crimes that cannot simply be ignored and buried. Bringing these atrocities to the light of day, however, is not the only role of the book. Allende notes that for every "torturer you have a thousand people who have risked their lives for freedom, for justice, to help each other" (Montenegro 262). And so the heroic acts of Irene, Francisco, José, Sergeant Rivera, Mario, and the others balance out the evil of the likes of Lieutenant Ramírez and the General.

In this view, the love story between Irene and Francisco is as natural a response to the Los Riscos atrocity as the demonstrations and military trial. Their relationship is not simply prompted by a chance shared encounter with the specter of evil, but in a very real way immortalized by that despair. Like the sphinx rising from the ashes, their new love reaffirms life and hope amidst the rubble of a terrorized country. It does not seem so strange, then, that when Irene and Francisco first confront the gruesome reality of the buried bodies, their immediate response to visceral mortality is a night of lovemaking. The "shadows" or shades of the dead hover over the birth of this couple's future together. Later, as Irene lies in the hospital fighting for her life, Francisco attempts to use the light of love to conquer the darkness of encroaching death by conjuring up his brightest memories of their lovemaking. And when Irene escapes the hospital, she is disguised as a pregnant woman. Resurrected from her deathbed, Irene represents corporeally the promise of a new beginning that she and Francisco will create out of their exile.

A second important emphasis of the novel is on class difference, in particular how social disparities contribute to the injustices perpetrated in the country. While this theme can be interpreted in marxist terms (see the following section), the class divisions can also be viewed more generally as a further dichotomy in a book of doubles. One example compares the two mother figures in Irene's life—her natural mother, Beatriz, who lives in upper class circles removed from the everyday troubles of the country, and Irene's Nana Rosa who has spent her life serving the narcissistic woman. On the surface, Rosa would seem to be the naïve one, living an uneducated and underprivileged life. It is, in fact, Beatriz who must be sheltered from the hard realities of the authoritarian regime and its many victims. Believing categorically in the General's words, Beatriz prefers not to question the government's actions. The narrator describes Beatriz as one of those who adjusted quickly to military rule, as "[i]gnorance was indispensable to peace of mind" (237). Beatriz understands that her own life is better—no more standing in line "to buy a miserable chicken" (221)—and so she prefers not to question whether the lives of her countrymen have improved. Instead, her energy and money go into preserving her looks against the ravages of age, a full-time job rewarded by the young lover who meets her for bacchanalian vacations around the globe. Should Beatriz question even for a moment the behavior of her superiors, she need only look at the luxuries enjoyed by everyone she knows to assure herself that life is far better than it was before. Even Mario, who himself lives surrounded by luxury but uses it like the Leals to serve the needy, finds himself repelled by Beatriz, whom he feels has "lost her place in the world" (255).

Standing in contrast to this blind matriarch, the housekeeper, Rosa, lives with her eyes open. Perhaps because she lives in closer kinship to the needy and victimized, Rosa has a heart able to comprehend danger and injustice. On one level, the Beltráns' servant is merely a type, like the jolly black mammies that figure in U.S. literature of the pre–Civil War South. So large she is unable to cross her legs, Rosa seems to exist solely to nourish the bodies and spirits of her mistress' family. Faced with any difficulties or inconsistencies in life, Rosa answers each with a simplistic proverb or axiom that effectively ends further discussion. Listening to melodramatic *novelas* (soap operas) on the radio all day, the housekeeper appears satisfied to live through these imaginary characters and the family she serves rather than to claim a life and identity of her own. The only hint that Rosa's world extends beyond the Beltrán kitchen occurs when Irene is a small child and witnesses the aftermath of an illegitimate pregnancy. Coming home from school, the little Irene is unable to find her Nana anywhere. She eventually discovers Rosa in her room, covered in blood, with the lifeless body of a tiny blue baby at her feet. Rosa tells Irene that the baby "fell in through the skylight" and that they must keep this secret from the family (138). The well-read Irene can tell that this is a six- or seven-month fetus that was likely stillborn, but she keeps her Nana's secret and helps Rosa give the baby a clandestine burial in the garden. For years, the women keep silent, except to tend the forget-me-nots that mark the baby's spot. Later, they speak casually of the baby-that-fell-through-the-skylight, sharing this secret that speaks to the darker realities of life. In the end, Rosa proves a much more resilient woman than her mistress, able to comprehend Irene's danger, the true corruption of the government, and the extent to which buried bodies—in mines and gardens—represent far more than the tranquil surfaces of life might suggest.

HISTORICAL BACKGROUND

As one reads *Of Love and Shadows,* there is little doubt that the stratified society critiqued in the novel is a thinly veiled depiction of Chile in its early years under dictatorial rule. When General Augusto Pinochet led the military coup that overthrew President Allende's government on September 11, 1973, he ushered in a seventeen-year reign characterized by poverty, terror, and corruption. Pinochet disbanded Congress and prohibited political parties, shut down liberal newspapers, purged universities, and imposed a strict after-dark curfew across the country. Dissidents and previous Allende supporters were rounded up into detention centers, tens of thousands were involuntarily exiled, and several thousand more "disappeared" without a trace. To control a populace accustomed to more democratic leadership, Pinochet relied on fear, coercion, and persecution. His secret police, called the *Dirección de Inteligencia Nacional* (Directorate of National Intelligence) or DINA, were responsible for many of the incidents of torture documented during the years of the dictatorship (Collier and Sater 359–360). In Allende's novel, Lieutenant

Ramírez is a member of a police force that behaves with much the same impunity as the DINA. He menaces the Flores family for a minor breach, specifically, their participation in an agricultural cooperative much like the Agrarian Reform established by President Allende's socialist administration. Just as the Flores family is decimated by the dictatorship, the middle-class Leals in the novel have paid dearly for their political affiliations since the junta takeover; they are blacklisted from academic posts and left to survive any way they can.

While *Of Love and Shadows* documents many abuses attributed to the oppressive government, Allende is particularly focused on bearing witness to the *desaparecidos* of Chile, those who were taken away by military personnel or kidnapped by the DINA and never seen again. Though exact numbers are disputed, historians agree that during the early months of the regime, local military and DINA used their authority to eliminate potential enemies that numbered in the thousands. Often, these were minor political figures or powerless peasants who had participated in oppositional activities or joined unions. Many political prisoners were held for months or years in detention centers, where they were coerced into fingering other "traitors" or becoming DINA informants. Other victims were subjected to fatal rounds of torture or killed outright and buried in hidden graves. Because family members were given no information on imprisoned relatives, were not allowed to bury their remains, and in many cases never learned the true fate of their loved ones, these prisoners came to be known as *desaparecidos,* or the ones who have disappeared without a trace. Mothers, wives, and daughters spent countless hours at police headquarters, government bureaus, and Catholic agencies trying to gain the tiniest clues that might offer them closure. Many participated in rallies and demonstrations, holding pictures of their lost relatives and demanding answers. Like Señora Flores and Digna Ranquileo in the novel, these women were often urged to sign paperwork acknowledging their relatives' deaths and warned to stop meddling in war crimes.

While the village of Los Riscos and its victimized inhabitants in *Of Love and Shadows* are fictional, the larger story of the mass grave and military cover-up is based on the kinds of real incidents involving *desaparecidos* that occurred during the first five years of the military occupation of Chile. In particular, the narrative echoes public accounts of the mass grave discovered in 1978 in Lonquén, outside of Santiago. The Catholic Church used its relative authority to help uncover the corpses of fifteen *campesinos* who had been missing from the rural community of

Isla de Maipo since the first month of the coup. The men had been assassinated and left in two brick ovens at an abandoned mining site. For almost the first time since the coup, the press was given some freedom to publish details of the crime and the subsequent trial (Moody, "On Shadows" 51–52). Allende made use of newspaper articles, her own experiences as a journalist, and interviews with Chilean exiles in Venezuela to piece together the historical elements of the story (Rodden, "Introduction" 10). She based Señora Flores on an actual woman, Purisima Munõz de Maureira, who lost her husband and four sons in the Lonquén massacre. And like the fictional Evangelina Flores who bravely faces the war crimes tribunal and goes on to give worldwide testimony of Chilean abuses, one of the real-life Maureira daughters traveled to Geneva to speak at the Commission on Human Rights in an effort to win justice for victims like her murdered siblings (Moody, "On Shadows" 53). In fact, the addition of Evangelina Ranquileo's mutilated body to the concealed grave site is one of the few instances of artistic license Allende takes in the retelling of this atrocity.

The novel also maintains historical accuracy in its representation of the Catholic Church. In describing the perilous activities that José Leal and his fellow priests engage in to promote human rights, Allende does not exaggerate the important function of the Church in protecting the country's disenfranchised. Unlike most institutions in Chile that were either disbanded or cowed into submission, the Catholic Church retained a relatively autonomous position throughout military rule. The honorable Cardinal Raúl Silva Henríquez, whose fictional counterpart figures prominently in Allende's novel, played a key role in developing a Peace Committee to monitor human rights violations in Chile. When General Pinochet forced its closure, the Church countered with the "Vicariate of Solidarity" that provided humanitarian and legal aid to the oppressed (Collier and Sater 362). In the novel, José's underground activities are greatly abetted by his religious profession, which grants him a certain amount of immunity from police brutality. Likewise in the novel, the Cardinal, with the help of the Vicariate, manages to arrange the exhumation of the mass grave despite close surveillance, in large part because any threat to the Cardinal's safety would be met with a nationwide uproar. In characterizing the selflessness of José and the Cardinal in her novel, Allende pays appropriate tribute to the courage of the Catholic Church in bringing to light the crimes hidden at Lonquén.

ALTERNATIVE PERSPECTIVE: MARXIST CRITICISM

Marxist theorists interpret social issues through an economic lens that views all organized societies as engaged in a perpetual class struggle, a fight for power between the dominant ruling class at the top of the social strata and the mass of laborers at the bottom. Based on the political theories of German philosopher Karl Marx (1818–1883) and his longtime colleague Friedrich Engels (1820–1885), Marxism identifies these segments of society as the bourgeoisie and the proletariat, two warring sides that ironically must work together to produce the material goods for a society's survival. Marxist literary criticism essentially argues that all language expression, including literature, is a representation of this historical struggle, an ideological mirror of class attitudes and beliefs. This shared and maintained ideology typically favors the "status quo," the present state of society that derives from and is fiercely protected by the dominant class. That is, cultural artifacts produced during any given period will articulate the values of a society's wealthiest and most educated members, the bourgeoisie, and reveal the extent to which the status quo is secure or threatened at that time in history. In general terms, a marxist view argues that all literature is shaped by such historical, social, and economic forces, and that its content regularly reflects the tensions inherent in those forces.

While early practitioners of marxist literary criticism held that the ruling class almost exclusively influences a society's cultural and intellectual products, socialist critics of the last twenty years, including Terry Eagleton and Fredric Jameson, have argued that an author with sufficient political awareness can write against the status quo and produce a text that defies the ruling ideology. Eagleton argues that literature in this view should be seen as transformative in the broadest historical sense, "concerned with people's political situations as a whole—rather than narrowly abstract, concerned only with the immediate interpersonal relations" of any single individual within society (208). As Jameson explains in his seminal work, *The Political Unconscious* (1981), an author always writes with the political in mind, however unconscious the writer's motives might be. In marrying marxist criticism with a psychoanalytic view, Jameson suggests that literature can never suppress historical truth. A novel is itself an artifact of historical significance given that "history is inaccessible to us except in textual form" (81). The views of Eagleton and Jameson together with other contemporary marxist critics suggest that all literature is polemical; in positioning itself within a political argument, the subtext of any novel either reinforces the status quo or works to overturn it.

Allende's *Of Love and Shadows*, then, can be read not solely as a love story, a murder mystery, or a historical novel, but also as a political treatise deriding dictatorial rule and embracing socialist reform. In this interpretation, Professor Leal is the dominant voice, subscribing first to a marxist ideology and then to a reformed philosophy that denounces all governmental control. As a young man, Professor Leal has fled Franco's Spain a staunch marxist, but his disappointment in Soviet leadership and what he views as the failed socialist experiment has led him gradually to abandon the Communist Party to embrace an anarchist philosophy with a socialist bent. He argues that governments are "intrinsically corrupt" because they "guarantee the freedom of the rich, based on property, and they enslave the rest in misery" (92). For the same reason, the professor denounces nationalism as a dangerous form of propaganda used primarily for oppression and control of the lower classes. While Professor Leal is bourgeois in his background, education, and cultural interests, he participates in the political activities and revolutionary views of the intelligentsia rather than the leisured lifestyle of the idly rich. This relegates him to the fringes of society, reduced in economic means and blacklisted from academic posts. Though he and his sons are, in fact, better educated than Beatriz Beltrán, their personal values and radical politics align them with the proletariat.

Beatriz Beltrán and her absent husband, Eusebio, on the other hand, represent the worst kind of bourgeoisie in this South American society. In them, Allende offers a critique of the irresponsible rich who allow the military free reign and merely enjoy the profits of the corrupt government. Beatriz lives in an enclosed world represented accurately by the separate entrance she has added to her own residence to effectively ignore even the needy under her own roof. She has succeeded, through marriage, in climbing the social ladder to the very height of fashionable society and refuses to allow even dire financial troubles to threaten that hard-won station. Like most of her wealthy countrymen who disbelieve the rumors about the poor, Beatriz prefers to suppose them "loafers" who do not wish to work (168). She rejects socialist sentiments, even deliberately identifying Francisco as Irene's "colleague" because she cannot "tolerate the revolutionary implications of the word *compañero*" (36). A shadowy figure in the novel, Eusebio also subscribes to a feckless existence of wasteful living. A man with a weakness for beautiful women and extravagant living, Eusebio squanders his inheritance in foreign lands like a veritable prodigal son. Upon his return, he impetuously marries Beatriz and begins a life of foolish business dealings and regular domestic squabbles. Eusebio often dabbles in silly inventions, like a coconut-harvesting machine, though he has never seen a coconut palm in his life. For the second time in his life, Eusebio finds himself in dire debt and saddled with thousands of pounds of worthless sheep meat when the Arab company he is working for discovers that he has disobeyed their strict food preparation guidelines. When he is subjected to death threats for his "Philanthropic Butcher Shop" (a scheme to give the meat away before it rots), Eusebio simply disappears, only to reappear at the novel's close living in leisure on a Caribbean island, safe from old debts and nagging wives.

In a marxist reading of Allende's novel, the prevailing hope in the narrative is that the lower class will rise up against the oppressive dictatorship and the upper class that keeps it in power. The members of the proletariat have sufficient motivation for such a revolutionary uprising. The government controls their production (the Farmers Union has been disbanded and some participants murdered), it monitors their cultural activities (newspapers, magazines, and television stations are all carefully censored), and it limits their mobility. The society is essentially static with little movement between classes. While a social climber like Beatriz may claw her way into the upper class, most of the middle-class families like the Leals are limited by occupation, political connections, and finances. In a like manner, the lowest classes—laborers, farmers, and unemployed peasants—have no means by which to establish economic independence. They are chained to the system that punishes them. The country is in essence "two countries . . . functioning within the same national boundaries: one for a golden and powerful elite, the other for the excluded and silent masses" (168). Yet, the injustice exists even less in the inequitable distribution of wealth as it does in the imbalance of power that allows the authorities to torture and murder their citizens with impunity.

Though no overt revolution has developed by the novel's close, some expectations remain. The two protagonists, a middle-class intellectual and an upper-class society woman, have moved away from their privileged positions in society to reject the status quo and serve the laboring class. The rich hairstylist Mario has succeeded in joining the underground revolutionary activities. He has risen from the lowest class to achieve a privileged position from which he can use his wealth surreptitiously to smuggle refugees from the country. While Beatriz, like the upper class she represents, has refused to believe in injustice outside her doors, José Leal will continue to fight for the rights of the poor. The Floreses have gained a certain amount of justice, and their daughter Evangelina will go out into the world to claim more. Most promising of all, Irene and Francisco leave with the decision to fight from the outside, and then to return. Just as marxist literary criticism argues that a book does not simply reflect but can also challenge and change an existing ideology through introducing new ideas, Allende's *Of Love and Shadows* gives the working poor of Chile a voice with which to tell the world their stories, and perhaps overturn the injustices to which they have been subjected.

5

Eva Luna
(1988)

By the time Isabel Allende began writing the manuscript that would become her third novel, *Eva Luna*, she was enjoying international recognition with two best-selling books and finally felt ready to call herself a writer and the words she was writing, a novel. In fact, she has explained that *Eva Luna* was a more carefully planned narrative than the first two books, due in large part to this conscious shift in self-perception. Allende wanted the story to be read not only as a "picaresque novel, but also as a story about writing, about storytelling, about being a woman" (Ross 99). For this reason, critics often regard the title character, Eva Luna, as a reasonably accurate fictional representation of Allende herself. The day that Eva takes out a clean sheet of paper, places it in her typewriter, and becomes a full-time writer, her feelings that "that page had been waiting for me for more than twenty years" (224) could describe Allende's experience when she first picked up the writer's pen at age thirty-nine. In the same way that Allende began to record the voices of family members whose stories had been tucked away in her memory for almost four decades, Eva Luna discovers her characters as they step out of hiding and begin to people the stories that have been locked in her imaginative universe. Allende creates in Eva Luna a strong female artist, a woman true to herself and to her creativity. While critics are quick to point out these parallels between Allende and Eva Luna, Allende has called this extraordinary character, not a self-portrait, but a wishful one, her "dreamself" (Manguel 273).

In the novel, Eva Luna is a resourceful woman who survives because of her single talent—telling marvelous stories. Her ability to enchant others by weaving words reflects her heroine, Scheherazade of *The Thousand and One Nights*. Just as Scheherazade tells magical stories nightly to preserve her life, Eva Luna exchanges her own stories "first for food and shelter, later for friendship, and finally for love" (Cruz et al. 205), when she seduces a prospective lover with a fireside tale. Eva Luna's life unfolds in an unnamed Caribbean country, whose exotic Amazon jungle, beautiful mountains, and humid coast mirror those of Venezuela, Allende's adopted nation after her exile from Chile. While the clever heroine of *Eva Luna* does not offer the overt magical realism that Allende does in her first novel, Eva weaves a fairy-tale-like story nonetheless, one whose fanciful plot twists begin to blend with the *telenovela* scripts she writes for a living until the two narratives become almost indistinguishable. Eva has learned this method of storytelling from her mother, a woman who embraces an Allende-influenced philosophy that "reality is not only what we see on the surface; it has a magical dimension as well and, if we so desire, it is legitimate to enhance it and color it to make our journey through life less trying" (21). If Eva Luna's remarkable journey is any example, this method of concocting alternate lives can prove an unquestionably rewarding one.

PLOT

The story of Eva Luna begins with the childhood of her mother, Consuelo, a woman of unknown origins who, as an abandoned toddler, wanders out of the Caribbean jungle one day and is adopted by missionaries. When she reaches puberty, Consuelo is sent to a convent in the city where she learns basic domestic skills. After three years of a very cloistered life, the orphan is hired as a housekeeper in the home of the foreign doctor Professor Jones. An imposing personage, the professor spends his days perfecting embalming solutions that have the unique ability to preserve a human body intact for decades. Consuelo lives for years in this household, secluded from political uprisings in the nation and only briefly touched by the dictator's death when she and the professor are summoned to embalm his body. This ritual is blocked, however, by the dictator's military brother, who prefers that the ruler be buried expediently rather than be immortalized. One day, the professor's Indian gardener is bitten by a venomous viper. Consuelo attempts to save the life of the strong, silent man, but when she sees that he will surely die, she resolves to live true to her name and "console this man in his misfortune" (18). They make love on his deathbed, and in the process conceive Eva Luna. Then, to the surprise of the professor and the snake experts, the Indian gradually gets better. Eventually he says good-bye to his lover and goes away. Consuelo says nothing when she begins to show the signs of pregnancy, and Professor Jones never dreams that his housekeeper might be in such a condition. The solitary housekeeper gives birth to the breach baby in her room alone, with the African cook arriving afterward to help clean up the infant. Consuelo determines to name the child Eva, "so she will love life," and Luna, after the baby's Indian father, whose tribe is called the "Children of the Moon" (20). The cook insists that Eva Luna be properly baptized, taking it upon herself to save the money necessary for the ceremony. When she finds that she still does not have enough money after three months, the cook cleans the church from top to bottom to ensure that the child will be baptized as she deserves. Through these special attentions, the cook becomes Eva's *madrina,* or godmother.

Though Consuelo is a silent woman in the world, her creative imagination brims with words and stories whenever she is alone with her child. For Eva, her mother invents a universe full of wonderful tales, characters, and magic. Under Consuelo's tender care, Eva thrives in the professor's unconventional household. Then one Christmas, when Eva is only six years old, her mother dies from swallowing a chicken bone that has accidentally made its way into a *hallaca* (a holiday dish of corn-meal tamales stuffed with meats and boiled in plantain leaves). Consuelo leaves Eva in the care of her *madrina,* the African cook. The cook, though coarse and unexpressive, loves Eva in her own way. Eva continues to grow up under the strict, if unorthodox, attentions of her adoptive godmother. When Professor Jones becomes ill and is finally on his deathbed, the little girl befriends him and they spend his last days in each other's company. When the professor dies, the cook tells seven-year-old Eva that she is old enough to go out and make a living.

Put out to domestic service, Eva finds herself in a bleak household governed by a shrill spinster and her gambling bachelor brother. Eva's only friend in her new home is the affable cook, Elvira. They tell each other stories and the elder woman protects her "little bird" by feeding her extra scraps and taking the heaviest work from her (53). At night,

Eva sneaks into Elvira's bed, offering to tell her a story if the cook will allow her to stay. For the first time, Eva discovers the bartering power of her special talent. One day, Eva runs away after rebelling against the *doña*, who won't allow her to look at a painting in the house. Eva encounters a poet reciting verses in a singsong voice in a plaza. She thus discovers the value of rhyme in remembering stories. In the same plaza, Eva also meets a little boy named Huberto Naranjo, who lives in the street and makes money by picking pockets and defrauding onlookers. Eva looks forward briefly by telling us that, later, Naranjo will lead a street gang and eventually end up a rebel in the mountains. This evening, though, Naranjo shows his new little charge how to barter for food. When they curl up for the night in a parking garage, Eva offers to pay him back with a story. In one of the only two stories transcribed word for word in the novel, Eva weaves a tale about a bandit whose sweetheart lives in fear of him until, one day, she opens a parlor and achieves personal freedom through economic independence. Naranjo finds the story ridiculous, foreshadowing his macho view of women—a perspective that will color the pair's relationship in later years. After a couple days of street life, Eva asks to return to her *madrina,* who beats her and delivers her back to the *doña's* house. Now Eva senses that she has won some fight and each evening, when her work is finished, she gazes unmolested at the painting that represents "the door to freedom" (62).

Eva's life remains the same for many years. She calls Elvira her *abuela* and dearly loves the funny old woman who sleeps every night in a coffin to "become accustomed to it" (63). Together the woman and girl listen to the radio all day, with Eva learning the songs and listening to the *telenovelas* (soap operas) that give her many ideas for stories. Eva learns little about the outside world except for what Elvira tells her. Through the cook, she discovers that the country is controlled by a dictator and has opened its borders to immigrants fleeing postwar Europe. Eva's *patrones* show their loyalty to the General by placing his portrait in a prominent place in their living room. At the same time, Elvira confides to Eva that a rebellion is brewing against the regime.

Halfway across the world, in a small Austrian village, lives the Carlé family, headed by the sadistic schoolmaster Lukas Carlé. He torments his wife and children, including his sons, Rolf and Jochen, and mentally feeble daughter, Katharina. One day, Lukas Carlé is found hanging from a tree with a severe head injury. Five of his students, who were the last to see him as they went for their annual outing in the forest, claim they have no idea how he was killed. Rolf and his mother feel only relief and peace at his passing, but the students who murdered him cannot bear to have the deed go unrecognized. They form a secret society and wear a circle of white cloth on their jacket sleeves, a symbol the meaning of which all the townspeople eventually guess. For twenty-seven days Rolf suffers in silence, until he collapses from nervous exhaustion brought on by the guilt of wishing he had done the deed himself. When his mother begins to fear for his life, she packs a bag and sends Rolf to live with his Uncle Rupert and Aunt Burgel in a Caribbean country in South America, where the family has fled to avoid the war.

On the voyage overseas, Rolf overcomes his depression and arrives a healthy, excited young man. His Uncle Rupert, Aunt Burgel, and their two pretty daughters meet him and bring him to a "fairy-tale village" founded by European colonists to be a utopian replica of their homeland (79). It is based on the Colonia Tovar, a German settlement where Bavarians lived in seclusion from the rest of Venezuela until a road was built in 1961. The village in which Rolf finds himself offers a home of simple tastes, generous people, and a "naïve dreamworld" in which he can heal from his terrorized childhood (83). As Rolf is welcomed into his aunt and uncle's household and begins to help with the tourist inn they run, he also receives amorous encouragement from his two cousins. Uncertain which girl to choose, Rolf engages in erotic romps with both. While the cousins find him delightful, they pragmatically decide to marry two rich heirs in the village and keep Rolf "in reserve as a lover and, when feasible, as father of their children, thus avoiding the risk of boredom" (88). Though Rolf's scruples argue against this immoral arrangement, he continues as the young women's lover for three years. A weekly visitor to the inn, the newspaperman and filmmaker Señor Aravena, befriends Rolf during this period and encourages him to consider a world beyond La Colonia. Through Aravena's influence, Rolf decides to move to the capital and study cinematography at the university.

Meanwhile, Eva is growing up in the household of her *patrones* under the protection of Elvira. Through the cook's "scandal sheet," Eva discovers that her *madrina* has given birth to a monstrous two-headed baby with the extreme feature that "one head was white by race, and the other black" (93). Giving birth alone in a deserted building, the woman has fearfully dropped the fetus down an incinerator shoot and is later called a murderess for the act until the coroner proves that the baby was stillborn. Eventually, Eva's *madrina* is driven mad by her own suffering and alcohol. She roams the streets and occasionally shows up to ask for Eva's wages. When the *patrona* can no longer stand the harassment, she fires

Eva, who is sorry only to leave her *abuela* Elvira, though the two find a way to see each other occasionally.

Eva begins to move from house to house, as her *madrina* attempts to find her better domestic positions and higher wages. Among her new employers is a Yugoslavian immigrant, who creates sculptures out of a special clay mixture she calls "Universal Matter" (97–98). Eva likes this *patrona* but soon moves on to a cabinet minister who lives in a colonial mansion. One of her few duties there is to empty his chamber pot, a Victorian vessel that sits under an antique armchair with a hole in the seat. Eva is offended by this humiliating job, wondering why the minister cannot use the bathroom like the rest of the household. On the fifth day, she loses her patience and dumps the contents of the pot over his head, walking out of that household for good. When she cannot locate Elvira and is too fearful to call her *madrina*, Eva heads for the plaza where, years before, she had encountered Hubert Naranjo. She asks around for him, but, having no luck, falls asleep in a doorway. Eva is awakened by a grown Naranjo, who drops his tough pose when he recognizes his old friend. Though Eva hopes to live on the streets with Naranjo, he takes her instead to the home of a prostitute, La Señora. Naranjo asks the woman to take her in, assuring her that he will pay Eva's keep and that she can entertain the woman with stories. La Señora takes the thirteen-year-old girl into her home, and bathes and clothes her. She then introduces Eva to her best friend, an Italian transvestite named Melesio who works as a quiet language professor by day and performs as a cabaret star by night. Eva lives in this unorthodox home but does not become one of La Señora's girls, the high-class prostitutes who work for the most distinguished men in the country. Together Melesio, La Señora, and her girls share a pact to keep Eva pure and innocent. Naranjo also insists that La Señora teach Eva to read, but there is rarely time for that pursuit.

For many months, Eva lives a blissful existence with the prostitutes. Then a new sergeant arrives in the neighborhood. He begins a raid that lands Melesio in jail and chases La Señora and Eva from their home in the night. Eva finds herself deserted when La Señora fears she will be caught with the girl and arrested for corrupting a minor. The "Revolt of the Whores," a four-day citywide riot that results in much looting and some deaths, also leaves Eva penniless and without a home while the nation demonstrates against the General, whose men have murdered a publisher for allowing publication of caricatures of the dictator that implicate him in the scandal. Eva wanders the streets for days, turning into a "filthy urchin" who must scavenge for food and hide from the Security Force (121).

One day, Eva runs into Riad Halabí, a middle-aged Turkish man with a severe cleft palate. When Eva tries to back away, she is overcome by a deep fatigue. Riad feeds her and then tucks her into a truck loaded with boxes. They drive through the night to a little town called Agua Santa, stopping in front of Riad's shop, where Eva is invited to make her new home. Agua Santa is a sleepy town and its only excitement is the changing of the guard each week from the local penal colony on the island of Santa María. On Saturday, the guards come into town to amuse themselves at the whorehouse and to raise a general racket. Likewise, the Indians arrive on that day to beg for handouts.

At this point, the narrative flashes back to Riad Halabí's arrival in the town ten years earlier, an event that has brought a few changes to the sleepy hamlet. In an otherwise insular community, Riad has become an accepted citizen largely due to the unusual circumstances that transpired on his first day there. The day Riad arrived in Agua Santa, the town was paralyzed by the murder of the schoolteacher's son. The boy had stolen mangoes from a rich outsider who owned a hacienda there and the *patrón* had taken matters into his own hands. Riad immediately took control of the situation, placing the child's body on an improvised bier and serving coffee to the mourners. The next day, he organized the burial and then suggested a way for the mourners to assuage their fury. They collected all the mangoes in the village and filled the rich man's house from top to bottom. The murderer fled the town, and Riad settled in at Agua Santa as an accepted native. Prior to Riad's arrival, the town had had little contact with the outside world. When Riad proposed that passing truck drivers be enlisted to carry the town's produce and crafts into the city, his idea began to bring money into Agua Santa. Using this improvised trade route, Riad developed a thriving shop and gradually became a prosperous businessman. Eventually, when Riad had reached a sufficient level of prosperity, he returned to Turkey to claim the bride his mother had found for him, observing the full seven days of proper ceremony. Unfortunately, Zulema is repulsed by her husband's deformity and hates her new life in South America, "stuffing herself with food and growing increasingly fat and bored" (133).

When Eva arrives, Riad and his wife, Zulema, have achieved a life of comfort, but not genuine wealth, from running their successful shop, "The Pearl of the Orient." Eva discovers that Riad wishes to bring her into the home to keep his wife company while he is away on his regular journeys. After a few moments of indifference, Zulema responds with warmth to her new "daughter." Eva adapts well to her new life, feeling as if she has always lived with the Halabís. She enjoys the new life that permits her to come and go as she pleases, learn the world of commerce, and enjoy private lessons with the schoolteacher. For Eva, learning to read and write is a special blessing because it allows her to make up more complex stories. Eva reads *A Thousand and One Nights* with a fervor and learns all the stories. She adds embellishments and special twists of her own until Zulema, enchanted by the storyteller in her household, learns Spanish. While Zulema continues to turn from her husband's ugly mouth, Eva loves him like a father and sees "his imperfection as a gift of birth, something that made him different from others—unique in this world" (137). They spend special time together, playing games, singing, and dancing. Riad gives Eva her two most important gifts in life, "writing, and proof of existence" (141). In addition to ensuring the girl's private school lessons, Riad finds a way to bribe the authorities to get official documents drawn up for Eva so that she is finally registered as a real person.

After Eva has lived with the Halabís for a year and a half, one of Riad's cousins comes to join them. The twenty-five-year-old Kamal becomes Riad's close companion and Eva is edged out of their previous friendship. It is Eva's job to teach the newcomer Spanish, a chore that tortures her in part because she is completely infatuated with the older boy. Kamal seems to bewitch all the young girls of the village and they drop by the shop with any excuse to flirt with him. Eva, now fifteen years old and ready for love, suffers from the sight of these interactions and her first pangs of jealousy. Even Zulema finds the boy attractive, awakening "from a lethargy of almost forty years" (144). With shameless precision, Zulema waits for one of Riad's journeys in order to seduce Kamal and bring him to her bed. Eva watches everything from her jealous post in the doorway. The next day during the siesta, Kamal secretly packs his suitcase and sneaks from the house. Zulema waits up all night, making Eva stay with her, believing less and less with each hour that her lover will return. When Riad arrives home, he finds his wife suffering from a deep lovesickness that he cannot acknowledge without shaming himself. Instead, he returns to his old friendly ways with Eva and they never mention Kamal's name again.

During this period, Rolf Carlé spends his weeks learning moviemaking at the university and his weekends with his aunt and uncle in La Colonia. Under Aravena's tutelage, Rolf develops not only the skill for making documentaries but also the boldness to record the political unrest in the country. After the gross corruption of the most recent election, the dictatorship has begun to crumble. The head of the Security Force escapes to Europe. Many officials follow suit, fleeing the country before they can be killed. Finally, military captains get involved in the conspiracy and the government falls, with the dictator and his family narrowly escaping the country. Mobs descend on the General's mansion, the barracks of the Security Force, and the shops and homes of those believed to have profited from the General's policies. During the wild days following the fall of the government, Rolf films all the events around him, daring to go where other journalists fear to go and earning a reputation for his work. At the end of the commotion, "the dust settled, the noise diminished, and the first day of democracy dawned" (158). Despite these momentous changes, many in the nation remain untouched by the altered politics, including Eva in the relatively secluded haven of Agua Santa. During the next two years, university students in the capital, feeling betrayed by a government they believe has capitulated to the interests of the United States, begin to follow the lead of revolutionaries in Cuba to develop a guerrilla movement in the mountains. When Rolf Carlé insists on filming them, he ultimately meets Huberto Naranjo.

As the respected leader of the street gang La Peste, Naranjo has been recruited by the guerrilla movement, beginning as a trainee with small missions and gradually working his way to explosives training and, ultimately, to frontline fighting from mountain outposts. When Naranjo finally completes his training and joins the secluded forces, he discovers that the guerrilla movement is small, with groups of ten to twenty young men scattered throughout the mountains. He also discovers that daily life within these groups is filled with hunger and physical discomfort. Naranjo's street life has prepared him well for a routine of privation, however, and he rises rapidly through the guerrilla ranks, eventually becoming Comandante Rogelio, a commander with influence over many troops and special authority over new recruits.

Eva matures into a young woman under Riad Halabí's careful tutelage. She continues to help him care for Zulema, who has drifted into an invalid state since Kamal's departure. One weekend in Eva's seventeenth year, after Riad leaves for a typical buying expedition, Zulema shoots herself with his pistol. When Eva discovers the dead woman in the morning, she dutifully cleans the body, returns the gun to its hiding place, and tidies the room. The result of her efforts is that the police immediately suspect her of murder, arresting her and taking her away in handcuffs. At the police station, Eva is tortured in order to coerce her into a false confession, which she refuses to offer. The newspapers publish

Eva's picture with a story about how she has killed her mistress. When the news travels by word of mouth to the capital, Riad rushes home and demands to see the girl. He is outraged by her woeful condition—beaten and bruised, her legs covered in cigarette burns. Riad pays off the lieutenant and takes Eva back to his home, supported by the townspeople who believe her innocence. Three months later, however, when she is still living under his roof with no female chaperone, rumors spread through the village. Riad tells her she must leave him and move to the capital to escape the scandal. In Eva's sorrow, she approaches this man with whom she has spent five happy years and embraces him, kissing him on his misshapen mouth where he has never been touched. They end up spending a wonderful night making love together, after which Eva begs Riad to allow her to stay as his companion. Certain that the townspeople will never give them peace, Riad insists that Eva leave, offering her Zulema's buried jewels for a dowry whenever she needs one and delivering her to the bus stop the next morning.

When Eva arrives in the capital, a student riot is in full progress. She finds a hotel and tries to get work, but when she is swept up into one of the street demonstrations, she seeks refuge in a church. There she meets up with Melesio, the Italian transvestite who has become Mimí since the two separated many years ago on the chaotic day of the Revolt of the Whores. Arrested and jailed, Melesio had been saved by La Señora's loyalty. By illegally exporting prostitutes overseas, La Señora gradually earned enough money to bribe the judges overseeing Melesio's case, but then had to flee the country to protect herself. Melesio, now Mimí, offers to take Eva in for awhile, encouraging her to explore ways to use her single talent of storytelling. Eva stays with Mimí for several years, developing into a woman and gradually overcoming her strong attachment to Riad Halabí. Mimí becomes a famous actress, wanted by all the best families to grace their guest lists, and her celebrity brings tremendous wealth. Eva and Mimí find themselves living in the most exclusive neighborhood in the capital, with a beautifully appointed home and a full social life. Eva completes her bachelor's degree and continues to write her stories every night. She looks up her *madrina* and discovers a sick old woman who cannot recall the past. When the *madrina* attempts suicide, Eva has her placed into a private clinic and works at a secretarial job to pay the expenses.

One day Eva runs into Huberto Naranjo, barely recognizing the weather-beaten but businesslike revolutionary. Eva finds herself instantly in love, not understanding the full extent of Naranjo's new life.

They begin a relationship that involves Naranjo's sudden appearances at sporadic intervals, brief trysts in hotels, and his equally sudden departures into the anonymous streets. A couple years into the unorthodox relationship, Eva still does not know about Naranjo's surreptitious activities. Then two policemen are killed near her factory and, on the same day, Naranjo meets her at the bus stop after work. Finally, Eva realizes that her lover may be involved in the underground guerrilla movement. She criticizes the acts as "murder," to which Naranjo corrects her by explaining that the police were "executed" by the people for violence that originated with the government (206). Though the two disagree on the effectiveness of terrorism, they continue to see each other.

During the same years, Rolf Carlé has become a celebrated newsman, working for Señor Aravena's television network and traveling the world filming historic events. Only in his occasional retreats to La Colonia does Rolf find rest from the "world's atrocities" (195). When the guerrilla movement begins to expand its work, Rolf Carlé is assigned to renew his connection to Huberto Naranjo and to attempt to interview and film the revolutionaries in action. Rolf approaches one of Naranjo's contacts, El Negro, who gradually drops his guard after a month of entreaties. When the revolutionaries decide this famous journalist might be useful to them, Rolf goes underground, smuggled into the mountains through a circuitous route and ultimately delivered to Comandante Rogelio's troops, where he spends several months observing the workings of the movement and filming the men's training and subversive activities. Rolf Carlé begins to lose focus, fearing that he may be losing his sanity, and yet he does not leave for several months. When he finally has all the footage he can use, Rolf attempts to cover the other side of the story, visiting army operations centers and interviewing the soldiers fighting for the government. When Aravena warns him that the government knows about his film footage and will want to obtain it, Rolf Carlé takes the film to La Colonia and has his aunt and uncle hide it for him.

Eva continues working at the factory, a regimented workplace overseen by the military. When she catches the eye of Colonel Tolomeo Rodríguez, Eva is not sure whether to be flattered or frightened by this enemy of Naranjo. When she dines with him, Eva asks forthrightly whether he wishes to sleep with her. The colonel is offended by her candor, but admits that he hopes they can strike up an intimate relationship. When Eva proposes that they get it over with that night and be done with it, her proposal is met with fury and the colonel leaves it to her to seek him out at a later date. Fearing that she may bring trouble to herself or Mimí, Eva resigns her job immediately and sets to work to become a full-time writer. Mimí encourages her by purchasing a typewriter and urging Eva to try her hand at the *telenovelas* that have become so popular in the country. Eva writes obsessively for days, only stopping to accompany Mimí to Aravena's office, where they are received with little interest. In a desperate attempt to gain attention for her friend's manuscript, Mimí invites the famed producer to dinner with the express purpose of seducing him. Aravena arrives accompanied by Rolf Carlé, who finds himself enthralled by one of Eva's entertaining stories.

Shortly after, a storm covers the city streets with floodwaters, and Eva hears on the news of an old woman who has floated down the street in a coffin. Eva rushes to the emergency shelter to claim Elvira, her adopted *abuela* from long ago. She and Mimí make arrangements for the elderly woman to live with them. At the same time, Rolf Carlé attempts to uncover a massacre at one of the army operations centers, where demonstrating prisoners have been summarily executed. When Aravena refuses to put Rolf's material on television, the newsman uses the photographs and films to influence the parliament, which in turn pressures the president into making some changes, including the transfer of nine political prisoners to a heavily guarded section of the penal colony on Santa María. Eva is recruited by Naranjo to draw plans of the factory to aid one of his operations, and Mimí reluctantly helps them in the endeavor, more to free her friend of Naranjo's influence than to forward the revolution. Naranjo also determines to release the nine prisoners on Santa María, and the women help him plan this impossible attack.

Naranjo sets the date for the prisoners' release, with Eva participating in one part of the plan. Driving into Agua Santa, Eva cannot resist disobeying orders and stops in at The Pearl of the Orient where she speaks briefly to Riad Halabí, who does not recognize her. She discovers that he has married a pretty young girl. Eva stays in the town only long enough to dig up the small cache of jewels that Riad Halabí had offered her years before and that she had buried according to Zulema's orders before her death. Then she heads with El Negro to an Indian encampment where they are to wait for the others. A group of guerrillas arrive, as well as Rolf Carlé, who has been asked by Naranjo to film the events. As the others finish arrangements for the ambush, Eva sets about preparing a large batch of Universal Matter from the recipe that her former eccentric Yugoslavian employer had created. Eva uses this clay mixture to shape a set of fake grenades. In the evening, Rolf Carlé sees her anxiety and asks Eva to tell him a story, one that she has "never told anyone" (249). Eva describes a female storyteller who makes her living from sharing her tales. One day a warrior with a devastating past comes to ask her for a new history, a *"novel of his life"* that will erase the melancholy (249). At the end of the long night of storytelling, the woman realizes that she has told him her story and saved nothing for herself; she decides that she will now have *"the pleasure of blending with him into a single story"* (250). The story is meant to be suggestive, one of the only times in the novel that Eva uses her stories to seduce a listener. From that point on, Eva's attraction to Rolf Carlé grows while her relationship with Naranjo slips into a friendly sisterly affection. She also discovers the next morning that her menstruation has begun again after stopping the night of Zulema's death. She believes that her body has finally "overcome its fear of love" (253). Just as the raid is about to begin, Eva returns by bus to the capital and her home.

Eva finds Mimí and Elvira waiting for her, with no official word on any uprising at the prison. The next morning, Rolf Carlé arrives at the door with the euphoric news that the escape has been successful. Then he takes Eva to La Colonia where he believes she will be safe from any military reprisals. While there, Rolf Carlé describes the successful attack and his alternate plan should his films be censored—that Eva should write a *telenovela* about what happened at Santa María. He argues that the military will have to leave her TV program alone or admit that the events are true. When she returns home, Eva begins to write this new soap opera based on her own life and the many stories entangled with hers. One day she is summoned to the Ministry of Defense. Fearing that she is finally to be punished for preparing the grenades, Eva finds herself face to face with Colonel Tolomeo Rodríguez, now a general. The general explains that he knows about Eva's relationship with Rolf Carlé and has read her newest script with its remarkably detailed plot regarding the escaped guerrillas. He wants her to urge Comandante Rogelio to accept amnesty and end the guerrilla warfare, with the hope that his men will follow their leader's decision. Eva pretends that she will consider the proposal, never planning to deliver her old lover into enemy hands. She leaves the military offices with a gracious good-bye and returns to Rolf Carlé with whom she hopes to share a new and joyous love.

CHARACTER DEVELOPMENT

As in her previous novels, Allende makes women the central actors in *Eva Luna*, even including the memorable addition of a man-turned-woman in the figure of Melesio/Mimí. The book's title character and narrator, however, is the most important figure in the novel. Eva Luna, whose name invokes the first woman and whose mother hopes she will affirm and celebrate the "life" of her name (3), lives many lives before the final pages of the novel. Eva Luna can be a difficult character to decipher, as she reveals less about herself than she does about those she encounters. Her love affairs, which are not numerous but tend toward the dramatic, arrive with little warning and offer still less to shape her character. A few early scenes, however, distinguish Eva Luna as a woman to be reckoned with. The first occurs during her early years working for the spinster *patrona* in the capital. When the *patrona* purposely drops a vase to distract Eva from gazing at a painting and demands that she clean up the mess, the headstrong girl simply snatches the woman's wig off her head and flees from the house. She spends a couple of days roaming the city with her new friend Naranjo before finding her *madrina,* who returns her forcibly to domestic servitude. In a second instance, Eva dumps a chamber pot over the cabinet minister's head as he sits in his stately bishop's armchair with the hole in the seat, "liberating [herself] from humiliation" (101) in that one gesture. These episodes demonstrate Eva's strong sense of self, despite her uncertain origins and orphaned status.

Eva Luna has a powerful gift of storytelling, which she uses most often as fair barter to gain the goods and services she needs to survive. On only two occasions does Eva employ her skill to seduce or entrance her listener: the first is the tale she shares with Huberto Naranjo to keep him with her through the long night on the street; the second is the story she offers Rolf Carlé during their dark night by the campfire waiting to aid the prison escape. In both cases, Eva divulges the plot of the story for her readers as well, even narrating the second tale in its entirety. In these two stories, Eva reveals much about her personality and her ability to foretell the future: the first describes a woman who extricates herself from her outlaw husband to live an independent life, just as Eva will ultimately break from Naranjo and his macho code; the second tells of a professional storyteller who replaces a troubled wanderer's memories with a new and peaceful past, a promise Eva silently makes to the defensive Rolf who becomes captivated by that liberating plot and its enchanting narrator. Ultimately, Eva Luna has the power to narrate her own future, a power she exercises in the final pages of the novel when she first reports that her love for Rolf Carlé eventually "wore thin and nothing was left but shreds." She then alters the story, revising their love into one she did not have to "invent" but which was an "exceptional

love" that could endure (271). Like any artful storyteller, Eva Luna leaves
it to the reader to decide which conclusion satisfies.

A number of women serve as mother figures to Eva Luna, as well as
midwives to her art. The foremost, of course, is her actual mother Consuelo, whose mysterious origins lend a measure of fantasy to both
women's lives. Consuelo organizes her world through storytelling and
so demonstrates to her child that "[w]ords are free" (21), and one of the
few pleasures that people of all stations might enjoy alike. Eva's original
talent is received from her mother; its development is nurtured by others.
The cook, Elvira, offers a ready audience, entreating Eva for new stories
each evening. Eva explains that gaining her adopted *abuela*'s favor and
a safe place to sleep was how the budding storyteller "learned to barter
words for goods" (63). Likewise, the eccentric old cook introduces Eva
to the radio serials that offer the girl a template for thousands of stories.
Through the schoolteacher Inés, hired by Riad Halabí, Eva learns to
write, a skill that accelerates her storytelling now that she can transcribe
her creations and craft them into lengthy epics. Though Zulema does
little more than serve as passive listener, Eva spends years telling her
stories and so develops a keen ear for plot and development. Later, Mimí
offers a gift that proves priceless—she provides the typewriter, financial
stability, and encouragement that finally motivate Eva to make a living
off her stories. Through Mimí's suggestion, Eva turns her melodramatic
tales into material for the popular *telenovelas* that dominate the television
stations. Finally, Eva has found an avenue for her talent that provides
sustenance and satisfaction. Her mother's long-ago gift has become her
independence.

Three male characters in the book merit attention, both for the special
relationships they have with Eva and for the male types they characterize
or counter. The first, Huberto Naranjo, is merely a wily street urchin
when Eva meets him. He lives by his wits and by the friendships he
develops with others living on the margins of society. As an adolescent,
he organizes a feared street gang called La Peste. Though they gain no-
toriety for their lawlessness, the members of La Peste originally band
together not to prey on innocents but to fight the middle-class street
gangs who dress in leather jackets and cruise the neighborhoods on expensive motorcycles. Naranjo's early fight for justice against these
wealthy truants foreshadows his lifelong devotion to the national rebel
movement that claims his adult years. When Naranjo is recruited by the
guerrilla forces, he begins to "see clearly the schisms that determine
men's lives from birth" (161) and resolves to channel all his rage into

the underground movement. In the first terrible months of deprivation and suffering in the mountains, Naranjo grows harder on the surface but internally exchanges his rage for a newfound compassion. Transformed into Comandante Rogelio, he welcomes new recruits with a pounding heart and a "lump in his throat" (211). This sensitivity wrapped in a stern exterior explains Naranjo's special devotion to protecting Eva, both when she is a homeless girl ensconced in La Señora's household and when she is a comfortable writer aiding the guerrillas. The couple's parting words of sincere, concerned care for each other demonstrate Naranjo's sensitivity despite his hard exterior.

Although Eva Luna's father disappears from the novel in the first pages, Riad Halabí plays a key paternal role in her life. A man marked by the deformity of his cleft lip, he is described as a member of the tribe of persons "undone by their own compassion" (125). In Riad's case, this includes exhibiting genuine solicitude for others, taking pity on the needy, and being careful not to offend anyone with his distracting deformity. Riad becomes a salesman primarily to engage in bargaining, a formalized social interaction under whose guise he can nurture a deeply felt need to connect to others. When he proves too "honest and unambitious" to be successful in the capital, his acquaintances urge him to move to the small towns "where people were more ingenuous" (126). Shaped less by his ethnicity as a Turk than by his disfigurement, Riad's character is drawn as a deliberate antithesis to the stereotypical *machismo* of the Latin American male, encouraging Eva Luna's education and feigning ignorance when Zulema has an affair with his cousin. Finally, thanks to his boundless thoughtfulness, Riad is so attuned to the needs of his partner that he is characterized as the perfect lover.

Rolf Carlé is eight years Eva's senior, born in Austria to a sadistic schoolmaster who abuses his children and despises his wife. Rolf's life is marked by death and despair. During World War II, he and his fellow villagers are forced by the occupying Russian soldiers to bury the dead bodies at a local prison camp, thus burning the images of the ovens and gallows into their memories. Rolf's father returns after the war to abuse his family further, compelling the mentally disabled Katharina to retreat fearfully under the dining room table. Lukas Carlé occasionally forces his terrified wife to strut naked in red patent-leather stiletto-heeled boots for his pleasure. When Rolf finally escapes after his father's murder and his own banishment to South America, he is a young man with many skills but little ability to give or accept affection. Almost the only love he demonstrates is toward the pups his uncle breeds for the rich. Just as the novel follows Eva Luna's journey to independence and artistry, so does it chart Rolf's gradual healing and introduction into the world of filmmaking, which will be his refuge. The book's close features Rolf as the classic hero, whisking Eva Luna to safety in La Colonia and settling with her into a life of love that mimics the storybook endings of her most illustrious characters.

THEMES

With *Eva Luna*, Allende returns to subjects she has emphasized in her previous novels while weaving in a new theme that reflects the Caribbean landscape. Like the female protagonists in *The House of the Spirits* and *Of Love and Shadows*, Eva Luna uses her memory and imagination to defend against forgetting, using the written text as the primary receptacle for preserving the past. The importance of writing is foregrounded here in a way that it has not been in the previous books, as Eva Luna spends most of her younger years untaught and fully dependent on oral expression. To be able to write, then, is viewed as a gift that characters such as Clara the Clairvoyant and Irene Beltrán take for granted. Where *Eva Luna* diverges most from its predecessors, however, is in the way the narrative celebrates life. In the face of difficulties, characters still embrace their existence, love each other with exuberance, and welcome the future, reflecting a world released at least in part from the burden of history.

Critics have noted the important role that memory plays in the novel, both as a literary device and as a method for resurrecting the lost. First, Consuelo promises Eva on her deathbed that she will stay alive as long as the girl remembers her. Not only do Eva's powerful recollections keep her mother's memory alive, but Eva also finds herself able to resurrect her mother corporeally in times of trouble. Later, Eva remarks that her stories arise from the "genetic memory" passed to her from her maternal ancestors before her birth (224). Likewise, she has the power to erase, modify, and manufacture memories for her listeners, and even, by the novel's close, for herself. One critic comments, "Allende's long, allusive meditations on Latin American literary history ensure that this history, too, will remain alive" (Diamond-Nigh 42). Eva wields a dangerous power—she can change life with her words. The men in the novel who find themselves enthralled by Eva Luna seem often to be attracted as much to the magical power of her stories as they are to her presence.

Interestingly, Eva's ability to salvage, embellish, and even invent memories is characterized as a female attribute alone. While Eva's mother, too, has the storytelling gift, only Rolf Carlé comes close to Eva Luna's talent in his ability to create stories—and his offerings remain in the concrete realm of factual journalistic artifacts, including interviews, film footage, and historical documentaries. Ultimately, the restorative effect of Eva's remade tales is hers alone.

In addition to preserving memories, the physical act of writing itself has a palpable value for Eva Luna. Born not only a pauper but also a female, Eva Luna is doubly barred from the luxury of education, though she spends much of her childhood immersed in storytelling in the forms of oral folklore and radio serials. Despite her inability to recognize a single letter of the alphabet, Eva Luna understands the value of words. When Naranjo leaves her with La Señora, the worldly madam advises Eva Luna that looks are important for women and that she must lift her head and smile. Eva answers back wisely, "I'd rather learn to read" (106). She is not destined to do so, however, until Riad Halabí adopts her into his household. The principled man secures Eva Luna's future when he ensures her literacy. For Eva Luna, a new world is opened, one in which she can invent more complex stories and delve into the minds of other writers. Riad's gift to her of the four-volume *A Thousand and One Nights* offers Eva Luna not only masses of fresh material but also a newfound sexuality that blasts into her life with the "force of a typhoon" (137). Just as words provide Eva Luna the means to gain sustenance during the desperate crises of her childhood, and then initiate her into the mysteries of her adult desires, so do they offer her one of the only avenues to historical documentation permitted in the police state. After the prison escape at Santa María, Eva Luna acts on Rolf Carlé's urging to write the facts of the revolt into *Bolero,* her daytime soap opera. Through this courageous move, Eva Luna single-handedly records a historical event that would otherwise face censorship or complete suppression, a triumph of free expression due not in small part to the artistry with language that is Eva's gift.

As numerous critics have noted, the novel as a whole seems infused with a sense of exuberance about life and its many sensual joys, despite inescapable hardships and cruelties. In a departure from the harsher backdrop of the previous South American novels, *Eva Luna* grows out of the lush Caribbean landscape that extends to its colorful characters. Even while Eva Luna herself lives an austere existence as a penniless servant, her world blooms with the beauty and adventure promised by the untamed wilderness around her. Civilization often seems an after-thought in the Caribbean setting, as exemplified by both the isolated La Colonia and the mission where Eva Luna's mother is raised, an outpost in the middle of an "expanse of voluptuous vegetation writhing and twisting from the banks of the river" (4). When Rolf Carlé glimpses the country for the first time, he is most struck by the riot of sights, sounds, and smells that assault him, chasing away the melancholy left by a war-torn Europe and an abusive father. Even the European transplants, Uncle Rupert, Aunt Burgel, and their daughters, embrace the voracious appe-tites of the region as they indulge in aphrodisiac stews and, in the case of the two cinnamon-scented girls, unorthodox bedroom play with their new cousin Rolf. Toward the end of the novel, as Eva Luna waits with the Indians to help effect the prison escape, the jungle's edge seems an exciting, dangerous place, a dark "temple" full of dangers hidden from human eyes (248) that yet inspires a blossoming love between Eva and Rolf Carlé. Whether the characters live cloistered in La Colonia or lurk on the edges of the jungle, they embrace the exotic and the sensual. Finally, unlike Allende's previous two novels, *Eva Luna* ends with a hopeful, exotic scene of life's promise: Eva Luna belly dancing with her lover, telling stories between "laughter and sips of wine" (271).

ALTERNATIVE PERSPECTIVE: FEMINIST CRITICISM

The memorable Eva Luna is one of Isabel Allende's favorite creations, a woman comfortable in her own skin despite cultural codes that attempt to belittle or discount her womanhood and her social status. For this reason, Eva Luna's story is one that lends itself to a feminist critique (see chapter 3 for an introduction to this literary term). Allende describes her headstrong character as a woman who "accepts her feminine essence from the time that she is born; she never questions her own femininity . . . " (Cruz et al. 217). Birthed into a community of female servants, Eva Luna spends her life aligned to women. Even at her birth, Eva's mother comments that the "father's name isn't important" (20), despite a culture that counts paternity of sole importance. Throughout her growing years, Eva Luna rebels against the adults who attempt to contain her. When her *patrona* washes her mouth out with baking soda to keep her from talking out loud to her mother's ghost, Eva continues doing it secretly. Likewise, even after she is beaten for running away from that house, Eva asserts her right to gaze at the *patrona*'s painting of the sea, "never asking permission or offering an explanation" (62). Later, she baptizes the cabinet minister with his own urine to free herself permanently from degrading servitude. In these public and private acts of defiance, Eva Luna challenges the image of the obedient, submissive female that her society demands.

Counter to Eva Luna's fierce independence and confident initiative, Riad Halabí's wife, Zulema, exhibits the height of coddled femininity and indolence. She does not love her husband but stays with him out of safety and habit. Eva observes that Zulema fears all negative possibilities and lives in a state of inertia. She performs no role within the household and has no interests except "gold and jewels" (139). Riad spends much of his income on such gifts, only to have them buried in the yard due to Zulema's fear that they will be stolen. Like these hidden baubles, Zulema keeps her sexuality concealed from her devoted husband, indulging herself in pampered baths and the affair with Kamal. Though she enjoys Eva like a kind of "lapdog" (139), Zulema thrives most on the girl's stories, particularly those with handsome heroes whose good looks and strong bodies satisfy her sexual longings. Contributing nothing to her household or society and thwarted in her one foray into illicit romance, Zulema ultimately ends her own life and nearly destroys Eva Luna's at the same time. Zulema's suicide reads like an act of cowardice because she has been so utterly pampered and her husband requests so little from her. The narrative of Zulema represents a kind of cautionary tale to warn a society bent on infantilizing its women to the point of uselessness.

Zulema's helpless lethargy is hardly the norm in the novel, however. Many of the unmarried women in the book live industrious, independent lives with few prohibitions against their lifestyles or sexuality. The prostitutes enjoy a relatively independent and satisfying existence. The Austrian cousins manage to avoid strictures on even their most adventurous sexual activities. Eva feels little concern over her tryst with her guardian, Riad Halabí, or her relations with later male characters. Even Eva Luna's convent-trained mother suffers no serious consequences from her spontaneous sexual union with the snakebitten gardener. On the contrary, these women seem in control of their sexual relationships and, to a lesser extent, the direction of their lives. In a society ruled by patriarchal conventions and macho stereotypes, however, the self-reliant women who characterize Eva Luna make their choices and assert their autonomy largely on the edges of society with the major events still within male control.

The negative effects of a male-dominated culture shadow the entire novel. From Rolf Carlé's masochistic father, who magnifies the evils wrought during the Nazi regime, to the lieutenant who beats Eva Luna senseless in the prison, examples of unchecked male power color the episodes in which women claim back their lives. Even Eva's relationship with Naranjo is shaped by these characteristics. The same "noble" machismo that causes Naranjo to protect Eva, that urges him to feed and clothe her while keeping her from prostitution, also causes him to withhold guerilla secrets from her and bar her from the rebel movement. Eva quotes Naranjo's motto, "If you want to get ahead, you have to be macho" (58). She calls this his "crutch" and seems not to hold to the traditional views of her society. In fact, Eva ultimately realizes that the revolution Naranjo is fighting will achieve little for her or the community of women to which she belongs because they are not allowed to participate in any broad decision-making or future leadership plans. Though she supports the rebel effort and risks everything to aid the prison escape, Eva Luna understands her limited position and depends only on herself and her writing abilities to gain financial and emotional independence. When Colonel Tolomeo Rodríguez propositions Eva, she takes the upper hand, urging them to go to bed at once and "get this over with tonight" (222). Even in such a vulnerable position, Eva Luna finds a way to assert herself and ultimately to triumph over the oppressive culture.

In a like way, Melesio, the transvestite who eventually becomes Mimí, plays a special role in the novel's exploration of male and female roles. Allende imagined the character as a type of Latin American antithesis, a parodic figure to "question many aspects of machismo" (Cruz et al. 221). In her newly fashioned female body, Mimí enjoys the trappings of being female but seems always to end up with a "tough, macho type, who . . . would exploit her" (189). Eventually, even Mimí comes into her own. As a celebrated soap opera actress, she finally enjoys the life of a wealthy, beautiful woman who depends on no one. She uses her charms to seduce Aravena, the TV director, and reaps not only a key role for herself and a soap opera option for Eva Luna, but also a devoted partner who worships her womanliness. In an exaggerated way, Mimí offers a small revolution of her own—that men can throw off the chains of macho culture and embrace what is feminine in themselves, to the betterment of the entire society.

6

The Infinite Plan
(1993)

Only three months after Isabel Allende divorced her husband of twenty-five years, she met William Gordon, a San Francisco lawyer whose life read like a novel (*P* 299). Nearing the end of a lecture tour, Allende found herself at dinner with a handsome man who had read *Of Love and Shadows* and wanted to meet its author. During the meal, Allende asked the reticent stranger to share his life story—a trick she uses to save herself "the effort of making conversation" (*P* 299). Captivated by this man's unlikely narrative, filled with eccentric family members and an unconventional childhood in a Los Angeles barrio, Allende found herself intrigued enough for a second date and ultimately a permanent relationship. Noting that she perhaps mentally began writing *The Infinite Plan* her first evening with Willie, Allende often quips that she had no choice but to marry such a valuable literary resource. Though the novel is undeniably fictional, its main character, Gregory Reeves, bears a marked resemblance to Allende's husband, and the complicated journey of the imaginary California native follows many of the same twists and turns as that of his real-life counterpart.

A major challenge for Allende in moving the setting of one of her novels from the familiar landscapes of Chile and Venezuela to the urban streets of Los Angeles involved recreating images of a life in California that she had never experienced firsthand. In order to produce a narrative that would ring true to its American readership, Allende had to rely on her training as a journalist to guide her through rigorous research. Specifically, Allende needed to understand better the firsthand experiences of Vietnam veterans, first, fighting in an unwinnable war, and then, returning to an unsympathetic country. At the same time, she explored the counterculture of Berkeley in the 1960s and tried to understand the New Age world of 1970s California and the "Me" decade that followed in the 1980s. Allende explains, "I went to all the places, I 'researched' California: there really *is* a man who invented a religion called 'The Infinite Plan' " (Rodden 436). Though some critics have commented that these sections of the book can feel remote, the faded images of West Coast culture are also meant to conjure up a world that has passed, and one that Gregory Reeves must somehow learn to survive and grow beyond.

PLOT

The book opens on a curious picture of a poor yet dignified homeless family near the end of World War II. Charles Reeves, who titles himself a Doctor in Divine Sciences, is little more than a charismatic fraud, but even he nearly believes his own tale of mystical conversion. During his purported vision, Reeves claims that the Master of the Universe came to him and revealed the mystery of the universe, otherwise known as the Infinite Plan. Since that revelation, Reeves has taken it upon himself to travel American back roads in a rattletrap truck painted with colorful symbols of his celestial system in order to share this wisdom with the searching. Reeves earns his meager living through the fees incurred for his speeches and books and by painting cheap renditions of *National Geographic* pictures on demand. His traveling companions include his wife Nora, a middle-aged schoolteacher resigned to spinsterhood who fell in love with him one night at a public lecture, and their two children, Judy and Gregory. Olga, the fifth member of the party, is an old friend of Nora's from Russia who contributes to the family income by telling fortunes and delivering babies in the tiny towns where they set up their temporary camps. Though the family lives on the tightest of incomes for a number of years, Charles Reeves regulates their little universe with strict rules and steadfast order.

For Gregory, the first years of his life spent traveling the back roads of America are the only secure and peaceful ones of his childhood. His earliest memories include watching a peaceful sunset on an open hillside and meeting a black soldier named King Benedict, who hitches a ride with the family one day and then disappears from the story, and Gregory's life, for many years. The family's fortunes take a drastic turn at the end of World War II. First, Nora falls into a deep depression precipitated by the atom bombs dropped on Japan, and she uses this as a reason to withdraw even more from the others. Then Charles Reeves falls gravely ill, losing weight and breaking into fever. For a time, Olga nurses the failing patriarch and takes his place as the head of the family. When it becomes clear that Charles Reeves will not be getting better, the family delivers him to a hospital in Los Angeles and then takes refuge in the home of Pedro Morales, a devotee of the Doctor in Divine Sciences who feels honored to serve his wise teacher. Pedro and his gentle wife, Inmaculada, become Gregory's second parents, welcoming him into their clan of six children as if he had been born to them. The Morales children initiate Gregory and Judy into the ways of the barrio, teaching them to speak the hybrid "Spanglish" of Los Angeles and to survive on the mean streets of the neighborhood. Gregory becomes fast friends with the second daughter, Carmen, a year younger than him but "much better informed" (48). When Charles Reeves is released from the hospital, the Morales family and their relatives help to repair an old house on the edge of the barrio for the Reeves to make a more permanent home.

For Gregory, the family's sedentary life is not a happy one. The ill and raging Charles Reeves drinks too much and beats his children. Gregory is also taunted and persecuted by the older boys of the barrio because he looks and speaks differently from them. The steady Olga, who had offered some security to the unstable family, removes herself to separate lodgings where she makes her living telling fortunes and entertaining male visitors. Reeves continues to fail and sink into depravity until he finally succumbs to his illness, leaving a bewildered Nora with neither the fortitude nor the practical skills to raise her children. Under Pedro Morales's guidance, she signs up for welfare and then tries on two occasions to give away her difficult son. Refused at the orphanage, and then running away from the farm family that offers to adopt him, Gregory finally convinces his mother to keep him, answered by her appeal that he "grow up soon" (82). Finding home an unpredictable shelter, Gregory becomes obsessed with making money, first shining shoes and then performing street entertainment with Carmen. He continues to be tormented by the older barrio boys, until one day he is cornered and raped by a boy named Martínez, one of the leaders of the Carniceros gang. Gregory feels such despair over his solitary and persecuted life that he wishes to die.

The novel moves forward to Gregory at sixteen, now attending high school and learning about socialist political systems from the communist elevator operator at the library. Outside school and work, Gregory's time is spent dancing at every opportunity, with Carmen as his adept partner, in an attempt to relieve himself of the agony produced by riotous hormones. One day Olga, whom Gregory has continued to visit all these years, takes pity on his pubescent suffering and makes Gregory her lover. For months, she initiates her charge into the mysteries of sexual love. At the same time, Gregory's nemesis, Martínez, begins to threaten Carmen, and so Gregory challenges the barrio bully to a "duel to the death" (100)—a race against the train that runs behind the tire factory. Gregory practices in secret and counts on Martínez's macho to keep the older boy from preparing properly, backing down, or in any way showing fear. Gregory's calculations prove correct, as he wins the duel and Martínez is killed by the passing train. The death of his enemy and the lessons learned in Olga's bed bring a close to Gregory's boyhood.

After the legendary train incident, Gregory becomes a favorite in his high school, winning the class presidency and attempting to foster unity among the races, at least in his small corner of the barrio. Encouraged by his library friend Cyrus and Olga to attend college, Gregory instead accepts the "invisible ceiling" (115) of barrio youths and takes a series of labor jobs that leave him injured and bored. When Cyrus falls fatally ill, he makes the young man promise to attend college, even leaving a sum of money to get him started. Gregory uses the cash instead to procure a respectful funeral for his old friend and then makes good on his promise by heading north to Berkeley to finish his education.

After twenty years of "routine, fatigue, and asphyxia," Gregory finds Berkeley intoxicating, "the cradle of radical movements and audacious forms of rebellion" (125). Overwhelmed by the university bureaucracy and the urgency of finding work and housing, Gregory is relieved to befriend a handsome student named Timothy Duane, who offers to share his lodging. Gregory enrolls in classes and finds work, also joining the ROTC for the full four years and attaining the rank of officer. He travels home rarely, though he does manage to return for Judy's marriage to a persistent red-haired factory foreman whom she weds in order to fulfill her desire for children. Carmen takes Gregory's absence the hardest and ends up in a relationship with a freethinking newspaperman, who leaves town before she discovers she is pregnant. Carmen agonizes over the decision to end her pregnancy and is quite far along by the time she seeks Olga's assistance. When she begins to hemorrhage, Olga calls on Gregory, who flies down to Los Angeles and gets Carmen to a hospital.

The Moraleses discover what has happened when police arrive at their house to question them about the illegal abortion. Although they do not inform on Olga, she retreats to Puerto Rico for a time. Meanwhile, Pedro Morales dons a black armband and makes it known that, for him, his daughter no longer exists. The disinherited Carmen, barren from the botched abortion, retreats to Mexico City to find work in a jewelry factory.

Thriving in college, Gregory graduates with honors and then transfers to a law school in San Francisco, both because he is attracted to the profession and because he hopes to avoid military service for a time. Gregory's initial attraction to the ROTC uniform has soured with the instigation of the Vietnam War. At the same time, he begins earnestly courting a woman he has met in college, the rich but empty Samantha Ernst. Despite their wildly disparate backgrounds and Samantha's cool demeanor toward him, Gregory convinces himself that she is the missing piece that could make him "part of a real family" (147). To make money, Gregory begins a child-sitting service where he watches a herd of youngsters after school. The work is exhausting but entrepreneurial, and Gregory makes a solid business of it. At about this time, Samantha's father produces an unsuccessful large-scale film and is ruined financially. Samantha's new state of penniless ness hastens her marriage to Gregory, who adds his new wife's many demands onto his long list of obligations.

The marriage is not a successful one, characterized by the same lack of communication exhibited during the couple's courtship and heightened by their proximity and a surprise pregnancy. Samantha loathes the idea of her body swelling and expelling a child, and she becomes indolent and depressed with the news. Gregory, on the other hand, sees his desire for a real family materializing in this child and so he puts up with Samantha's childishness. When baby Margaret arrives five weeks early, Samantha must undergo a caesarean section and can hardly endure the scar across her body or the tiny intruder in her life. She rarely touches the baby, only giving her the minimal care. Gregory is likewise reluctant to cuddle his daughter, burdened by the accusations his sister has made recently about his father's sexual abuse and wondering if such a vulgar predilection could be inherited. Margaret develops slowly under her parents' inattention, and a pediatrician recommends classes to teach them fundamental parenting skills. Margaret gradually becomes a strange little girl, quiet and withdrawn, who washes her hands compulsively.

The marriage reaches a crisis when Margaret is two years old. Gregory comes home to find a neighbor leading his daughter by the hand; she has apparently wandered almost two miles from the house. With her usual lethargy, Samantha evades responsibility, and the couple gets into a loud fight. That night during a "wife-swapping" party, Gregory discovers that Samantha has been sleeping with several of his friends. He stays away from the house for five nights, takes his bar exam, and then reports immediately to the army. After a grueling basic training, Gregory is selected for language study and learns Vietnamese in two months. Then he leaves for Vietnam.

Gregory's tour in Vietnam proves a relentless nightmare. To calm his terrors and dull the suffering caused by cold, bad food, and mosquitoes, Gregory takes many kinds of drugs by the handful. Though he goes overseas to "live recklessly, to give meaning to my life" (184), the horrors of a brutal war strip Gregory of all but one goal: to survive. By impossible coincidence, he runs into Juan José Morales one day on the beach. They reminisce on their boyhood spent as brothers and the ten-year separation since, including Gregory's wife and daughter and Juan José's Vietnamese sweetheart, Thui. Shortly after that meeting, Juan José is mortally wounded in battle and sends his scapular of the Virgin of Guadalupe to Gregory for good luck. For Gregory, the height of terror during his Vietnam tour is a night spent trying to defend a mountaintop. When a scared young man from Kansas is mortally wounded, Gregory feels something inside him break. He throws his weapon aside and begins screaming over the roar of the guns. Then he turns and begins to collect wounded men, carrying them fearlessly through heavy gunfire to safety. Gregory's nerves collapse at the end of the night, and he ends up restrained in an army hospital. Nevertheless, he receives a Silver Star for valiantly saving eleven soldiers.

Ultimately, Gregory is given an assignment to collect intelligence in a mountain village. Teaching English to the villagers is meant merely to be his cover, but this mission becomes far more important to Gregory than the gathering of meaningless and rare information. Several months pass in relative peace, but then Gregory begins to suffer from what seems to be a severe case of dysentery. Treating himself with a variety of medications, it finally becomes apparent that he is desperately ill and the army transfers him to a hospital in Hawaii. During the weeks spent recovering, Gregory faces his life squarely and decides he has little to live for except to become rich and powerful. He determines that with prestige and wealth, no one in or out of the barrio will be able to look down on him with disdain. After three weeks' recovery, an incredulous

Gregory is sent back to Saigon. During a two-day leave, he asks his friend Leo Galupi, a veteran who served two years and then decided to stay permanently, to locate Juan José's girlfriend, Thui. As it turns out, she has already heard of her lover's death and assures Gregory mysteriously that she has all she needs.

While Gregory is trying to complete his tour of duty unscathed, Carmen is experiencing adventures of her own. She spends the second half of her four years in Mexico City living with an anthropologist who alternately educates her in the ways of past cultures and abuses her in drunken rages. When Gregory discovers the oppressive environment to which Carmen has subjected herself, he sends her money and she escapes to Europe, where she travels the continent and pays her expenses by making jewelry. Finally, she settles in Barcelona to study the history of jewelry-making and eventually sets up house with a Japanese lover, who forces her to submit and serve, much like her previous partner. Because he does not beat her, Carmen persuades herself that this is an acceptable relationship with mere cultural differences. Then a telegram from her mother arrives announcing that Pedro Morales has become ill; Carmen decides the family estrangement has gone on long enough and she leaves for home after seven years away. Though momentarily shocked by the wild gypsy who enters his home, Pedro embraces his daughter, and Inmaculada invites the neighbors over for a celebration. After a few weeks, it becomes apparent that Carmen has outgrown the barrio and she moves to Berkeley with the blessing and financial help of her father. There she finds her natural environment, a free community that embraces her independence, her exotic jewelry, and her new identity, "Tamar."

Gregory returns to San Francisco but tells no one for two weeks. Attempting to purge himself of the war, he burns his war souvenirs and resolves neither to remain addicted to the drugs and alcohol that had dulled his terror nor to become "hooked forever on the nostalgia" of that time in his life as so many others had (233). During this period, his nightmares begin, fearful images of that night on the mountaintop and other horrors of war that will continue for many years. Meeting Samantha at last, Gregory realizes that their marriage is over and that his daughter Margaret is a stranger. He returns to Los Angeles to a distant mother and preoccupied older sister and does not feel welcomed until he finally returns to the Morales's home to describe for them Juan José's last moments. Back in San Francisco, Gregory reunites with Carmen who has set herself up selling jewelry on the streets. The two meet in a torrent of pent-up emotions, find a motel room, and make love desperately.

Despite this show of intense need, however, they gradually discover that each has changed in irreversible ways and they part awkwardly, losing touch for the next two years.

Essentially freed from past attachments, Gregory sets all his attention on becoming a powerful lawyer. His first stroke of luck occurs at a dinner given by Timothy Duane's parents where he meets one of the most powerful lawyers in California and lands a position in his firm. For the next seven years, Gregory works long hours and battles his way up the hierarchy of the firm. He pays Samantha alimony and visits Margaret at longer and longer intervals. As his fortunes change, Gregory also begins an obsession with procuring the accoutrements of his new life, including a string of beautiful women, a yacht, a Porsche, expensive furnishings, and impeccable clothes. Though most of these purchases are acquired on credit, Gregory feels, nonetheless, that he has begun to effect the lifestyle he has dreamed of for himself since his barrio days. Likewise, in his pursuit of women, Gregory settles for "quantity, not quality" (254) and ends up feeling emptier after each encounter.

A couple years go by, and then Carmen gets a letter from Vietnam. In it Juan José's girlfriend, Thui, explains that she is very ill and needs to send her twenty-one-month-old son, Dai, to America. Carmen immediately elicits Gregory's help in getting her overseas so that she can, at long last, become a mother. In Saigon, Carmen is met by Gregory's old friend Leo Galupi, a resourceful man who makes his living in Vietnam through underhanded business dealings. Unlike any other, Leo knows how to maneuver the system and manages to speed the adoption through as Carmen spends time with Thui and little Dai. Toward the end, however, Leo deliberately stalls the proceedings in order to keep this intriguing woman in his life for a few extra weeks. When Carmen recognizes her old lover Tom Clayton at an embassy dinner, Leo surmises a deeper story. After they return to his apartment, Carmen shares her life story, talking long into the night, and a friendship is cemented between the two Americans. At last, Dai's papers come through and Carmen leaves with him for the United States. There the boy suffers from terrible loneliness, never speaks, and eats almost nothing. At Olga's advice, Carmen tells him that his mother is now a "tiny translucent fairy" watching over him (273). With this information, Dai eats his first meal. A year later, he smiles for the first time, and a year after that, he speaks his first words in English. For Carmen, Dai is like the vindication for her lost child a decade before; she feels content and peaceful for the first time in years.

Under the able instruction of an excellent and shrewd lawyer, Gregory continues to excel in his profession and live a madcap bachelor life that draws him deeper and deeper into debt. During this time, a new receptionist arrives at the firm. Shannon is a twenty-two-year-old ingénue from Georgia with no money and few assets beyond her charms; nevertheless, her seeming innocence enchants Gregory, who pursues her with an adolescent fervor. To keep Shannon from a modeling career, Gregory invites her to live with him. Months later, he returns home to tell her that he has decided to open his own law office and she announces her pregnancy.

The case that catapults Gregory into independent practice involves the soldier who had hitchhiked a ride with his rambling family caravan many years before. King Benedict is the only son of Bel, the faithful housekeeper of Timothy Duane's parents. Now fifty-three, King has suffered a fall on a construction job that has rendered him amnesiac. Remembering nothing after his fourteenth year, King has effectively become a child again and depends wholly on his mother for protection. When Duane brings the case to his old college friend, Gregory believes he can successfully sue the insurance company for permanent disability. As the head of his firm scoffs at Gregory's plans, he decides it is time to go his own way. Borrowing yet again from his bank, Gregory goes deeper into debt to begin this venture at the same time that he marries Shannon and prepares for a new child. Renting a small office above a Chinese restaurant, Gregory meets the restaurant owner's son, Mike Tong, who becomes his frugal accountant and loyal first employee in a firm that grows to six lawyers in two years.

Gregory's marriage to Shannon proves as luckless as his first, as she rapidly loses interest in homemaking and child care. When Gregory learns that she has been kissing one of the young lawyers in his firm in public, he leaves her briefly, only to return to a repentant wife who almost immediately betrays him again. During this period, Gregory's teenage daughter, Margaret, runs away from home, eventually to be found in a bar wearing whorish clothes and showing evidence of heroin use. For the next nine years, her father will be unable to save her as she gradually spirals into drug addiction and prostitution. In a similar way, Gregory's life begins to spin out of control, as he finally admits defeat in a second marriage and divorces Shannon. When she deserts their hyperactive son, David, because she has a "right to live her life" (323), Gregory's life becomes even more chaotic as he juggles a busy law firm, heavy debts, and a traumatized child. Finally, the night of his mother's funeral, Gregory suffers a terrifying anxiety attack that he mistakes for a heart attack and finally admits that he needs help.

Carmen helps to keep Gregory from a breakdown by first providing him with a wonderful Dominican housekeeper. Daisy takes David as her special charge and transforms the household with her practical ways. Gregory decides it is time to face his own demons, gives up alcohol and women, and seeks therapy from a psychiatrist recommended by his friend Timothy Duane. For five years, Gregory attends his sessions and gradually overcomes his lifelong anxiety and guilt. He tries to help his daughter, Margaret, now ruined by heroin and prostitution, but when his efforts fail, he learns that he must let her go. Flanked by his unfailing accountant, Mike, and secretary, Tina, Gregory continues to pursue King Benedict's insurance case. He uncovers an earlier episode of childhood head injury and trauma that may account for the later amnesia. The insurance company settles during pretrial, and Gregory helps King and his mother invest the money for their future.

Gradually, both Carmen and Gregory simplify their lives, she by going overseas to propose marriage to Leo Galupi and he by getting rid of parasitic colleagues and reducing his expenses. Gregory still does not have the money to carry malpractice insurance, however, and when a disgruntled client brings a malpractice suit against him, the future of Gregory's law firm is in grave danger. When a jury finds Gregory at fault, he tells Mike and Tina that he is declaring bankruptcy. Gregory takes the blow with composure, telling himself that "there is no infinite plan, just the strife of living" (379). He reflects that all the struggles of his life have prepared him for such a dead end. Then, as he returns to the office to shut it down, Mike and Tina are there ahead of him. They announce that Carmen, in Rome with Leo, has lent the firm a large sum of money. One of Mike's uncles has extended a loan for the rest. Gregory realizes that the fight will continue and he smiles to meet the challenge.

CHARACTER DEVELOPMENT

Casting her main character as an American male is a radical departure for Allende, and one that succeeds surprisingly well. Gregory Reeves is an imperfect figure, a selfish egotist who takes as his central goals in life the pursuit of wealth and the seduction of women. However, at his core he is a sensitive man damaged by a difficult and brief childhood whose surface interests mask deeper unmet yearnings. In a review of *The Infinite*

Plan, Robert Bly suggests that the reader is never certain that "we know the interior life of any one of [Allende's] characters" (Bly 13). It is true that the narrator often seems to observe Gregory from a reserved distance, documenting his haphazard choices without revealing the internal motivation for those behaviors. Even during the first-person sections, Gregory seems habitually unable to articulate his feelings or motives. One example is the week Gregory spends deciding whether he should stay with unfaithful Samantha or join the Vietnam conflict. The reader learns little of his turmoil, only that during that period Gregory makes decisions that will help turn him into the "arrogant, frivolous, and greedy man" (178) who dominates the greater portion of the novel.

The obscurity that clouds Gregory's interior life seems appropriate rather than problematic here. Confused by the gap between his barrio background and privileged racial status, trapped in loveless relationships that he enters in a perpetual search for a substitute mother, and driven by the need to rectify inadequacies in both his parents and himself, Gregory regularly makes poor choices in an unconscious fashion. Thus, his seeming lack of selfhood is not a defect in the narrative but a flaw in his character. If Gregory were unredeemable, the book would be an empty exercise. In truth, however, Gregory has a deep sense of himself in relation to the universe, one that coalesces in the first pages of the novel. There, Gregory describes his earliest memory, an epiphany he experiences at four years old while urinating on a hilltop. At that moment, Gregory understands that he belongs to a "splendid place" where anything can happen and every event is purposeful (6). Throughout his life, when Gregory faces seemingly impossible difficulties and the infinite plan touted by his father turns ludicrous, he returns mentally to that memory that offers him a sense of well-being. In a sense, Gregory's journey through capsized relationships, war horrors, and legal contests brings him full circle to that sense of the stripped-bare meaning of life. At the novel's close, Gregory has reconciled himself to the relentless hardships of life and given up the empty pursuit of material wealth. In exchange, he believes he has claimed back his soul, left in the "quicksands" of his boyhood (381).

Gregory's parents take up minimal space in the book, but their roles in shaping the main character's destiny reach across the entire novel. Charles Reeves, the disseminator of the "Infinite Plan," is a mysterious figure. Considered a wise teacher and present-day prophet by his wife, son, and numerous disciples, Reeves looms large in Gregory's early childhood as the family's authoritarian but dependable leader whose

chief end in life is to unravel the mysteries of the universe for his fol-
lowers. To his young son, Charles appears omniscient, watching his clan
"like the eye of God" (6). Though Gregory clings to the memory of his
father as a benevolent, if stern, man, his sister Judy characterizes the
patriarch as a counterfeit preacher, an egomaniac, and a child abuser.
While Gregory remembers only one cruel episode in which his father
burns his hand as punishment for petty stealing, Judy argues that the
violence was always there, haunting her brother with beatings and
haunting her with incest—abuse that escalates with their father's illness.
In his final days, the father is maniacal, an image that becomes a source
of nightmares for Gregory who envisions his father as a dark skeleton
with a snake coiled around his legs (53).

The children's mother does little to protect them against mistreatment,
looking on impassively as little Gregory's hand is burned and respond-
ing to the beatings with silence. With a powerful husband controlling
her life, the reserved Russian immigrant Nora "gradually faded from the
world, turning into a shadow" (22). She is an impassive person whom
Gregory tries to reach again and again. He finally decides that she cannot
feel true love toward anyone, even her own children. After years of raging against her indifference, the adult Gregory finally decides to be
thankful for the three gifts she gave him: "love for music, tolerance, and
a sense of honor" (23). After the loss of her husband, Nora begins to
fade from reality, lapsing into a quiet madness. As her husband escapes
through death, so does Nora withdraw from the world despite the young
children left in her care.

Olga, a fellow Russian immigrant, knows Nora from years before and
steps into the family drama easily. Adventurous and independent, Olga
stands as a foil to the shrinking Nora and acts as an unconventional
mother figure to Judy and Gregory when their parents prove incapable
of the role. During Gregory's boyhood, Olga seems like a "grumbling
aunt" (19) who steps in when the family falls into crisis. Though the
mystery is never fully revealed, Olga also seems to be Charles Reeves's
secret lover, both when he falls ill and later when she no longer shares
the Reeveses' home. Unlike the other family members, Olga is not cowed
by the authoritarian patriarch but matches his intensity measure for measure. She also loves both the children as if they were her own, though
she separates herself enough from them emotionally to become Gregory's lover for a brief period in his adolescence. Despite hardships that
match and even surpass Nora's, Olga adapts to life's difficulties and
makes a home for herself in the Los Angeles barrio.

Gregory's older sister, Judy, does not fare as well. For the first years of Gregory's life, she is a comfort and a friend, rare qualities in his family. Then she inexplicably turns him away and becomes openly hostile to her entire family. It is only years later that Gregory discovers that the real reason for Judy's rejection stems from the incestuous abuse she has suffered at the hands of their father. A beauty in her youth, the sexually abused Judy becomes filled with self-loathing and ends up obese and angry. She seems incapable of loving any man despite three husbands and numerous lovers. She marries the red-haired foreman, Jim Morgan, solely to produce the children she yearns to bear. Because he gives her those, she ignores, for a time, his alcoholism and mistreatment, but then is relieved finally to divorce him. Only as a mother to her brood of children and to others that she adopts does Judy find a way to heal her brokenness and recover some of the tenderness of her younger years.

Standing in counterpoint to the dysfunctional Reeves family is the Mexican family that comes to their aid. The Morales clan offers an encouraging, if perhaps stereotypical, picture of the traditional Mexican immigrant family's trajectory from illegal aliens to established citizens. Even their surname "Morales" suggests the careful value system to which they adhere. Pedro, the ostensible rock of the family, has followed his dream to give his children a future in Los Angeles that is unavailable to them in Zacatecas, Mexico. With old country values and strict discipline, he succeeds in getting his four sons through high school and established in various jobs. Though he loses one son to Vietnam, he refuses to lose another to the barrio gangs, and forces his second son to work in his automobile repair shop until the boy is mature enough to manage his own garage. The two daughters are raised under the same authoritarian rule with mixed results. Inmaculada is the true rock of the family, a saintly woman and the "universal mother figure" (44) of the book who parents not only her own children but also Gregory Reeves and the entire barrio. Her gentle talents seem almost magical as she produces enough food from her simple kitchen for any number of visitors. Like the perfect matron, she takes on all the burdens of the household with never a complaint or word of self-pity. Pedro and Inmaculada jokingly call themselves "wire-cutting wetbacks" (41), seemingly untroubled by their struggle as aliens in an unforgiving country. By gradually gaining legal status and financial independence, they also succeed in achieving a lifestyle that, as the narrator points out, so many immigrants fail to attain. After years in his adoptive country, Pedro finds himself at the end of his days "surrounded by grandchildren who spoke no word of Spanish" (73) and, in a scene that the narrator paints with wistful irony, he seems satisfied with what he has accomplished.

The Moraleses' second daughter Carmen is the classic second-generation immigrant. Acclimated to her place in barrio society, she is also ready to move beyond her doorstep into an American world where women have more opportunities and more space to breathe. She is the one who urges Gregory Reeves to play their street act in the wealthier business district and tourist areas of Los Angeles instead of staying behind the invisible wall of the barrio. As a small girl, she announces her desire to do more than live her mother's life again, imagining herself as a circus performer or a professional dancer. When the young woman becomes enamored with a white newspaperman and finds herself pregnant, however, Carmen discovers the limits of her world; she becomes barren from a botched abortion and is disowned by her humiliated father. Alone first in Mexico City and then in Europe, Carmen becomes involved with a series of abusive men, but always returns to Gregory, who is her closest life companion, though never a successful love match. It is Dai, the Vietnamese boy fathered by Carmen's older brother, who saves the woman's life. Emancipated from a string of empty relationships and an uncertain career path, Carmen finds motherhood "calming for her soul" (276), and she gradually develops a healthy self-confidence as a parent and as a first-class jewelry designer. Carmen's journey to selfhood mirrors Gregory's in that they both must overcome the narrow opportunities offered by the barrio and the unhealthy pull of dangerous relationships. Carmen, however, is immune to the obsession with money that controls Gregory. Thus, when money begins to come her way, she maintains equilibrium as a parent and a professional in contrast to Gregory's failure in these areas.

The other women in Gregory's life mirror each other and echo Nora Reeves in their lack of moral and emotional substance. His first wife, Samantha Ernst, is little more than a spoiled Hollywood child who has grown up wealthy and privileged but ignored by the adults around her. Her father has been obsessed with his mistresses, and her mother has committed suicide. Though Samantha has few interests, Gregory mistakes her quiet boredom for an enigmatic depth of character. He courts Samantha because he sees in this tall, healthy woman a chance for a real family. Yet, Samantha is obsessed only with her body and what goes into it, living always in a "fantasy world in which there was no room for sorrow or ugliness" (235). Her absolute self-absorption makes no room for Gregory or a genuine future. Ultimately, their marriage cannot survive the experimental drugs and free love of the 1970s. When Gregory discovers that Samantha is sleeping with his friends, he feels utterly betrayed, explaining that "something fundamental in [his] soul was forever twisted" (177). His second wife, Shannon, proves a younger version of Samantha. Though Shannon has had the opposite upbringing, raised in devastating poverty in the South, she has been conditioned like Samantha to believe her beauty sets her apart. When she arrives like a "breath of fresh air" in Gregory's life (286), he seems eager for laughter and companionship. As with his first wife, Gregory seems to fall into marriage with Shannon, this time due to a carefully calculated pregnancy that Shannon uses to ensure her financial security. Like Samantha, Shannon rapidly loses interest in all things domestic, allowing the house to fall into disrepair and leaving the baby for longer and longer periods. Losing herself to the lure of alcohol and lovers, Shannon also becomes an unbearable partner, and Gregory extricates himself from a second failed marriage.

Three male characters act as important reflections of and foils for Gregory. Gregory's college friend Timothy Duane, like the central character himself, lives his life in reaction to his father. Supported by an inheritance, Duane is not required to work and takes a job as a pathologist to thwart his father's wishes that he become a doctor of the living. Scoffing openly at his rich parents and their high-minded causes, Duane surreptitiously gives to charities and supports political movements. While his "greatest delight lay in creating a scandal" (285), Duane secretly mourns the lack of genuine love in his life. His existence, without lasting commitments or personal satisfaction, reflects Gregory's emptiness and suggests that should Gregory obtain the riches of which he dreams, the gratification will be fleeting. Duane is not the only cautionary tale, however; King Benedict suggests a second futile alternative.

King Benedict appears as a soldier on furlough early in the novel and then resurfaces years later as an injured laborer needing legal counsel. Just as the rancor Gregory and Timothy harbor against their parents has contributed to their arrested development, King has suffered a trauma that has literally set him back forty years. Despite the rare opportunity to live his life again more successfully, King behaves instead like a "somnambulist trapped in a recurrent dream" (353). When Gregory asks King's mother with wonder how a man can end up making the same mistakes twice, she wisely answers that no one can live "two different fates" and must focus on bettering the future rather than remedying the past (354). The character who best exemplifies this useful philosophy is

Mike Tong, the faithful accountant in Gregory's law firm. A minor char-acter in the book, Mike nonetheless looms large as the steady, thoughtful figure Gregory might become. The accountant looks squarely at financial matters, treats his colleagues with genuine respect, and when the law firm is threatened with collapse, finds a solution and looks to the future. At the novel's close, Gregory has begun to follow the example of this steady man and pattern himself on the gentle integrity of his most faith-ful employee.

THEMES

Examining modern life through the eyes of a male hero rather than one of the dynamic women who typically dominate Allende's imaginative worlds, *The Infinite Plan* departs from her previous works not only in its perspective but also in its style and themes. Indeed, Allende draws on at least three literary conventions to conceive the life journey of Gregory Reeves. The first part of the book follows the pattern of a coming-of-age novel, taking as its theme the discoveries and foibles of a developing youth. When Gregory reaches adulthood, his portrait replicates the mod-ern anti-hero, a flawed character whose failings regularly create obstacles in his life. A third theme underscores the destructive force of war, in this instance its devastating influence on Gregory's psyche. Despite the novel's apparent emphasis on psychological themes, *The Infinite Plan* ech-oes Allende's earlier fiction in reaffirming the value of human relation-ships to heal personal injuries.

The convention used to characterize the young Gregory Reeves is often called a *Bildungsroman*, a German literary term that means "coming of age" or "formation novel." Traditionally, the term describes the upbring-ing and education of a male hero, though in modern literature the focus might just as likely be on a female's development. Highly popular in the late eighteenth and early nineteenth century, examples of the form exist to the present day. A *Bildungsroman* takes as its subject matter the for-tunes and misfortunes encountered by a character until he or she reaches maturity. Often, the novel will reveal a character's innocence and inex-perience, liabilities that are gradually transformed into wisdom after ex-posure to the harsh everyday world. Before this transformation can occur, however, the character must first make some foolish mistakes and forge some valuable friendships that will serve to help him or her to triumph in society and find a useful profession.

The life journey of Gregory Reeves, then, follows many of the conventions of the *Bildungsroman*. Brought up in near poverty in the barrio, the outsider Gregory must fight first for basic survival and then for a place in his society. A shrewd entrepreneur, he begins working at a very young age but at the same time demonstrates the imprudence that often characterizes the hero in this type of story. Beginning as a young man and continuing into adulthood, Gregory makes a series of mistakes in his personal life and his career path. He becomes enthralled with money and beautiful women, letting the first rule his legal career, and the second his home life. Only after two divorces and near bankruptcy can he begin to claim responsibility for his children and his law firm. As for his emotional life, Gregory must piece himself back together, as well, through a long course of therapy that finally banishes the ghosts of his miserable childhood and the fearful nightmares of the Vietnam War. Gregory's victory over personal demons and his final tenuous success as a lawyer are due in large part to a group of faithful friends, particularly Carmen and Mike, who stand firm in crisis. By the close of the novel, Gregory has gained the hard-won wisdom that epitomizes the genre.

At the same time that Gregory's story typifies the themes of the *Bildungsroman,* his character could be interpreted in modernist terms as an "anti-hero." The antithesis of the dashing and successful hero, the anti-hero displays negative characteristics that may range from incompetence to boorishness. With his good looks and legal skills, Gregory does not readily fit the image of the anti-hero. However, he also embodies many disagreeable traits, including greed, selfishness, irresponsibility, and egotism. He ignores his sister and mother, withdraws from his wives, abandons his children, engages in questionable law practices, and acquires unmanageable debt. Though Gregory earns a silver medal for valor in the Vietnam War, he does so only because he snaps and behaves irrationally during a battle. He is not in fact a hero but a deeply flawed product of neglectful parents and a money-driven society. In his pervasive superficiality, then, Gregory is rarely a generous figure with whom readers readily empathize. Rather, he illustrates the unattractive image of the contemporary male whose climb to success blocks out much of his humanity.

Like many novels of the twentieth century, *The Infinite Plan* is also—though not entirely—a war narrative. Through much of the latter part of the book, Gregory battles the physical and psychological demons of the Vietnam War, a protracted conflict that lasted from 1955 to 1975. Characterized by chaotic organization and unclear motives, the war had mixed support from civilians and gradually grew less popular as it stretched on. Viewed less as war heroes than as participants in a disgraceful conflict, many returning veterans felt betrayed by their country. For Gregory, his tour in Vietnam is in large part merely an escape from draining personal problems. At the same time, however, it is an opportunity to express the courage that has seemed to fail him in his lifetime. He explains that he goes "in search of my manhood, the myth of the macho, the definition of masculinity" (184). Yet, this illusive machismo proves to be the same swaggering fiction it was in the barrio, only here propped up by amphetamines, sleeping pills, alcohol, and marijuana. The emptiness of the killing and the hopelessness of proving that one does not need to feel cause Gregory to weep. He says, "I will have a wail stuck in my throat as long as I live" (186). When any man in the squadron touches him out of sympathy or tenderness, he feels embarrassed, repeating the litany that "men don't hold hands, men don't cry, men don't feel pity" (196). The futility of his tour in Vietnam echoes throughout the novel, as Gregory attempts to find authenticity in life and suffers through long nights of reimagined war terrors.

The Vietnam War, coming as it does at the center of the novel, also serves to reiterate the theme of racial equality that runs throughout. Gregory notes that he cannot seem to find the hatred for his enemy that is required of him. He blames this on his mother's Baha'i teachings and on his months spent in the mountain village, both of which taught him to focus on the similarities that all humans share. This philosophy is key to Gregory's later partial redemption as a lawyer who serves the disenfranchised, the ignored underclass, and the minority groups that suffer daily indignities despite protective legislation. While Gregory is hardly an altruistic character, his desire for social justice echoes throughout the narrative.

Similar to Allende's first novels, *The Infinite Plan* also reiterates the importance of family and friends for survival. Gregory's lack of a supportive nuclear family inflicts lasting damage on him as an adult. At the same time, his loving friendship to Carmen acts as a balm against that hurt and serves as a thread of normalcy through the ups and downs of his adult life. The lover/writer addressed at the novel's close likewise promises continued acceptance and liberation for Gregory. Carmen, too, is healed, first by her father's forgiveness and acceptance, and then by her redemption through surrogate motherhood and her realization of true love in Leo Galupi. Even Timothy Duane achieves peace through the affection of the wise Dr. Ming. Each character's salvation arrives in the shape of a faithful partner, underscoring the value of relationships in Allende's worldview.

ALTERNATIVE PERSPECTIVE: PSYCHOANALYTIC CRITICISM

In its broadest terms, psychoanalytic theory offers a language for scholars to interpret the inner psyche and draw connections between a person's internal motivations and his or her outward actions. Applied to literature, this type of criticism may examine the relationship between the artist and his or her work of art, viewing the art as a product of the artist's unconscious suppression. Alternatively, psychoanalytic concepts can be used to elucidate the complex development of a character within a novel or story, interpreting that character's behavior by relating internal motivation to external behavior. Taking many forms in contemporary literary criticism, psychoanalytic theory has its roots in the conceptual models and treatment techniques developed by Sigmund Freud (1856–1939). Considered the father of modern psychology, Freud broke new ground in nearly every area of the social sciences with his seminal work examining and interpreting the dreams of his patients. Freud shaped many of his principles around novel models of human development, the most famous of which he called the "Oedipus complex." Using the Greek tragedy of Oedipus as his archetype, Freud argued that all boys experience a strong attachment to their mothers, seeing their fathers as rivals whom they fantasize about destroying. Eventually, boys recognize the powerful role of the father and associate themselves instead with that parent and suppress their sexual feelings for their mother, thus resolving the complex. In Freud's view, a boy who does not move beyond that crisis and align himself with his father will grow into manhood with an unnatural attraction to his mother and an unresolved resentment toward his father.

Gregory Reeves, a character haunted by his childhood privations and war horrors, demonstrates the classic arrested development described by psychoanalytic theory. The offspring of a remote mother and controlling father, the young Gregory experiences each stage of the Oedipal crisis. He views his father as an all-powerful figure for whom he feels both attraction and repulsion. Although Charles's illness makes him belligerent and deranged, Gregory continues to believe in him and imagines how he can help his father complete the room full of "unfinished works"

(52), a metaphor for his father's curtailed dreams and goals. When Charles realizes his life is drawing to a close, he decides that he needs to plant a tree to fulfill the last of a series of essential life tasks. Gregory is made to dig the hole for the tree, though the boy feels anxiety about contributing to his father's death. As if in answer to his apprehension, the very day that the weeping willow puts out its first new shoots, Charles succumbs to his illness. Though outwardly, Gregory expresses deep grief at the loss of his father, a psychoanalytic reading of his behavior points to an unconscious wish fulfillment that frees Gregory from the dominant force of the father and leaves the widowed Nora fully available to her children.

In keeping with the Oedipal construct of mother-love, Gregory spends his life attempting to win his mother's heart, "captivated by the same curiosity" that his father had felt when meeting Nora for the first time. Like his father, Gregory finds little satisfaction in attempting to confirm his mother's love for him. When Charles burns the boy's hand for stealing, Gregory rages not against his punitive father but against his mother, whose "impassive gaze" permits the injury (23). His wish to win her affections is further thwarted each time she attempts to give him away, first to an orphanage and then to a farming family. Unable to understand Nora's rejection, Gregory withdraws from her early in life to protect himself. In adulthood, Gregory exhibits the immature development that results from that withdrawal, continually making inappropriate choices in his career path and his relationships. The similarities his wives share with his mother point as well to his Oedipal obsession. His first spouse, Samantha, exhibits many of the same traits as Nora. Like Nora, Samantha treats Gregory with indifference, showing him little genuine affection and betraying him with infidelities. Shannon, Gregory's second wife, proves no more faithful than his mother and Samantha have been. Likewise, both Samantha and Shannon parallel Nora in their unnatural mothering. They treat their children like playthings that have grown tiresome; in Shannon's case, when her son's behavior becomes too much to handle, she deserts him to pursue her own interests. For Gregory, this succession of unloving women only ends after he faces his private demons.

Gregory's year spent battling anxiety and night terrors echoes another area of psychoanalytic study. Carl Jung (1875–1961), a Swiss psychiatrist who collaborated with Freud for several years, broke away to develop his own system of psychotherapy that saw mental illness as a manifestation of a dark split in a person's psyche. Jung used the term "the shadow" to characterize those dark impulses, fears, and losses individuals repress in everyday life. Dealt with correctly, the shadow can be a source of insight and growth for a mentally healthy individual. If the shadow is ignored, however, the individual may experience a split psyche, burdened by depression or even psychosis. In a description that seems to rely heavily on Jungian symbolism, Gregory's first anxiety attack is portrayed as an episode of such splitting. Visiting his dying mother, Gregory is deeply pained that she does not recognize him, and he sees this as just one more way she has managed to "erase him from her heart" (332). That evening Gregory rehearses all the regrets of his life, from his failed marriages to his broken children. Gradually, his heart tightens and he feels pain rip through his body. When he comes to consciousness, he finds himself face to face with a figure much like the Jungian shadow, which he calls the "beast" (335). In the face of the beast, Gregory sees an embodiment of all his fears—death, abandonment, and loneliness—that have dogged him throughout his life. For an entire year, Gregory faces the beast daily, suffering through anxiety attacks and nightmares that return him to the Vietnam mountaintop.

Though he makes every attempt to heal himself, Gregory finally pursues psychiatric treatment to overcome his nightly anxiety. During a first tentative session, he relays his recurring dream of the Vietnam skirmish and notices for the first time that all the soldiers share his face. Once Gregory has concluded that the enemy he battles is himself, he is prepared to enter a full course of psychoanalysis. For five years, the despondent man approaches his beastly shadow, learns to face his fears, and embraces his loneliness. With his doctor, Gregory enters the room of "unfinished machines" (380) and imposes some order. He accepts the myriad losses and griefs of his boyhood, emerging a whole person who can function as a parent and a lawyer without drowning in anxiety. In the final two pages of the book, Gregory addresses the listener/author as "you," the lover to whom he has shared his complex history. Grateful to his doctor and to this new woman in his life, Gregory declares himself in control of his destiny for the first time—a man reconciled to the shadows of his past.

7

Daughter of Fortune
(1999)

After the publication of *The Infinite Plan* in 1993, Isabel Allende did not write another novel for six years. Instead, her life took a tragic turn. On the book tour for that novel, Allende received word that her daughter Paula had been hospitalized for a blood disorder. After a year in a coma, Paula finally succumbed to the illness. Distraught and grieving, Allende turned her memoirs of that year into the best-selling *Paula*. Then she faced the worst writer's block of her career. It took over a year for Allende to pick up a pen. When she did return to her writing, it was to create the lighthearted anthology connecting sex and food called *Aphrodite: A Memoir of the Senses*. Writing that book revived Allende's zest for life and she decided to return to a project she had conceived before Paula fell ill. The project, a historical novel sweeping from Valparaíso, Chile to San Francisco, California and focusing on a spirited heroine named Eliza Sommers, proved a superlative comeback for the popular novelist.

Daughter of Fortune reveals a more mature writing style than that of Allende's previous novels. Though she still utilizes a large cast of characters, Allende spends more of the novel examining interior motivation and developing character portraits. The plot itself has a tighter shape than those of earlier works, with a carefully woven story line that ties up loose ends and connects characters inventively. Likewise, Allende's thorough research of the Gold Rush era in California enriches the setting and adds authenticity to her narrative. All these elements may help account for the novel's success. The single most important event that helped *Daughter of Fortune* gain wide readership, however, was Oprah Winfrey's selection of the novel for her Book Club. Although Oprah disbanded the feature in 2002, the nationwide "club" connected to her show for six years brought million-dollar sales to any fortunate author chosen. Allende was unusual in that hers was the first book in translation that Oprah selected and the first by a Hispanic author. During her appearance on Oprah Winfrey's afternoon talk show on March 28, 2000, Allende commented that *Daughter of Fortune* is not really a book about the quest for true love but rather about finding freedom. Just as the act of writing the novel released Allende from her mourning, so does the journey to California liberate her fictional heroine from the burdens of conventional womanhood and illusory first love.

PLOT

The novel opens in the British colony of Valparaíso, Chile in 1843. Eleven-year-old Eliza Sommers is being raised in the home of her spinster aunt, Rose, and bachelor uncle, Jeremy. Miss Rose and the housekeeper, Mama Fresia, are in dispute over the girl's mysterious origins. Miss Rose recalls the girl's arrival in a beautiful wicker basket with a note explaining the child's British origins, while Mama Fresia recalls a naked infant left on the doorstep in a soap crate. While Miss Rose assures Eliza that she has English blood, Mama Fresia warns the girl not to get any grand ideas with her "Indian hair" giving her away (4). The arrival of the infant is an irritation to the thirty-year-old Jeremy, who is trying to build a fortune and a future as an upstanding member of the British Import and Export Company, Ltd. His sister Rose, however, is already a woman "with a past" (7) at the age of twenty, living in a foreign land with few prospects, and aching for motherhood. Jeremy indulges her by allowing the baby to stay. Rose makes Eliza her plaything, showering her with affection and teaching her music and literature. When Rose becomes distracted, Mama Fresia steps in. Thus, Eliza spends as much time being a rich, pampered girl reciting English verses as she does being a barefoot peasant child speaking mestizo Spanish.

In 1843, Protestant preacher Jacob Todd arrives in Chile from London to evangelize to a local Indian tribe. Although he does not actually subscribe to the Christian religion, Jacob has enrolled with a missionary organization to attempt to win a drunken bet that he can sell three hundred Bibles in one year. Almost immediately, Jacob feels an overwhelming attraction to Rose and plants an impertinent kiss on her hand. On his second day, Jacob suffers a terrible bout of gripe and Rose sends Mama Fresia to "romance," or chase away, his illness, chanting mysterious charms over his ailing body (30). Before the reluctant missionary has time to court Rose in earnest, prodigious floods followed by earthquakes wreak havoc on the local villages. Jacob finds himself fascinated by the spectacle of religious Chileans parading around in great lament and flagellating their own backs in an attempt to absolve themselves of the sins that must surely have brought on these punishing acts of God. Eliza, separated from Mama Fresia in the crowded streets, approaches Jacob and he delivers her to the household. When the rains have abated, Jacob returns again to spend Wednesday evenings at the Sommers household, where he attempts to win Rose's hand, answered by regular refusals. His fine speaking ability wins over the local British Protestants, who help fund his half-hearted efforts to evangelize the Indians.

Two years pass by, during which time Jacob Todd becomes as comfortable in Chile as if he were a native. When he befriends a Chilean landowner, Agustín del Valle, Jacob gains access to the aristocracy of the country. Descendants of Spanish conquistadores, the del Valles hold to an ancient family code of patriarchy and reserve. Eliza befriends Paulina del Valle, a girl older than herself but one with the same playful manner. Otherwise, the women of the family live in the background, figures trapped in a world of customs that exclude their active participation. For Eliza, this is largely a convenient situation. She spends her days reading anything she can get her hands on, helping the servants with their daily chores, and remaining childlike in her stature and outlook. When Eliza begins to menstruate at thirteen, Rose informs her that she is no longer a girl and must attend a finishing school to learn proper behavior. Although Jeremy balks at the thought of the adopted, unpedigreed child attending Madame Colbert's school for girls, he relents under Rose's persistent requests and myriad sudden ailments.

Jacob Todd, although a relative newcomer to Chilean society, manages to get involved in a number of questionable activities. He first intervenes when Paulina del Valle, now a girl of marriageable age, falls in love with a gold miner. Feliciano Rodríguez de Santa Cruz is not acceptable to the del Valle family because his fortune is brand-new and his origins questionable. Agustín del Valle shaves his daughter's head and sends her to a convent to circumvent the love affair. With the help of Jacob Todd, Feliciano waits until Paulina is able to escape and then takes her to his mother's home. To avoid a scandal, the del Valles are forced to accept Feliciano and throw a lavish public wedding. Next, Jacob Todd befriends a young intellectual named Joaquín Andieta, who dreams of organizing the workers and giving land to the *campesinos*. Jacob Todd enjoys his interaction with the young revolutionary and his hours spent reading and writing philosophical treatises. Then the Anglican church sends a new pastor to Valparaíso, and Todd's hypocrisy is uncovered. He turns over what is left of the missionary money, but his reputation suffers irreparable damage. Eventually, the door to every respectable household in the city is closed to him, and Todd must take lodgings in an inconspicuous neighborhood near the ocean where he begins to drink. When the middle Sommers sibling, Captain John Sommers, arrives to unload his ship and pay a family visit, he urges Todd to join him on his voyage back to England by way of Hong Kong.

By age fifteen, Eliza has been trained in all the ways of a lady, prepared by her aunt for a good marriage to an upper-class gentleman. At the same time, the resourceful girl has become a self-taught cook who feels as comfortable in the kitchen up to her elbows in flour as she does in the parlor at the piano. Rose has plans to attach Eliza to a young officer in the English fleet, an uninteresting fellow from a good family. Rose's hard work goes awry when the young man proposes to her instead and then flees the house in embarrassment. On Eliza's part, she has already fallen in love with Joaquín Andieta, the intellectual sparring partner of Jacob Todd. Seeing him one day unloading goods into the Sommers home, Eliza becomes irrevocably smitten with the "devastating passion that would warp her life" (80). Joaquín feels swayed by the same deep emotion, but his narcissism suggests itself when he sees in Eliza's face "his own image" (81). Sick with desire, Eliza begins to waste away until a desperate Mama Fresia seeks the counsel of a *machi* healer who reveals the girl's diagnosis: a "fixation on love" for which there is no cure (84).

As Eliza's attraction for Joaquín becomes apparent, Rose hopes for a quick end to the matter at the same time that she dreams Eliza might live out her passion to its fullest. On her part, Eliza leaves nothing to chance, slipping the young man a letter with instructions to meet her. For a series of Wednesday nights, the young lovers meet for brief intervals of tentative caresses and conversations until they finally rendezvous one night at the Sommers home. Initiating each other into the mysteries of sexuality, the pair continues their secret love affair. Eliza falls deeply in love with Joaquín, or at least the idea of Joaquín that she perceives from the flowery, poetic letters he writes to her. In reality, he is a young man whose thoughts always seem to be elsewhere, who makes love hastily, and who leaves her unsatisfied. To reconcile these discrepancies, Eliza gradually idealizes her lover until he becomes an "obsession" (115).

Part Two of the novel opens in 1848, three months into Eliza and Joaquín's love affair. With his interest already waning, Joaquín is quick to plan a fortune-seeking journey when gold is discovered in California the following January. Like thousands of Chileans with the "souls of miners" (121), Joaquín tries to find a way to fund his voyage. When nothing presents itself, he steals guns from the dock and sells them on the black market, quickly procuring a third-class ticket and leaving for San Francisco. Six weeks later, Eliza discovers she is pregnant. Mama Fresia sets to work trying to rid Eliza of the baby. At the same time, John Sommers arrives in port for a visit. He has been hired by Chilean investors to captain a steamship. The investors turn out to be his old acquaintances Feliciano Rodríguez de Santa Cruz and his wife, Paulina del Valle. Feliciano has already been planning to leave for California, when Paulina points out to her husband that the real money will be in providing services to the miners. Thus, they decide to join the transport business and hire John as their top employee.

In John's few days home, he notices the changes in Eliza. One night, as she creeps downstairs to meet Mama Fresia, who is going to attempt an abortion, the unwitting but concerned John corners Eliza and takes her into the library. There, he proposes that she move to England with Miss Rose where the girl can be introduced to society and "make a good marriage" (137). Desperate to hide her pregnancy and find Joaquín, Eliza heads to the red-light district to discover a way to stow away on a ship to California. When drunken sailors at a bar begin to hassle her, it is Tao Chi'en, the Chinese cook recently released from John Sommers's ship, who arrives to rescue her. Reluctant to aid this young girl in dishonoring her family and his former employer, Tao Chi'en ultimately decides to help her in exchange for a pearl necklace.

Eliza invents a pretext to visit the del Valles at their hacienda and leaves her only home accompanied by Mama Fresia. The old woman has decided to return to her people in the south, since she is utterly unable to face her *patrona* after helping Eliza run away. Tao Chi'en hires a stevedore to smuggle Eliza on board his new employer's ship in a sack, which the quiet Chinese man arranges to be stored in the cargo hold of the ship. Because he is the only authorized person allowed in that area, Tao Chi'en has many opportunities to tend to Eliza's needs without fear

of discovery. Eliza is installed in a tiny hole where she lives for two
months in darkness, with only the company of a cat that slowly goes
crazy. Changing into a disguise before the detached gaze of Tao Chi'en,
Eliza has the sensation that she is entering the next stage of her life,
"beginning a new story in which she was both protagonist and narrator"
(152).

Eliza's protector is an important figure in the novel, as well. Born to
a poor family of healers and called simply "Fourth Son" for the first
eleven years of his life (153), Tao Chi'en distinguishes himself by learning
the healing trade swiftly and well. Unfortunately, in 1834, a series of
calamities strikes his family. First, the youngest daughter is scalded by
boiling water and dies of the wounds. Her grieving mother dies soon
after. Then the eldest son is killed by a rabid dog. Finally, the poor father
sells one daughter to a merchant and his fourth son into ten years of
servitude. Fatefully, Tao Chi'en is apprenticed to a famous physician and
acupuncturist in Canton, and his servitude earns him knowledge rather
than suffering. Given the name "Tao," which suggests the "journey of
life," Tao Chi'en is urged to follow his destiny "to ease pain and achieve
wisdom" (158). The master becomes attached to his bright apprentice,
harboring thoughts of adopting Tao Chi'en as a son should the boy remain faithful through adolescence.

When the Opium War between China and Great Britain breaks out in
1839, Tao Chi'en's mentor loses his spirit. With the signing of the treaty
of Nanking, which ceded Hong Kong to Great Britain, the master loses
his will to live and commits a ritualistic suicide in the garden. Having
died without adopting his apprentice, the master leaves Tao Chi'en des-
titute with the status of a mere servant. Others portion out the estate,
getting everything except a small amount of money and medical instru-
ments that Tao Chi'en thinks to hide for himself ahead of time. Twenty
years old with still a year left on his service contract, Tao Chi'en decides
to flee to Hong Kong. Now he is a *zhong yi,* a trained Chinese healer,
and ready to build an independent life. Tao Chi'en's first goal is to acquire a proper wife—beautiful with magnificent bound feet. However,
on his very first night in Hong Kong, Tao Chi'en disobeys one of his
master's principal lessons and goes to a gambling house. There he loses
all his money in only two hours. The next morning, a chastened Tao
Chi'en goes to a tattoo parlor to have the word "No" emblazoned on his
betting hand (174). Then, he offers a market woman afflicted with warts
a treatment for her hands in exchange for a month's worth of crab

lunches. Her successful cure helps establish Tao Chi'en's reputation and he builds a robust clientele over a period of six months.

After only a short time in Hong Kong, Tao Chi'en determines that the English hold the power and he decides to learn English. Shortly afterward, he meets Dr. Ebanizer Hobbs, a British expatriate hoping to learn the secrets of Eastern medicine. Exercising discretion to protect their mutual reputations, the physicians build a friendship and exchange knowledge about acupuncture and surgery. In a year, Tao Chi'en has finally accumulated the necessary savings to purchase a desirable wife and he weds Lin, a lovely and disarming woman recommended by the agents and the I Ching sticks used to foretell the future. A wonderful bride, Lin is also an unhealthy woman, made into a near invalid by her bound feet and her diseased lungs. During pregnancy, Lin's tuberculosis advances and Dr. Hobbs informs Tao Chi'en that she will not survive. After she delivers a stillborn daughter, Lin never returns to her former self. Tao Chi'en ignores the signs until the morning he awakens next to his dead wife. The widower sinks into "total despair" (187) and begins to drink heavily. Working half-heartedly until his patients stop coming, he loses all his possessions. One night, he goes into a bar to attempt to help a Chinese sailor whose head has been split open in a brawl. There, Tao Chi'en encounters the unfortunate man's captain, John Sommers, who expediently gets the doctor drunk in order to kidnap him as the ship's new cook. For two years, Tao Chi'en travels the globe under contract to Sommers. When he arrives in the port of Valparaíso in 1849, his two years of service are up. Captain Sommers grants Tao Chi'en his freedom and releases the physician-turned-cook. At Tao Chi'en's request, Captain Sommers furnishes him with a recommendation letter addressed to a Dutchman, whose sailing ship, the *Emilia,* will prove Eliza's salvation.

During her first weeks hidden in the storeroom, Eliza becomes gravely ill. Tao Chi'en does what he can to revive her with chicken broth and water, but he cannot understand why she does not become accustomed to the rocking ship like the other passengers. One day, the healer finds his patient lying in a pool of blood. When he revives her, Eliza admits that she is pregnant and falls again into unconsciousness. Resolving to leave her to her fate, Tao Chi'en tries to leave the hold, only to be confronted by the ghost of his wife Lin. The beautiful apparition tells her husband that she has come to remind him of "the duties of an honorable physician" (203). Tao Chi'en uses skill, laudanum, and acupuncture needles to complete the miscarriage and help nurse the girl through the night. He admits to himself that Eliza's "valiant determination," the "fragility of her body and the bold love" that she claims remind him of Lin. Eliza is still dangerously weak after the operation, so Tao Chi'en enlists one of the Chilean prostitutes on board to help him nurse her daily. Azucena Placeres grows fond of her patient, and Tao Chi'en administers opium to Eliza to help the time pass quickly. Once in San Francisco, Tao Chi'en dresses Eliza in the garb of a Chinese boy and she walks off the ship without attracting attention.

The shantytown of San Francisco is a chaotic mass of tents, hurriedly built structures, and muddy streets. Eliza begs Tao Chi'en not to desert her, so he brings her with him to the Chinese settlement called "Little Canton." Following an afternoon of information gathering, they find a ramshackle hotel in which to spend the night and then head to the Chilean barrio to look for Joaquín. There Eliza discovers that her lover has proceeded to Sacramento to search the placers for gold. She urges Tao Chi'en to accompany her, explaining that they are in "the land of opportunity" (232) and one surely in need of an excellent physician. Thus, the two book passage on a ship to Sacramento and arrive in a little city barely a year old. The first night in the Chinese district, Tao Chi'en has the opportunity to set a man's broken arm, already gaining attention as a useful doctor. With rumors that Joaquín has already headed up the river to mine, Tao Chi'en determines that the two must earn some money.

Using the one marketable skill he knows, Tao Chi'en sets up a physician's shack with Eliza posing as his deaf-mute brother, and he begins to develop a clientele. Helping her friend tend sick patients, Eliza finds herself attracted to the gentle, quiet man who behaves much older than his years. While Eliza expresses impatience to be on their way, Tao Chi'en secretly hopes to stay long enough for his wife's ghost to find him. He is also busy advancing his knowledge, discovering new medicinal plants and meeting with the Indian shamans who consider him a medicine man worthy of respect. He and Eliza also make trips to the Mexican *ranchos* where Eliza spends time with the women, speaking in Spanish while retaining her male disguise. At night, the two share a bed and enjoy the close proximity with each other, though by day "the secret spell of those embraces disappeared entirely and they were again brother and sister" (241). Years later, Eliza will ask herself why they did not admit then their attraction for each other. She decides that the racial barrier must have seemed insurmountable, underscoring a belief that "there was no place for a couple like them anywhere in the world" (242).

Once Eliza has accumulated enough money to support an excursion into the hills, she leaves Tao Chi'en to search for her lost lover.

While Eliza and Tao Chi'en are on their adventure, John Sommers is hired by Paulina del Valle and Feliciano Rodríguez de Santa Cruz to pilot their steamship down south to a glacier where he will fill the boat with ice, return for fresh produce, and then head to San Francisco to make a fortune in high-priced foodstuffs. It is not until Captain John returns to Valparaíso to pick up the produce that he hears of Eliza's escape. Miss Rose discovers during a visit to Joaquín's mother that he has left for California and she begins to understand that Eliza has followed him there. Rose begs her brother John to hide Joaquín's weapons theft from Jeremy. When Jeremy announces that the search must end, that Eliza will never be welcome in their home again because she is not family, Rose blurts out the truth—Eliza is John's daughter. A Chilean girl who had entertained him briefly while in port dropped the infant at the house wrapped in John's sweater, so that Rose would know immediately who had fathered her. John and Rose have conspired to protect the child all these years without raising their elder brother's suspicions and had been successful until this crisis.

Eliza, disguised as Elías Andieta in search of his brother, joins a group of Chilean miners on the banks of the American river. For several months, Eliza travels the mother lode in search of Joaquín. She always travels with other groups—salesmen, hunters, speculators—and joins any crowd that represents relative safety. Though the rumor of her search reaches the far corners of the hills, Joaquín continues to elude her and Eliza begins to consider Tao Chi'en's wise suggestion that her lover does not wish to be found. Still, Eliza relishes the adventurous life and the many characters she meets, gradually falling "in love with freedom" (275). She comes to embrace the pioneer spirit of the California wilds, a place where men are "inventing equality" (277). Yet, survival is difficult, and when Eliza loses her last forty dollars betting on a bear-baiting contest, she must find a new means of making a living. She discovers that writing letters for semi-literate miners is a lucrative business. When a traveling band of prostitutes arrives in town, Eliza earns money playing piano for the dancing girls. The madam, a mannish woman who calls herself Joe Bonecrusher, invites Eliza to join her circle. The roving bawdy house consists of four "soiled doves" (296) or prostitutes, a small Indian boy the madam has adopted and named Tom No-Tribe, and a giant dubbed Babalú the Bad, who protects the women. Eliza, still posing as

Elías, is taken for a homosexual, and so they never question the smooth beard and effeminate ways.

At the same time, John Sommers is experiencing phenomenal success carrying out Paulina's plan to transport delicacies on ice to San Francisco. During one of his trips, he runs into Jacob Todd, now Jacob Freemont, who has traveled there as a journalist to cover stories on the Gold Rush for various newspapers on the east coast and abroad. Todd also hopes that, like others, he will be able to start over there, leaving his scandalous past behind him. As a journalist with a keen eye for a story, Todd discovers that "in seeking anonymity he was finding celebrity" (293). Because Todd travels regularly through gold country, Captain John enlists him to keep an eye out for Eliza.

As winter descends on the California foothills, Joe Bonecrusher installs her caravan of women in a barn in a small town outside Sacramento. There they entertain male visitors and continue to ply their trade through the cold weather. When dysentery strikes the town, Joe proves a generous woman, nursing stricken miners and bringing the worst cases back to the barn for special treatment. Her resourcefulness proves priceless later, when so many in the town owe her their lives. During a terrible ice storm, a half-frozen Mexican shows up at the door, calling himself "Jack" and behaving like a fugitive of the law. Eliza feels uncomfortable around the suspicious character, thinking that he "smelled of evil" (306). When Jack's frostbitten fingers begin to gangrene, Eliza volunteers to perform an amputation, earning her the respect of her compatriots. The patient sneaks away one night when his hand has healed, and two weeks later Eliza finds a bag of gold dust outside the door. Shortly afterward, the sheriff organizes a group of vigilantes to go after the murderer of a miner found stabbed in his cabin. Eliza and her friends strongly suspect their night visitor. Later, when rumors circulate about a bandit named Joaquín Murieta and his counterpart, Three-Finger Jack, Eliza fears the worst of her old lover and the man whose life she saved. As Joaquín Murieta's mythology grows, Jacob Freemont follows the bandit's trail and prints a series of primarily fictionalized articles describing the activities of this infamous character. The articles serve to enflame the public's imagination and further Jacob's career.

As the winter comes to a close, the brothel's business begins to thrive again. Then one night in March, a fire breaks out during a lively evening. Everyone makes it out safely, until Eliza realizes that young Tom No-Tribe is missing. She risks her life to reenter the building, but is too weak to get the boy out and both must be rescued by Babalú. The town responds kindly to its homeless entertainers, returning the favor of their ceaseless nursing in the winter months with housing, fresh clothing, and food. Joe Bonecrusher uses the bag of gold dust to purchase a house for her girls and considers settling down in the community. At this point, Eliza begins to think about looking again for Joaquín, but when another bout of dysentery threatens her friends, she stays through the summer to help nurse the sick.

During this same period, Captain John Sommers arrives on his third voyage of the *Fortuna,* this time with Paulina Rodríguez de Santa Cruz aboard. She immediately sees the potential for San Francisco and determines to establish herself and Feliciano among its aristocracy. John, meanwhile, meets up with his old friend Jacob and they head to the red-light district for a night of relaxation. There, John recognizes Eliza's brooch on the breast of Azucena Placeres, who happens to be working that night. Pressing the woman for an explanation, John reveals that he is Eliza's father. Azucena decides to protect the shamed daughter, saying that Eliza bled to death during a miscarriage and was thrown overboard.

Meanwhile, Tao Chi'en is living a rather solitary life in Sacramento. He has befriended a fellow *zhong yi,* or Chinese medical practitioner, with whom Tao shares his medical expertise. Yet, he wonders how to cure his loneliness without a wife. His friend advises that no "cultivated and intelligent man would try to make [his wife] his companion" (317), but Tao Chi'en does not know how to explain what he enjoyed with Lin or even Eliza. Planning to make his way back to China, Tao Chi'en returns to San Francisco to work and raise money for his departure. Tao heads to Chinatown where he finds that the rumors are true—his fellow immigrants have created a city within a city that is a near-perfect replica of their homeland. Their presence in San Francisco is hardly welcomed, however. After a mugging in which thugs cut off his queue, Tao decides to dress as a Westerner. When he shows up at Eliza's door one day in December, she can hardly recognize her friend but agrees to follow him back to San Francisco, where Tao has a job to do.

As a newly established *zhong yi,* Tao Chi'en has enjoyed success in his first months in San Francisco. Then one night, he is sent to a brothel to declare death "due to natural causes" (346) for a prostitute who has clearly been poisoned. Tao Chi'en has long ignored the sad fate of the "singsong" girls who leave China thinking they have been promised in marriage, only to discover, when it is too late, that their brief lives in America will be spent, first auctioned to the highest bidder, then chained to a bed in a dark brothel to work for their owner's profit. Deeply disturbed by what he has seen, Tao spends the night in meditation, visited by both Lin and his first medical master. These spirits prompt Tao to change his destiny and help the poor women enslaved in the underworld of San Francisco's Chinatown red-light district.

With Eliza's help, Tao begins to take the singsong girls away from the brothels before they die, issuing a death certificate in advance to keep the madams happy. Most of the girls die anyway, but occasionally he manages to save one. He also attends the auctions when he has any money to spend and buys girls who would otherwise be sentenced to a short, ugly life of prostitution. Eliza uses her connections with the Quakers in the foothill town to create an underground railroad for the girls. Babalú the Bad acts as transporter, delivering the girls to "farms in Oregon, laundries in Canada, and craft studios in Mexico" (374) where they can learn honest work and live out peaceful lives. Tao Chi'en considers all in the prostitute trade his proven enemies. One of the most famous, Ah Toy, has built an empire out of her imported girls. Summoned one day to the famous madam's palatial brothel, Tao Chi'en briefly considers slipping her arsenic but instead performs his usual duties and leaves.

Eliza spends several years working for Tao Chi'en, learning a little Chinese, and helping nurse the prostitutes he saves. She leaves twice to look for Joaquín, but both trips prove fruitless. Finally, one day, she seeks out Jacob Freemont to learn more about Joaquín Murieta, somewhat convinced that this bandit may be her long lost lover. Eliza is shocked into silence when she recognizes Miss Rose's "perennial suitor" (371). Only after Eliza leaves the office does Jacob realize how he knows her. Jacob tells John about the meeting, and when Miss Rose hears of it she determines to find her adopted daughter. Likewise, Eliza has grown weary of her masquerade and wishes to put on dresses again and write to her family. At the same time, she begins to realize different feelings for Tao Chi'en, as if there is "something unfinished between them, something much more complex and fascinating than their old friendship" (393).

The novel closes with an ambiguous ending. Miss Rose has not yet arrived in San Francisco to find Eliza, yet it is clear that she will hear from the young woman. On her part, Eliza has determined to return to the garb of a woman. She goes with Tao Chi'en to have her portrait taken, first with Joaquín's love letters that she subsequently destroys, and then with the pearls Tao Chi'en has returned to her. During that summer of 1853, the governor issues a one-thousand-dollar reward for the death of Joaquín Murieta. A band of vigilantes searches for three months and then claims to have killed and captured him. His pickled head goes on display, and Eliza waits her turn to examine it. When Tao Chi'en asks her if the head is her former lover's, she answers simply, "I am free" (399). Whether Joaquín is truly dead or whether she has simply decided to release herself from following her ephemeral lover, Eliza places her hand in that of her loyal friend and moves toward a new life.

CHARACTER DEVELOPMENT

Eliza Sommers, the central female character of the novel, has two prominent traits: "a good sense of smell and a good memory" (3). These features seem insignificant in Eliza's protected girlhood where she is "clad in the impenetrable armor of good manners and conventions" and "bound by corset, routines, social norms, and fear" (275). Only later, when Eliza's determined will sets her on a journey that will take her from Valparaíso forever, does the value of her special traits emerge. With the ability to sniff out the ingredients in almost any dish, the resourceful Eliza becomes an excellent cook to help pay her way in the wild settlements of California. Likewise, her memory serves her well when she needs to recall piano music from her childhood in order to provide entertainment for the brothel. Because Eliza spends nearly half the novel masquerading as someone else for long stretches of narrative, most often as a male and only occasionally as a Chilean, the reader alone knows her true identity. In the eyes of her brothel-house companions in California, Eliza is a quiet "Chile Boy" (295) with a compassionate heart. For Tao Chi'en, she is a big-footed *fan wey* (205), a "white ghost" with an irreproachably optimistic attitude. To the reader, Eliza is a resourceful and determined young woman who sets her mind on a single goal and allows it to drive her for four years. During all that time, she spends the warm summers traveling by foot or mule to search for her first love. Long after Joaquín has begun to emerge as a cad or worse, Eliza remains true to her heart, which she believes to be undeniably attached to her gold-seeking lover.

Eliza's character is a complex one, however, in that she is driven by more than the conventional desire to attach herself to her sweetheart. When she discovers her pregnancy and believes she can hear the baby crying out for its "right to live" (134), Eliza's most powerful sensation is that she is trapped. Her voyage to California is appealing, then, not simply because Joaquín is there but because the "land is a blank page" where she can be "born again" (280). After many months depending on her wits and curbing her natural fears, Eliza comes to love her freedom, strength, and newfound boldness. She tells Tao in a letter that she has left her old self behind, that she wants to be like the adventurers around her, men who have become "masters of their destiny" (277). Even so, the independence that she craves does not transform Eliza into a heartless fortune-seeker like so many others but rather accentuates the qualities that Tao Chi'en comes to love in her. She passes no judgment on the "soiled doves" (280) who make up Joe Bonecrusher's party, and she works tirelessly with Tao to free the enslaved singsong girls. Tending to her friends, Eliza often forgets the very reason she has voyaged all that distance from home. Shedding the trappings of femininity during her search for Joaquín, Eliza casts off all that had been fraudulent about the well-trained young lady she used to be in Valparaíso, allowing a powerful new woman to emerge—one uniquely suited to the new world she has joined.

In counterpoint to Eliza's adventurous spirit, the three Sommers siblings share a civilized, subdued exterior that hides their private cares. Though they live in Chile, they retain all the characteristics of their homeland and spurn all but the most upper-class natives. Jeremy is described as a "ghost trapped in eternal winter" (17) who approaches all matters in life with the same chilly manner. A steady man, the patriarchal Jeremy never acts on emotion and shows little outward affection to any of his relations. Rose is more high-strung than her elder brother; however, he puts up with her eccentricities because of the grace and polish she brings to Jeremy's otherwise bachelor household. John is more expansive than his siblings, having sailed all over the world and developed a mind open to diverse cultures and customs. A robust adventurer, John acts as Rose's confidante and window to the world. Inseparable as children, the two adults wait eagerly for their time together when John is in port; between visits, they harbor each other's deepest secrets. For John, the secret is his daughter Eliza, the result of a drunken tryst with a prostitute on a Valparaíso beach. For Rose, it is the erotic fiction she produces under a pen name for John to sell, as well as the lost love that has condemned her to spinsterhood.

Rose's anxiety as she watches Eliza suffer for an "unworthy" suitor grows out of her own ill-fated tryst years before with a Viennese opera singer. Only sixteen, Rose had become involved with an experienced lover who professed himself equally smitten. They spent the opera season meeting in secret and planning to run away together. When the couple went to the seaside for a long weekend, Jeremy followed them there and announced that the tenor was in fact married with two children. Jeremy installed his sister in an aunt's home in Scotland until it could be determined that she was not pregnant. Then Rose returned to London society looking outwardly unchanged but inwardly harboring a "vast fresco of her memories of love" (98). When Jeremy decides the family should move to Valparaíso, Rose views her exile as a punishment that must be endured silently. Eighteen months later, baby Eliza enters their lives and Rose embraces motherhood, choosing to remain a spinster with cherished memories of a secret romance rather than marrying any of the suitors who approach her in Chile.

The most persistent devotee, Jacob Todd, shares numerous parallels with Rose's character. Like her, he has come to Chile under false pretenses, his being to distribute Bibles to win a bet. Just as Rose surrounds herself with music lovers in her makeshift Wednesday evening salons, Jacob finds stimulation by penning philosophical pamphlets and debating revolutionary issues with other intellectuals. When his missionary ruse is discovered, Jacob leaves Chile in shame just as Rose had to leave England years before. Jacob's new persona in California, writing as the journalist Jacob Freemont, also mimics Rose's chosen pastime; whereas she spends her private time writing erotic fiction, he spends his composing elaborate tales about the mythical outlaw Joaquín Murieta, thus using his talent for prevarication to "pull an imaginary outlaw from his sleeve" (342). The character of Joaquín himself has little substance beyond the "fanciful and heroic biography" (342) Jacob fabricates about him for newspaper readers.

The most authentic and fully realized male character of the novel is Eliza's protector and wise friend Tao Chi'en. On the surface, this quiet immigrant embodies a number of stereotypes attached to the Chinese. He is deferential and earnest, skillful with a knife, and an excellent cook. At times he moves so quickly and silently that he seems to "have vanished like smoke" (148). "[S]hanghaied" by John Sommers for his ship (146), Tao Chi'en proves, nonetheless, a faithful employee and seems characteristically dependable and discreet. Yet, Tao Chi'en is a far more complicated character than he appears on the surface. Dissatisfaction at being nothing more than "Fourth Son," and practically valueless to his family, breeds in Tao Chi'en a special independence and curiosity about the world. With a name that means the "journey of life" (158), Tao fulfills his *zhong yi* master's prophecy that he will spend his life easing pain and achieving wisdom (158). Like Eliza, who travels thousands of miles to shed her foolish girlhood, Tao journeys around the world to find his destiny and the insight that comes with it.

Through years of discipline and error, Tao Chi'en learns to tame his two vices—women and gambling—and acts shrewdly in the face of gold fever. Like Eliza, Tao Chi'en is a survivor and a faithful lover. For years, he remains true to his beloved wife Lin, fearing that her ghost will not be able to find him in California. Through Lin and Eliza, Tao develops a new perspective on female companionship, seeing marriage not as a convenient arrangement of household labor but as a genuine partnership of minds and hearts. Central to Tao's development is his transformation into an American. Though he encounters numerous trials and setbacks, Tao recognizes opportunity at each turn, reestablishing his medical practice, developing a faithful clientele, and seeking out medical colleagues to help expand his knowledge. His life's work to smuggle Chinese prostitutes from sex slavery to independent life also stands as an important symbol in the novel, serving as an emblem of all the shapes taken by freedom for the adventurers who seek it.

THEMES

On January 24, 1848, James Marshall found a gold nugget at Sutter's Mill and sparked a worldwide frenzy that changed the shape of California forever. Within a year, throngs of prospectors had arrived to seek their fortunes, even as the easy gold was already diminishing. In truth, most miners would go home empty-handed as large companies came in to strip-mine. Nevertheless, by the time gold-rush fever had begun to subside in 1852, the non-native population of California, which had been a mere 14,000 before 1848, had grown to well over 200,000. Gold fever represented more than just the promise of wealth and the entrepreneurial spirit of those who sought it. The Gold Rush also symbolized the possibilities of adventure and freedom, a characterization that the territory on the westernmost edge of the continent never lost. Not only communities from across the United States but also visionaries on other continents sent their young men to seek their fortunes and fulfill their dreams. *Daughter of Fortune*, set as it is in the promising landscape of gold country, reflects the themes in its narrative about hopes lost and found.

With the Gold Rush as a central plot event, the theme of adventure plays prominently in the novel. The thousands of men who seek their fortune in California create a temporary city overnight on the hills surrounding San Francisco bay. They are a greedy, chaotic band developing a haphazard government in which frontier justice rules and "no one was affected by one more dead man" (224). Jacob Todd notes that the "ethic of hard work" upon which America was founded was erased by the Gold Rush, which revealed "greed and violence" (234) on every side. The rumors of gold nuggets the "size of a shoe" (228) strewn across the riverbeds for any persistent fellow to gather prove predictably false. In truth, very few of the argonauts who journeyed months to California became millionaires. The majority of successful "gold-diggers" during the California Gold Rush turned out not to be those who mined for gold. Rather, they were the business-minded prospectors who came to sell shovels, metal pans, food, and other necessities at exorbitant prices to the disadvantaged miners.

Paulina del Valle, with her brilliant scheme to ship in sumptuous delicacies on ice, symbolizes this entrepreneurial spirit that brought a bold and spirited type of adventurer to the West. Though not a major character in the novel, Paulina synthesizes the important dual themes of opportunism and freedom. In realizing a need ahead of others, Paulina represents historical figures such as Sam Brannan, who sold mining tools and hard-to-find fresh food at high prices in order to become California's first millionaire. Yet, Paulina's character is more than a shrewd businesswoman; she is also a disgraced daughter of a prominent Chilean family. Adding to that, she is married to a man below her station and promises Feliciano that only in San Francisco can he join the aristocracy that is barred to him in Chile. While inventing a new life for herself in California, Paulina revels in the fact that "eccentricity was welcomed and guilt did not exist" (356). Freedom and respectability are available for purchase in a way that was unknown in her homeland. The blank page that attracts Eliza leads Paulina and Feliciano, as well, to transplant their entire household to the burgeoning city of San Francisco, where they can help build a new society over which they might reign supreme.

For many who came west in search of gold, the months-long voyage to California came to be seen as a symbolic quest to follow one's dreams; for most, those broken dreams resulted in bitter disillusionment. Allende notes that by September 1850, gold-rush fever had begun to "take the shape of enormous collective disillusion" as "ninety thousand" prospectors headed for home (318). The exchange of illusions for reality takes many forms in *Daughter of Fortune*, few related directly to gold in the hills. For Eliza, the dream that carries her to California is one of finding true love and sustaining it in the face of hardship and heartbreak. She nourishes her first infatuation with romantic novels and Joaquín's florid love letters. Failing to see the "discrepancy between those inflamed declarations and the real person of Joaquín Andieta" (114), she invents the "perfect lover" and "obstinately nurture[s] that illusion" (115). Tao Chi'en argues that Eliza's endless pursuit of her lover is a kind of "madness, like gold fever" (363). Her friend's wise remarks help Eliza see that she has become trapped again, this time in the "morass of a legendary passion with no link to reality" (370). After viewing the head of the supposedly murdered Joaquín Murieta, she makes her choice, announcing at the novel's close that she is "free" as she grips Tao's hand and leaves the illusions of the past behind.

For Tao Chi'en, the dream that California promises comes clear over time as he attempts to develop his medical talents and save the singsong girls who suffer in the alleyways behind bars in Chinatown. The girls remind him always of his sister, who likely met the same fate when she was sold into prostitution. Unlike Eliza, Tao discards his illusions early, threatening instead to sink into despair over the seemingly unsolvable problem of the enslaved prostitutes. The discarded girls, poisoned and near death, haunt the doctor because he can so rarely save them. The healthy women he buys at auction disturb him because they represent hundreds of others he is powerless to save. As he suffers under this personal burden, Lin's ghost gently chides Tao that "the sage is always joyful because he accepts reality" (362). In his faithfulness, first to Lin's spirit, then to the pregnant and ill Eliza on the ship, and finally to the despondent singsong girls, Tao's character connects many of the novel's themes together. He demonstrates a spirit of adventure tempered by a clear view of reality and a fidelity to loved ones that, unlike Joaquín's temporal devotion, survives years, miles, and even death.

ALTERNATIVE PERSPECTIVE: POSTCOLONIAL CRITICISM

Postcolonial theory began to gain prominence in the late 1970s as a mode to study historical and literary representations of European nations and the societies they colonized in the modern period. In his 1978 book *Orientalism*, critic Edward Said launched postcolonial literary studies in earnest with his influential critique of Western interpretations of the Orient. In that study, Said underscores the idea that the "Oriental" as a figure of fantasy had to be invented in Western literature in order to create an artificial differentiation between the colonizer and the colonized. Specifically, the "Oriental" was characterized as passive and weak, needing the direction of his patriarchal colonizer. Postcolonial theorists, then, expose such false representations of the non-Westerner. In 1984, Homi K. Bhabha helped further establish postcolonial criticism with his important essay "Representation and the Colonial Text," followed in 1994 by his landmark analysis *The Location of Culture*. In those studies, Bhabha helped establish a new language for postcolonial studies, introducing in particular the idea of hybridity as an uneasy experience of the colonized subject, who becomes an amalgam of the native culture and the one imposed upon him. Gayatri Spivak was another major voice in developing this theoretical view, asking in one of her well-known essays whether the "subaltern," or subordinate person in a colonized state, can have a voice—a question answered by postcolonial novelists who write to resist the homogenous and negative image of the "other." Then, in 1989, *The Empire Writes Back: Theory and Practice in Post-Colonial Literatures*, written by Bill Ashcroft, Gareth Griffiths, and Helen Tiffin, gave full shape to this novel way of considering personhood in history and literature.

As the critical studies cited above demonstrate, postcolonial studies originally focused almost exclusively on the British Empire and its colonial subjects. For decades, narratives had maintained a Eurocentric view, in which the consciousness of the native was neither acknowledged nor entertained as a valid perspective. Indigenous people in the colonized countries of the Eastern world and the West Indies were considered "outsiders" and rarely given subjectivity in literature. In other words, literary characters from these cultural groups were not viewed as capable of controlling their own lives or of making complex choices. Treated more like stock characters, they played small parts or enacted predictable behaviors in narratives that underscored the dominant, colonizing culture. In a radical unveiling of this privileged perspective, postcolonial criticism gave voice to the "other," showing how canonized literature had established a cultural bias against colonized subjects. Not limited by the loci of European conquests, postcolonial theory has been applied to American literature of the "marginalized," including readings of African American, Asian American, Chicano, and Native American literature. Likewise, postcolonial theorists often share the focus of feminist scholars to give a voice to silenced women in history and literature.

In *Daughter of Fortune*, Allende includes many narrative elements that can be examined usefully through the lens of postcolonial theory. First is her treatment of British colonizers as they affect both Chile during years of trade and China during the Opium War. As the prototypical European, Jeremy Sommers epitomizes the character of his countrymen who arrived in Chile to make their fortunes but, finding it a country of mestizos and uneducated farmers, proceeded to "form a small nation within the country" (15). They could then follow familiar customs unhampered by outsiders. British colonists like Jeremy and his sister Rose keep to themselves, only associating with the highest level of Chilean society and establishing an island of "civility" (15) in Valparaíso. If any of the Sommers family, besides Eliza, questions England's right to establish its colonies throughout the world, it is Captain John. He explains that the British have conquered more than half the world through "naval power, greed, and discipline" (195). He adds that after all his travels, he is no longer "proud of being English" (195).

Captain John's ambivalence echoes that of the narrator, who describes England's pursuit of opium wealth later in the book. Never masking their feelings of "racial superiority" (177) in their dealings with China, the British sent their missionaries to evangelize the savages, rewarding "conversions with rice" (178). Allende makes it a point in her novel to describe the damage done to Chinese society through the Opium War of 1839, during which time the imperial army fell to "the powerful and well-disciplined English fleet" (166). After four years of fighting, China admitted defeat and had to relinquish Hong Kong to the British and allow them to set up "concessions" within the country (166). These were small foreign bases inside China from which the British controlled trade, primarily in opium. Like their counterparts in Chile and other English outposts, the British in Hong Kong lived in comfortable lodgings within protected areas guarded by British troops. The expatriates remained cloistered in their English-speaking compounds, only communicating with the wealthiest Chinese in order to conduct business with them. The open trade lines controlled by the British created a frenzy of interest in England for anything Chinese, including silk for clothing, miniature pagodas to decorate gardens, and knickknacks to accent Oriental-style drawing rooms. The worst problem was that the English flooded the Chinese markets with opium, making it cheap and accessible to the point that it weakened all sectors of the society, "causing it to crumble like stale bread" (177). Echoing the ethnic distortions Said describes in *Orientalism*, the exotic artifacts of Chinese civilization became a fashionable commodity to the Westerners while the "others" themselves had no identity beyond their opiate consumption.

The British are by no means the only antagonists in Allende's narrative, however. As she describes the convergence of the outside world on California in pursuit of easy gold, Allende is careful to document the considerable violations committed against the indigenous peoples of North America and their landscape. In fact, the Gold Rush itself is described as a kind of colonizing act in the novel, with the narrator critiquing that "where gold was found, the idyllic land, which had remained untouched since the beginning of time, was turned into a lunar nightmare" (272). The chief casualties of this land rape are, of course, the Native Americans. While they do not have a major role in the novel, the native people are characterized as the victims of greed, their numbers diminished dramatically as a result of disease and maltreatment. Allende's urgency in sharing the story from a new angle comes into focus in an interview:

> First of all you have to know [California] was Mexican territory until nine days after they discovered gold. People spoke Spanish there: it was a place that was totally Hispanic until Mexico lost the war against the United States and lost Texas, Arizona, Utah, half of Colorado, New Mexico and California. So, at the beginning, in 1848, it was mainly people of color who were mining. And then the 49ers came and they took over and it became an American territory. (Richards, par. 27)

Even Allende's characterization of the shadowy figure of Joaquín Murieta reflects her sympathy toward the Hispanics abused by the American land grab. Though Murieta's true story remains largely veiled by Jacob Todd's fictionalized account, the narrator hints at the bandit's partial innocence, his victimization and right to seek revenge for injustices against his family.

Whereas traditional historical narratives about the Gold Rush cast American men as heroic adventurers seeking their fortunes in unclaimed territory, Allende makes an effort in her novel to show the unfair treatment they imposed on all non-U.S. citizens, especially those who worked harder and achieved more than their American counterparts. Ironically, the "outsiders" who came to mine the land from other countries often traveled no farther than the whites who journeyed around the tip of South America. However, the whites felt resentful of the many Chileans and Peruvians who shipped out with them and found ways to discourage their foreign competitors. One penalty levied against diligent non-American miners came in the form of the Foreign Miners Tax, instituted in 1850, which charged every foreign prospector $20 per month. As Allende notes, "The whites made many rules against the people of color. Especially against the Chinese. The worst abuses were against the Chinese" (Richards, par. 28). Allende documents numerous racial conflicts not only against the Chinese but also between Yankee miners and prospectors from Chile, tensions that often erupted in court battles and vigilante lynchings. While the Chinese tried to keep to themselves, the Chileans formed "gangs of marauders, as many Mexicans had done" (304–305), to exact some revenge. Unfortunately, there was little else the foreigners could do to protect themselves from ill treatment. According to Allende's account, "An American was never sentenced for crimes against another race; still worse, a white criminal often could choose his own jury" (328). In documenting the myriad injustices to non-Americans, Allende's narrative resists the romantic stereotype of the rugged, gold-seeking pioneer whose "rightful" place in the placers is decreed by might and hasty land treaties.

Finally, Eliza herself can be interpreted as an archetype of postcolonial hybridity. As the daughter of a British seaman and a Chilean native, Eliza has the telltale "Indian hair" that sets her apart from the rest of her well-bred English family. John Sommers fathered her on a beach, in a tryst with a young woman he can barely recall except to say that she was a "girl from the port" and "very pretty" (258). The Sommerses raise Eliza to think of herself as a fortunate orphan rescued from the obscure masses, a woman whose alter ego might have been a voiceless, nameless prostitute like the mother she has never known. Instead, she is saved by the privileged blood that runs in her veins and by the expensive dresses and jewels that announce her lucky fate. Yet, as soon as Eliza leaves the stronghold of her British clan, she relinquishes the clothing and pawns the jewels, almost immediately taking on the features of the "other." Watching her in the ship, Tao Chi'en discerns a "slightly Oriental air" (205) about her almond-shaped eyes and long, black hair.

Paralleling the subjective role of the "other" in most colonial narratives, Eliza secures anonymity through her non-Western features, but in this case, such an end allows her to masquerade freely throughout the rest of the novel as one kind of marginal figure or another. First, she escapes from the ship dressed as a little Chinese "deaf mute" (221). Later, she joins a group of Chileans, disguised as a young man looking for his brother. Concealed in male attire, Eliza also learns to imitate the accents of Peruvians and Mexicans so that she can blend into the background of many groups. Dressed as anyone other than the white, well-bred Englishwoman she is, Eliza is able to wander invisibly through the outposts of the West. Overturning the supposed subjectivity of the other, Eliza gains liberty through her slippery origins, a hybrid self that gives her power beyond the circumscribed female role her British background can offer. At the end of the novel, when Eliza dons dresses once more, it is not to retreat into the safe world of the colonizer but to embark on a new adventure, an unprecedented relationship between a Chilean woman and a Chinese man. In this partnership, the unlikely couple forms a new kind of hybrid that represents the unorthodox, multicultural land to which they have arrived.

8

Portrait in Sepia
(2001)

Following the extraordinary success of *Daughter of Fortune,* Isabel Allende's protracted writer's block seemed finally to be behind her. Just two years after her best-selling fifth novel, Allende published *Portrait in Sepia,* something of a sequel to the previous book. Allende did not originally plan to write a continuation to *Daughter of Fortune.* In her research into California history, Allende had discovered a wealth of information about the development of the fledgling state following the Gold Rush. At the same time, she had renewed her fascination with the history of her Chilean homeland, a country torn by war during the same period that California was undergoing rapid development. As Allende began the narrative that she had envisioned to incorporate these dual histories, she discovered that her story could also complete the chronicle of Eliza Sommers and Tao Chi'en's romance, a desire expressed by many curious readers. With her new vision for *Portrait in Sepia,* Allende was able to create a trilogy out of three novels, one that begins in Chile in 1843, takes its readers to the developing California frontier, returns to Chile during the second half of the nineteenth century, and finishes a century later with the military coup in 1973. An engrossing narrative even when read independently of the other books, *Portrait in Sepia* also brings Allende's fiction full circle by introducing the eldest figures of the del Valle family, who launch the saga of *The House of the Spirits,* her first and most well-known work.

As in the majority of her novels, Allende uses a strong female voice to narrate *Portrait in Sepia,* a heroine whose desire to document the past and understand her mysterious childhood resembles the impulses of her author. Aurora del Valle, a Californian of mixed race who lives much of her life in a foreign country, spends her early adult years trying to piece together the mysterious parts of her past. Like Allende herself, Aurora has an absent father about whom she learns nothing until she is nearly grown. She also suffers from nightmares regarding a dark event about which she has no conscious memories. She photographs her world and writes her story ultimately to understand her own shadowy past. In her epilogue, Aurora writes almost as if she were Allende herself: "I write to elucidate the ancient secrets of my childhood, to define my identity, to create my own legend" (304). Explaining that her precursors are essential to her story, Aurora begins the novel with a description of her birth and then backs up almost twenty years to trace the origins of her life. She cautions the reader that her long story "requires patience in the telling and even more in the listening" (3). Some critics have suggested that Aurora's story becomes eclipsed by the illustrious characters on her family tree, and certainly her family is as colorful as most found in Allende's fictional universe. Philip Graham, in his review of *Portrait in Sepia* in the *New Leader,* describes Aurora as a "wallflower in her own narrative" in the face of her formidable and far more fully fleshed out family members (38). Eventually, however, the strands of the narrative come together to complete the tapestry of Aurora del Valle's life. Thus, the novel replicates the effect of a portrait developing in the darkroom, gradually revealing the mysterious faces hidden within.

PLOT

Aurora del Valle, the narrator and heroine of *Portrait in Sepia,* opens the story with a brief description of her birth in 1880 and reveals that thirty years have passed since that day. However, she immediately shifts to 1862 to tell the first part of her life story, a narrative contained in Part I of the novel that encompasses 1862 to 1880. The story of Aurora's origins begins with the arrival of a gargantuan Florentine bed ordered by the indomitable Paulina del Valle to shame her philandering husband Feliciano. Captain John Sommers, Aurora's great-grandfather, has been appointed to deliver the extravagant piece of furniture, after first parading it in front of the home of Feliciano's mistress, Amanda Lowell. After the bed has made its journey from the port to Paulina's mansion on Nob Hill, Captain John vows that he has had enough of his capricious employer and determines to remove himself from her service. He then heads to Chinatown to visit his daughter, Eliza, and her husband, Tao Chi'en. At this point, the reader learns the fate of these central characters from *Daughter of Fortune*. They have raised two children, continued Tao Chi'en's medical practice, and opened a successful tearoom and pastry shop. Captain John's sister, Rose, the adoptive mother of Eliza, has moved to London at the event of their brother's death. There, she writes romance novels with tremendous success and lives as she pleases. Tao Chi'en greets his father-in-law with deep respect. It has been fifteen years since the Chinese man served as cook on Captain John's ship. After a brief medical exam, Tao confirms Captain John's suspicion that he is dying of liver disease and has very little time left. They agree to keep the upsetting information from Eliza. Three weeks later, John chooses to slip quietly over the side of his ship rather than suffer through a long final illness.

The narrative then moves forward a decade, to introduce young Severo del Valle. One of Paulina's nephews, Severo has visited San Francisco once before in 1872. During that trip, his aunt takes him to Eliza's tearoom where Severo catches a glimpse of Lynn Sommers. Twelve years old, the girl is already a stunning beauty for whom Severo falls instantly in love. Though he will not see her again for several years, Severo never forgets the angelic face of Eliza's daughter. The next four years in Chile are difficult ones for Severo. After the sudden death of his father, he is sent, first, to boarding school and then to military service. When the bohemian young man proves too much for his widowed mother, Severo is packed off to Paulina in San Francisco where she encourages him to learn the legal profession. He leaves little behind him in Valparaíso except his cousin and childhood love Nívea to whom he has pledged his heart. By the end of 1876, the nineteen-year-old Severo finds himself living a luxurious life on Nob Hill, installed in the best legal firm in the city and sharing a mansion with his aunt Paulina, her self-indulgent eldest son Matías, their faithful and inscrutable butler Frederick Williams, and an army of servants.

The cousins Severo and Matías strike up a tentative friendship, despite their radically different temperaments and interests. One night Severo is awakened by Williams, who discloses that Matías is in trouble. The two men find the dissipated gentleman passed out in an opium den in the center of Chinatown. The ever-discreet Williams asks Severo to help him deposit Matías safely in his private apartment, where the reckless man spends a week recovering from his opium binge. A couple years later, Matías invites Severo back to his *garçonnière*, a bachelor's room in the attic of his apartment, to meet the prettiest girl in San Francisco. Matías describes her virginity as the girl's one "detestable defect" (42) and has placed bets with his friends to see who might be the first to seduce her. The girl in question turns out to be Lynn Sommers, the long-ago beauty from Severo's visit to Eliza's tearoom. At twenty years old, Lynn has read many romance novels and awaits her handsome prince. She decides Matías is that man simply because he is the only one who does not pay attention to her. When Lynn shows up at Matías's apartment, Severo feels as offended by her stupidity as by his cousin's vulgarity. The improprieties that the tactless "artists" impose on the naïve girl bring her to tears, attracting Matías just long enough for him to seduce the girl and begin a three-month affair with her.

During this period, Severo receives word that Chile has gone to war against Bolivia and Peru. He determines to leave immediately to help defend his country. As he packs, Paulina receives a visit from Tao Chi'en and Eliza Sommers, who explain that Lynn is pregnant with Matías's child and wishes to marry. When Matías denies the tryst, Lynn goes into seclusion. Deeply ashamed of his ignoble cousin and still pining for the unfortunate beauty, Severo begins visiting the Sommers household regularly, carrying with him gifts for Lynn and the coming baby. The mildly remorseful Matías begins to suffer acute health symptoms and flees to Europe to escape Lynn, his parents, and numerous gambling debts. Severo subsequently proposes to Lynn, promising to give her baby a name and an inheritance before he heads to the war in Chile; they marry a month later. The baby, Aurora, arrives too early during a difficult birth that causes Lynn to hemorrhage and die a few hours later. A distraught Severo gives guardianship to Eliza and Tao Chi'en, and then leaves immediately for Chile. Paulina, seeing her chance to procure a daughter, offers to take Aurora in Matías's name, but Eliza stands firm against the raging woman's threats and tantrums.

Like Part I, the second part of the novel opens in the present day with Aurora musing about her past and the mysterious events apparently revealed in the few photographs that she has accumulated. She is attempting to piece together the past erased by her stubborn grandmother Paulina. Aurora has one picture of herself dressed in costume for the Chinese New Year. Likewise, she has numerous photographs of her mother posing for calendars and postcards. She has few memories of her early childhood, but the most vivid is of her gentle grandfather Tao Chi'en with an "expression of unremitting goodness in his almond-shaped eyes" (94). Aurora describes the recurring nightmare that has tormented her since she was a child. She is walking in a strange city, holding the hand of a person she cannot see, when they are surrounded by children in black pajamas dancing wildly. Someone pulls Aurora away from the hand and she awakens alone and terrified. She credits those frightful night terrors with inspiring her interest in photography; she imagined as a girl that she might capture the dancing children on film and be free of them forever. As she has grown, her quest as a photographer has developed into a desire to capture the elusive, the essence of a person or event. Aurora seeks in her art not only freedom from her demons but also the "truth and beauty" (98) that have eluded her troubled dreams.

The narrative returns to the weeks after Aurora's birth, including Severo's leaving to fight the war in Chile. Met on the dock by his fiancé, Nívea, Severo discovers that the butler Williams has told her all the details of his marriage, Lynn's death, and the arrival of the infant. Nívea reveals that she has waited all her life for Severo and hopes that in the end she will be his wife. At the battlefront, Severo encounters bloody skirmishes and is changed by the brutality around him. During the battle to take Lima, he receives a dangerous foot injury inflicted by a village girl brandishing a machete. Severo uses his bayonet to gut her "like a sheep" (109) before he realizes that his attacker is a female civilian. Without benefit of anesthesia or a sterile hospital, Severo undergoes surgery to have his leg amputated below the knee and then fights against shock and blood loss to survive. Nívea has him transferred to a private home in Valparaíso where she can nurse him back to health. There they are married in a private ceremony and sneak many wonderful nights together, against doctor's orders, before Severo's leg is healed. Nívea discovers happily that their first child is on the way.

In San Francisco a few years later, Paulina's husband Feliciano dies, leaving the woman depressed and not as rich as she had believed. As she tries to decide how to control her profligate sons and regain her position in high society, Paulina receives a visit from Eliza Sommers and five-year-old Aurora. Eliza reveals that Tao Chi'en has died and that she must leave the little girl with Paulina so that she can go to China with his body. The two grandmothers agree that Aurora will be raised completely as a del Valle, with no mention of her early years in Chinatown. Terrified to find herself alone with this strange woman in her gargantuan house, Aurora spends the first day hiding under a table and then runs away at the first opportunity. Making her way to Chinatown, Aurora is captured by a madam who plans to prepare her for a life of prostitution. When her Uncle Lucky finds her and pays for her release, he returns the girl to Paulina, and Aurora sees nothing of her maternal relatives for twenty years. Frightened by Aurora's dangerous adventure and frustrated by her own shrinking fortune, Paulina determines to uproot the household and return to Chile. A week before her departure, Williams approaches his mistress with the unusual proposal that they marry and arrive in Chile as husband and wife. Because Williams suggests the match as a business proposition, raising his status and freeing her from widowhood, Paulina finds the suggestion appealing and introduces him thereafter as British nobility.

The del Valle entourage spends a year traveling by ship to Chile, with a long visit to Europe to pick up provisions and a trek by mule train over the Andes. By the end of the voyage, Aurora has grown more accustomed to her unorthodox grandmother and has begun to forget her life in Chinatown. In Europe, Aurora meets Matías, an unmemorable gentleman whom she believes is simply one of her many uncles. By this time Matías's health has deteriorated, the result of the syphilis he hides from his family by claiming to be arthritic. Once in Chile, Aurora is introduced to a multitude of del Valle relatives, including Severo and Nívea, who welcome her warmly. A strong bond gradually grows between Aurora and Paulina as they settle into life in Santiago. After Aurora escapes from several private boarding schools, her indulgent grandmother relents and allows the girl to be tutored at home. Aurora's favorite teacher is the liberal feminist and suffragette Señorita Matilde Pineda. Señorita Pineda is instrumental in prompting Paulina to begin a ladies' club to establish financial backing for entrepreneurial women of the poorer classes. Aurora spends hours listening to her unusual teacher and her aunt Nívea in their impassioned debates to better society, as well as to their friend and bookshop owner Don Pedro Tey, who develops the women's debating skills. Paulina, now required by social protocol to attend mass and live less ostentatiously than she has been used to in California, adapts less quickly to her dramatic change in lifestyle. For Aurora, the mansion in Santiago is like a "fortress" (151) where she can feel safe for the first time since losing her grandparents, Eliza and Tao Chi'en.

Aurora enjoys a happy childhood until January 1891, when a civil war breaks out in Chile. Severo immediately heads north to fight, leaving his pregnant wife, Nívea, and their brood of children under Paulina's protection. Nívea secretly works for the opposition from Paulina's home. In a back room, Williams and Señorita Pineda set up a printing press where they publish revolutionary pamphlets to distribute house to house. Conservatives and liberals alike join in their hatred of the dictatorship, uniting the politically disparate arms of the del Valle family. One night, Señorita Pineda bursts into Paulina's mansion to announce that the bookseller Don Pedro Tey has been arrested by the president's political police. Williams and Nívea confess that they have been producing revolutionary documents under Paulina's roof. The woman grows wild with anger and fear, dismissing Señorita Pineda as Aurora's teacher and leaving Williams to settle the problem while the family waits anxiously through the night to see if they will be arrested along with Don Pedro Tey. The next morning they leave Santiago for the del Valle estate in the country, though Williams insists on staying to guard the house. Aurora enjoys her weeks in the country, renewing her friendship with her many cousins and exploring the fields around the estate. When Nívea's contractions begin, Aurora ignores her grandmother's threats and sneaks into the hall to watch Nívea give birth to twin boys, a bloody scene that haunts the young girl (169). Finally, in August Williams arrives to tell the family that Don Pedro Tey did not implicate the del Valles under torture and that it is safe to return to Santiago.

Back in Santiago, the political battle reaches a climax when one of Aurora's male cousins participates in a revolutionary meeting that is ambushed. The frenzied soldiers end up slaughtering all the young men present. The massacre inflames the revolutionary army, which marches into Valparaíso and occupies the city, defeating the president's troops. While citizens celebrate in the streets, the president seeks asylum in the Argentine embassy, eventually committing suicide and becoming, in later years, a "symbol of freedom and democracy" (178). In Paulina's household, life begins to return to normal, although Aurora experiences the first confusing signs of adolescence and Paulina begins to suffer from age and obesity. They learn that Matías is returning to Chile and go to Valparaíso to meet him. The sickly man shocks his mother by arriving accompanied by Amanda Lowell, his father's old mistress, who has been his loyal companion for fifteen years. Seeing Amanda's faithful friendship to her dying son, Paulina releases her years of rancor and the two middle-aged women make their peace. Matías is installed in the del Valle mansion to await his death. Aurora overcomes her fear of the stranger and gradually spends more time in his room, eventually learning that

Matías is her father. In those long conversations, Matías gives his daughter the gift of memory, telling her about Lynn and especially about Tao Chi'en and Eliza, shadowy figures who haunt Aurora's memory.

After her father's death, Aurora suffers her usual nightmare with even more intensity. On her thirteenth birthday, Severo gives her a camera with which to photograph her night terrors and "in the task of deciphering that nightmare" Aurora ends up "in love with the world" (192). Paulina apprentices her to a famous photographer, Don Juan Ribero, and Aurora begins to learn the artistry of capturing vivid images on film. Meanwhile, Paulina and Williams embark on a wine-making enterprise, making Severo a partner when he shows interest in the vineyards. Aurora is now sixteen, and Paulina announces that they must travel to Europe to prepare the girl's bridal trousseau. Paulina also hopes to get medical help for her rapidly deteriorating health, caused by a gastrointestinal tumor.

Part III of the novel opens in 1896, with Paulina and Aurora settled in England to seek medical care at the clinic founded by Ebanizer Hobbs, an old colleague of Tao Chi'en. Out of modesty, Paulina sends Williams ahead to France to seek wine-making advice so that he will not be present to witness her surgery. During Paulina's operation and recovery, Aurora meets another surgeon at the clinic, a brusque but approachable Chilean named Iván Radovic who speaks straightforwardly about her grandmother's condition. Against Paulina's wishes, Aurora contacts Williams, who rushes back to London to be at Paulina's side during her recovery. As soon as the woman is able, the little family heads to Paris where their friendship with Amanda Lowell opens many artists' studios to them. There they begin to prepare Aurora for marriage through ladies' classes and trousseau shopping.

One evening at a ball given by the Chilean legation, Aurora meets the dashing Diego Domínguez, a twenty-three-year-old young man from an established family. In the paragraphs that introduce her suitor, Aurora explains that she has changed the man's name to protect his family and adds that she has "forgiven him" (214). Thus, the reader understands before the romance has even begun that this relationship will have a tragic outcome for our heroine. With Paulina's approval, Diego begins to court Aurora in earnest. Only Williams objects, making the level-headed point that Aurora need not select the very first man to present himself to her. When Diego asks for Aurora's hand, Williams again expresses concern that the young man is "unfeeling" (217), but the women ignore his admonitions and set about furiously shopping and preparing for the voyage home.

On the steamship back to Chile, Aurora and Diego learn little of each other, though he reveals that her hobby of photography neither interests nor bothers him. Aurora spends time on the lower decks photographing the interesting groups of third-class passengers bound for the Americas. There she runs into Iván Radovic, a second-class passenger who has finished his term at the Hobbs clinic and is returning to a hospital in Chile. Paulina, Williams, and Aurora arrive in Chile in December 1898, finding a "country in full moral crisis" (220). In two years, Aurora has turned into a young lady, barely recognizable to her Chilean relatives. Awaiting her September wedding, Aurora writes ardent letters to Diego who responds with "calm chronicles" of farm life and promises of a future spent in the bosom of his family. When the Domínguez clan comes to Santiago to meet Aurora, they seem intimidated by the ostentatious wealth of Paulina's household. Still, Aurora believes she will be happy among these unpretentious people. The wedding is moved to mid-April after Diego's mother suffers a heart attack and wants to see her son married before something more serious happens to her. For days before the marriage, Williams secretly urges Aurora not to wed if she has doubts, but she goes ahead with the ceremony.

From her first unhappy night with Diego, Aurora finds only disappointment in her marriage. An innocent nineteen-year-old, she wishes to run back to her grandmother but determines to face her life as an adult. After their one-day honeymoon, Aurora and Diego head to his family home to begin their marriage. Life at the Domínguez estate is run on ageless principles and religious laws. The entire extended family takes daily meals together, just as they worship and work as a unit. Diego's father bans novels as potentially sinful but does allow Aurora to continue her photography. Early on, Aurora notices strange behavior on the part of Diego, who treats her formally in public but ignores her when they are alone. Her sister-in-law Susana is similarly peculiar, complaining of severe headaches that banish her to her bedroom for hours at a time. Only Diego's brother Eduardo attempts to make Aurora comfortable. In this stifling environment that threatens to engulf Aurora in loneliness, the twentieth century arrives with little fanfare.

Hearing that Paulina's health has deteriorated seriously, Aurora requests an opportunity to travel to Santiago, a request that Diego grants without delay. Accompanied by Diego's sister Adela, Aurora arrives at her grandmother's to find the elderly woman in extremely poor health and the mansion in equally shabby condition. Paulina's sole doctor is Iván Radovic, with whom Aurora renews her old friendship. Radovic shows much interest in Aurora's photographs and they spend an afternoon looking through her work. Radovic asks whether Diego and Susana are married, planting in Aurora's mind for the first time that something is amiss within the Domínguez family. Upon her return to the estate, the new home for Aurora and Diego is finally ready and Aurora is startled to discover that Diego has furnished the bedroom with two single beds. Her desolation becomes obvious to Diego's mother, who counsels Aurora to pray, both for her marriage and for a child to bolster it. Then one night Aurora follows Diego on one of his nocturnal outings and discovers him making love to Susana in the barn. Diego does not defend his illicit love, but only tells Aurora that she must stay in their marriage to protect his mother.

In her desperate grief and rage, Aurora rides her horse all day in a driving rain. Her ride brings on a near-fatal case of pneumonia that installs Aurora in a hospital for many weeks. When she returns to the Diego estate, Aurora requests a bedroom in the main house with Diego's mother to nurse her. The affectionate love from that good woman begins to heal Aurora's fury and helps her understand the "inexorable fatalism" (266) of Diego and Susana's love. For the sake of not only Diego's mother but also his brother Eduardo, Aurora determines to hold her tongue forever. She tells Diego that she will stay until his mother's death and then she must be allowed to leave unfettered. Just as Aurora reaches full health and must face returning to her little house with Diego, she receives a telegram from Iván Radovic that her grandmother is near death. With relief, Aurora says good-bye to the Domínguez clan and heads to Santiago. There she finds the mansion and its mistress equally diminished, with much of the art and fine furniture sent to the Catholic Church. Williams has been a faithful husband, however, and has taken care of the family affairs with prudence and integrity.

Stepping away from the present narrative briefly, Aurora explains that nine years have passed since that day, and that she feels both her grandmother Paulina and the Chinese grandfather she lost years before hovering near her. At the moment of Paulina's death, however, the loss of this singular parental figure threatens to overwhelm the fragile Aurora. She locks her emotions inside her "like a huge block of ice" (271) until Williams gently prods Aurora to tell him everything. Listening to the sordid tale of Diego's betrayal, Williams urges Aurora to stay with him until Diego's mother passes on. He also reveals to her his secret that he is not British nobility but in fact an escaped convict, a secret that he had previously shared only with Paulina. Making an unlikely pair, Williams and Aurora buy a home in the country outside Santiago and set up a peaceful existence of gardening, dog breeding, and photography. A year after Paulina's death, Aurora becomes reacquainted with Iván Radovic and the two begin a love affair that seems strengthened by the obstacle of Aurora's marriage and the freedom the couple has to live separate lives.

Two years pass with Aurora living under Williams's protection and pursuing her relationship with Iván. One day Eliza Sommers, Aurora's maternal grandmother, shows up at her door. Finally, Aurora receives the answers she has always sought about her first five years. Eliza tells her about Lynn's death, which left Tao Chi'en feeling guilty and devastated. To save her husband's spirit, Eliza handed him the newborn orphan, claiming that she was too tired after twenty years of parenting to raise the baby. Tao Chi'en became Aurora's sole caretaker, slinging the infant in a pouch around his neck and becoming utterly attached to his granddaughter. He determined that Lai Ming would be "the first female *zhong-yi* in history" (290) and puffed up with pride at the cleverness of the little girl. For five years, the grandfather and granddaughter were an inseparable pair in Chinatown, and Aurora spent that time feeling loved and protected by her beloved Tao Chi'en.

One day Tao Chi'en was visited by Presbyterian missionaries who wanted to help in the cause of the singsong girls, the child prostitutes that Tao had spent his life trying to free. Lucky believed that his father was making a terrible mistake by informing whites about the clandestine activities of Chinatown, and the son's predictions proved true. The missionaries began to invade brothel after brothel, causing an uproar in the San Francisco quarter. Tao Chi'en was brutalized at the hands of a powerful madam's henchmen while he was out walking with his little granddaughter. Dressed in black garb, these are the men of Aurora's lifelong nightmares, the people she watched beat her beloved grandfather. Though Tao Chi'en survived the beating, his spine was broken and he could not bear to live paralyzed. Under his instructions, Eliza prepared a concoction that would end her husband's life quickly and painlessly. Left without Tao, Eliza felt she had no real love to give her son or granddaughter. Remembering how Paulina had yearned for the girl, Eliza decided to leave Aurora with her to grow up far from the miserable memories of Chinatown. At last, the mysteries of Aurora's life have been solved.

CHARACTER DEVELOPMENT

Aurora claims to be a woman shaped by those family members who came ahead of her, and in fact that is how her *Bildungsroman* unfolds (see chapter 6 for a definition of this type of narrative). The girl herself plays almost no part in her own life story until midway through the novel when she is six years old and traveling by ship to Chile with her grandmother Paulina. Before that time, she acts more like a third-person narrator and impartial observer of her rather eccentric relatives. Aurora as a tangible character begins to come into focus as she grows to womanhood in Chile. Even in these sections, she seems often detached from her own character, as if the space of nine years between the narrated events and her present life has softened the harsh outlines of her painful memories. The grown Aurora is the product of a coddled upbringing on the one hand and the influence of modernity on the other. These two forces help explain the conflict between her self-deprecating behavior during her marriage to Diego and her independent spirit after their separation. Describing her conservative marriage to the taciturn Diego, Aurora admits that she unabashedly served him and tried to make his life easy. It is only later, when Aurora experiences a genuine relationship with Iván Radovic, that she can see how she subjugated herself to an unfeeling person in an attempt to create her "dream of a domestic paradise" (239). By the novel's close, Aurora has shaken off the fetters of social provincialism and has begun to demonstrate the attributes that characterize the independent del Valle women.

A number of these women and their partners shape Aurora's destiny. With Lynn dying in childbirth and her lover Matías fleeing to Europe, the most important people in the girl's formative years become her grandparents. The maternal grandparents, Eliza Sommers and Tao Chi'en, play a minor role in the novel, though their influence on Aurora during her earliest years is long-lasting. The couple's love story begins at the close of *Daughter of Fortune,* as Eliza decides to free herself from her obsession with her first amour. Relinquishing the dream that has driven her for four years, Eliza chooses instead the friendship that has sustained her through that search. When Eliza enters Tao Chi'en's bedroom one night to find him waiting, they begin a lifelong romance of equals. Between Eliza's tearoom and Tao Chi'en's successful medical practice, the couple can support a household and continue to fund Tao's personal mission to free as many of the Chinatown singsong girls, or adolescent sex slaves, as his savings will allow. Eliza and Tao Chi'en have two children together, and give their offspring Eliza's last name to help protect the mixed-blood children from an intolerant society. Their son, Lucky, lives a long and full life, while their beautiful daughter, Lynn, does not meet the same happy fate. Named for Tao's beloved first wife Lin, the girl is a gorgeous mixture of English, Chilean, and Chinese lineage. Her one fault is a trusting naïveté that causes her to be easily flattered by the photographers and artists who select her as their model. While Lynn is unusually beautiful, she is not otherwise unique, and her relative simple-mindedness leaves her open to mistreatment by rogues like Matías del Valle and his companions.

Matías's mother, the colorful Paulina del Valle, is Aurora's paternal grandmother and the most powerful woman in the novel. Considering the era of the story, Paulina behaves more like a man than a woman, pursuing profitable business ventures at every turn in a society that typically relegated its women to throwing tea parties and managing the household. Barely literate, Paulina manages nonetheless to make her husband Feliciano astonishingly wealthy through numerous shrewd investments, including buying land parcels in towns where the new transcontinental railroad will pass through. Paulina loves Feliciano but has barred him from her bedroom out of an unspoken shame. While he has aged gracefully, she has grown larger each year until the obese woman presents a "prodigious spectacle" (11) dressed in her silks and jewels. Despite occasionally ruthless behavior, Paulina is not an unfeeling person but a shrewd one. She is also accustomed to getting what she wants, as evidenced by her behavior at Aurora's birth. Determined to acquire the infant girl at any cost, Paulina throws a fit in Eliza's tearoom when the wealthy socialite faces off against the immovable will of the quiet woman below her station. Screaming that she will not be stopped, Paulina sweeps fine china to the floor with a flourish and threatens all that Eliza and Tao Chi'en have left before she storms out. Paulina's tantrum proves unnecessary when outside forces remove Tao Chi'en and impel Eliza to relinquish the girl five years later. While Paulina does not shower the girl with sentimental affection, she proves a faithful and rather indulgent guardian who helps shape Aurora into an independent and creative young woman.

The other significant characters in the novel seem to be divided evenly between gentlemen and cads. A principal member of the first category is Severo del Valle, the high-minded nephew who comes under Paulina's influence. He has high aspirations and a sensible mind, making use of the opportunities that his aunt Paulina provides him. His finest act, and perhaps biggest folly, is to fall irretrievably in love with Lynn Sommers, exhibiting a devotion that remains steadfast despite the girl's affair with Matías. Severo's unconsummated week of marriage to the pregnant Lynn fills him with hope; he believes that Lynn will come to love him and they will raise Aurora together. In fact, when Severo holds the infant girl for the first time, he feels like a true father and ensures that she will have a legal name and financial support. Losing his beloved Lynn fills Severo with a deep despair that he attempts to assuage by joining the war effort in Chile. Military life threatens to damage Severo irreparably, however, as he becomes a "killing machine" (108) during one of the worst and final battles of the War of the Pacific. Fortunately, the solid influence of Nívea's steadfast love renews Severo and he recovers to become a well-known lawyer, successful vintner, and patriarch of a large family.

Paulina's eldest son, Matías, is Severo's foil, as "cynical, indolent, and libertine" as his Chilean cousin is "noble, fearless, and naïve" (39–40). A spoiled and insensitive young man, Matías focuses most of his attention on outfitting his exquisite wardrobe, entertaining his shiftless friends, and pampering his body, which suffers from the syphilis that marks his lifestyle. Yet, he is also a lover of poetry and the arts, often moved to tears when reciting verses from memory and inspired to produce "Dantesque paintings" (41) in his apartment. A "mixture of bohemian and dandy" (34), Matías cares little for his own reputation and even less for that of the family. While Severo studies diligently at law, Matías throws parties in his *garçonnière* in the attic of his private apartment. As a confirmed bachelor, Matías prefers the attentions of prostitutes to any demanding relationship with a woman of his station. While he experiences some surprisingly tender feelings toward Lynn, Matías is neither ready for her love nor prepared for a child. In a cowardly move, Matías heads to Europe to avoid his responsibilities. Only at the close of his life does the imprudent man feel some remorse, and he renews a tentative relationship with Aurora for the few months before his demise.

If Severo and Matías are the two male foils during the time of Aurora's childhood, Diego Domínguez and Iván Radovic are the contrasting men who dominate her adult life. If there is a villain in the novel, it is Aurora's husband, Diego. But even Aurora herself does not characterize him so harshly. More accurately, Diego is a man of false character. Marrying Aurora for little purpose except to hide his long-time affair with his sister-in-law Susana, Diego behaves like a selfish cad. When he begs Aurora not to create a scandal, Diego points out that she has made sacred vows, turning an astonishingly blind eye to his own transgressions. Yet,

Aurora attempts to understand the deepest heart of her chilly husband. Diego has been born into a family that holds God's laws in the highest regard; the man's destiny is laid out for him in the strictest form with no room for adventure. Unlike his older brother Eduardo, Diego would like to experience the wider world beyond the quiet rhythms of the Domínguez estate. In Diego's frustrated life, Susana is his most valuable possession. Aurora accurately interprets her husband's attachment to Susana as a love that has nothing to do with herself or Eduardo, and so she keeps the ugly secret. In contrast to Diego's indifference, Iván Radovic offers Aurora an authentic affection made stronger by the many obstacles the couple must face in Chile. Iván's forthrightness, first as Paulina's doctor and then as Aurora's lover, demonstrates his strength of character. Though his role in the book is minor, Iván offers Aurora a lasting love that helps to heal the deep wounds inflicted on her by her unfortunate marriage.

Providing a quiet example of gentlemanly behavior throughout the novel is Paulina's butler and husband, Frederick Williams, a man of dubious origins but with flawless integrity. Acting as a butler in San Francisco and an English lord in Santiago, Williams is in fact a convict from an Australian penal colony. When Severo helps Williams rescue Matías, the young man feels a bond grow between himself and this odd butler. Shrewdly perceptive of Severo's deepest desires, Williams often manages affairs unasked, including informing Nívea by telegram of Severo's difficult circumstances, an act that brings the betrothed cousins back together. Later, Williams shows his deep attachment to Paulina when he offers to become her husband prior to their move to Chile. Despite a difference in ages and attractions, the pair remains inseparable to Paulina's death. At that point, Williams again proves himself to be a sensible and honorable patriarch by taking the devastated Aurora under his care, freeing her to leave her husband and live in peace. Like Tao Chi'en, who guarded the five-year-old Aurora, Williams offers Aurora a safe haven so that she can pursue her budding relationship with Iván and her love of photography, shielded from the disapproving gaze of scandalized relatives.

THEMES

As with many of Allende's family sagas, *Portrait in Sepia* focuses on the intersections of memory, identity, and love. The protagonist Aurora struggles with the familiar dichotomy that characterizes her entire self-understanding. While she remembers pieces of her past, her identity is shaped primarily by a sense of orphanage that can be erased only by recalling her memories. Recovering the past, then, becomes the primary route to knowing the self. A secondary theme calls attention to the deleterious effects of counterfeit love set against the steadfastness of genuine affection. True love, as rare as it may be even in Allende's fictional universe, plays a key role in shaping the lives of its fortunate partakers. Finally, political turmoil has its part in the novel's themes, underscoring the universal dictum that there can be no peace without war. Surviving the worst of human cruelty and bloodshed, the characters of *Portrait in Sepia* prove that enduring is its own kind of victory.

With no recollection of her mother and father, Aurora feels disconnected from the world, an orphan troubled by nightmares that haunt her unconscious. She is especially damaged by the violent loss of her adored Tao Chi'en followed by the mysterious disappearance of Eliza on the day that Paulina takes over as guardian. Marked by these unexplained ruptures in her world, Aurora turns to an art medium that offers irrefutable evidence of reality. Her love of photography reflects Aurora's desire to capture the images of her life, arrested permanently in a form that can be studied for its veracity. This fascination with the fixed image is how Aurora discovers Diego's infidelity. It is also how she comes to understand the world, developing a connection with each of her subjects and capturing images that would have no interest to others, including the poor campesinos in the countryside. In her worst loneliness, Aurora turns the camera lens on herself, taking hundreds of self-portraits in which she sees little more than a "crepuscular sadness" (256). At the novel's close, Aurora explains the explicit connection between her art and her life, her use of photography to "conquer the transitory nature of [her] existence, to trap moments before they evanesce . . . " (303). She credits her collection of a thousand photographs with giving her the material to build her story, a tale that would otherwise be fashioned from little else than unreliable memories. Out of those pictures Aurora has pieced together a history that, if it has not silenced her nightmares, has at least reconciled her to her subconscious fears.

Gender identity is as important as personal identity in Aurora's development, and she has a number of positive models to follow in this regard. As Andrew Ervin points out, Aurora is surrounded by "many bigger-than-life women who . . . instill a sense of independence in her despite the inchoate feminism of 19th-century South America" (Ervin 32). Paulina del Valle, with her modern attitudes about property ownership and business matters, prepares Aurora unawares for the financially in-dependent life she will lead as a separated woman in Chile after her grandmother's death. In matters of feminist politics and sexual freedom, Severo's wife, Nívea, proves an invaluable resource. As a young woman, Nívea determines to spend her life fighting for women's suffrage even if she has to give up marriage to do so. As it turns out, she marries the crippled Severo and has fifteen children, although she supplies a nurse-maid for each one to free her for her suffragette work and energetic nightly trysts with her husband. Nívea becomes Aurora's chief counselor later in life, sending her reading material and advising her on matters of the heart. Even Eliza Sommers, who disappears early from Aurora's life, serves as a later example of female independence. When Eliza reap-pears, Aurora learns of her maternal grandmother's travels around the globe, her predilection for exotic locales, and her courage in the face of danger. A single woman like her granddaughter, Eliza has had no qualms about facing life alone. Since losing the only man she ever truly loved, she has had no desire to find another partner but lives with the assurance that her husband's spirit accompanies her in her worldly trav-els. Though Aurora never achieves the same remarkable autonomy, she learns to travel alone and pursue photography wherever it leads her.

Portrait in Sepia highlights another familiar subject in Allende's fiction, the theme of genuine love. Aurora's disastrous marriage to Diego is the exception rather than the rule in the narrative, which foregrounds nu-merous affectionate and successful relationships. The first, of course, is the unorthodox marriage of Eliza Sommers and Tao Chi'en. They battle impossible obstacles to maintain a union that defies every social conven-tion for over thirty years. Theirs is an erotic passion augmented by a sincere admiration for each other. Like them, Nívea and Severo share a unique relationship that begins under equally difficult circumstances but lasts a lifetime. Instructed by the erotic novels she has studied in her employer's library, Nívea brings a modern sensibility about sexual issues to her marriage and to her conversations with Aurora. The public kiss that Nívea shares with Severo after he returns from his long months at war marks Aurora forever. In fact, she searches for the kind of love that might produce such a kiss, finding it at last with Iván Radovic. A more unusual pairing is that of Paulina del Valle and Frederick Williams. When the genteel butler proposes to Paulina, he assures her that he does not expect to play the husband in any "sentimental area" (135) but looks only for more social respect and the opportunity to continue serving his mistress. Williams's actions, however, belie his self-interested assertion.

Having served Paulina for half his life, Williams seems to have grown quite attached to the woman and demonstrates his devotion to her and the del Valle clan in numerous acts of generosity and goodwill. On her part, Paulina begins to dress carefully for her husband from the day they are married. On her deathbed, Paulina recognizes no one but Williams, whose presence brings peace to her face. A strange union between two unlikely characters, the marriage is nonetheless one of the strongest in the novel.

Just as Aurora's photography mentor, Don Juan Ribero, advises that there is no "happiness without pain" (195), so there is no peace for the del Valle family without war. Military conflict and its damaging results is a subject within the novel that shapes its characters in the same way that the wars shaped the Chilean nation. The conflict that drives Severo from San Francisco back to his homeland is the War of the Pacific, a battle that flared up over territory disputes between Chile and its neighbors Bolivia and Peru in 1879 and lasted until 1883. During that conflict, Severo witnesses the worst of humanity, including acts of brutality committed by his countrymen. As Severo's primitive amputation attests, conditions were terrible for the troops, who battled much more than the enemy. With poor sanitation, unclean water, and primitive living conditions, the soldiers were laid low by small pox, typhus, and malaria (104), and many died from infections acquired in field hospitals (110). Severo survives his ordeal only by believing that Nívea will still love him despite a wounded body and soul.

The resolution of the War of the Pacific lasted only a few years before civil war broke out in Chile in 1891. Prompted by President Balmaceda's threats of dictatorship, the armed forces split, with the navy siding with congress and the army remaining loyal to the president. Women abandoned Balmaceda because he lacked support from the Church, support that was withdrawn when the President authorized civil marriages and the burial of non-Catholics. The middle class, which had benefited from Balmaceda's liberal ideas, also deserted him when it became clear that he would rule with the arrogance of "any other large landowner of the day" (155). Balmaceda closed down congress in order to declare himself dictator, and then appointed a pitiless henchman, Joaquín Godoy, to torture citizens who did not fall in line. Though the del Valle family is sheltered by their social status from the worst abuses, Nívea and Williams manage to create a temporary panic with their printing press. That crisis and the murder of Aurora's college-aged cousin for conspiracy are the two episodes that touch the del Valles during that difficult eight months, reminding them of their tenuous safety in a country where violence seems inevitably to erupt at regular intervals.

ALTERNATIVE PERSPECTIVE: MULTICULTURAL CRITICISM

Multicultural criticism is a relatively recent mode of literary inquiry, dating from the late 1960s and gaining prominence in the last twenty-five years. Scholars in this area focus on the diverse perspectives that shape social reality, examining race, class, and gender as the primary categories of difference. Much like marxist and feminist criticism, multicultural analysis highlights minority voices, in particular those authors writing from the margins of dominant cultures or from colonized or developing countries. This mode of inquiry explores the ways categories such as race and ethnicity influence how literature is written and understood. One important outcome of the rise in multicultural theory has been a sense of global literature and the development of a knowledgeable readership for exceptional lesser-known writers around the world. A broader objective of multicultural scholars is to deepen understanding of the social, political, and historical issues that divide cultures.

One way that multicultural critics highlight cultural influences is by calling into question the authority of the literary "canon." The canon is the name given to a group of books considered the "greats" of traditional literature. For centuries, the majority of authors on the list were European white males, such as William Shakespeare, Leo Tolstoy, and James Joyce. In the second half of the twentieth century, the canon became a disputed idea, especially among feminist scholars who wanted books by women writers to be valued and studied with the same attention as the "classics." Following the lead of their feminist counterparts, multicultural critics also began to question the validity of the canon, given the proclivity of its proponents to disregard the burgeoning literary offerings from non-European countries. Critic Laurie Grobman describes how this early alignment between feminist and multicultural scholars created joint concerns with "the oppressive and exclusionary nature of the Western and American critical and literary canon, the reevaluation and reinterpretation of such texts to reveal gender and/or racist biases and stereotypes, and the recovery of long-excluded voices and texts" (Grobman 229). Grobman suggests, however, that these important concerns should not cause readers to dismiss "traditional ways of reading, understanding, and evaluating multiethnic texts because these writers must negotiate within the numerous cultures intersecting the dominant one" (233). Ideally, a multicultural critic will balance the traditional perspectives and literary strategies that might help elucidate a non-canonical text— strategies including character and thematic analysis as well as the close reading and explication of key passages—without allowing these practices to eclipse other crucial perspectives unique to the cultural and historical realities that shaped the work.

Isabel Allende's *Portrait in Sepia* lends itself to a multicultural critique primarily in its attention to inequalities between sexes, races, and classes, as presented within the ethnically diverse societies of both California and Chile. In highlighting the social inequities that plagued the nineteenth century, and continued into the twentieth, the narrative offers the reader a uniquely varied multicultural perspective from within the lives of characters who reconcile their complicated mixed identities and learn to negotiate rigid social codes. In San Francisco, Paulina del Valle eats pastries at Eliza Sommers's tearoom nearly every day, and yet the women never meet outside that venue since they "belonged to separate worlds" (66). The former inhabits the upper echelons of San Francisco's high society, while the latter must work daily to earn her living. In addition, Eliza has broken a powerful social prohibition by living with a "Celestial," the racial slur given to the Chinese in California. When Eliza and Tao Chi'en appear in public, they stand apart, sit separately in theaters, and avoid drawing attention to themselves. Eliza and Tao Chi'en Anglicize the name of their daughter Lynn to make her life easier in the United States, where, as the narrator comments, the Chinese are "treated like dogs" (42). Aurora's one-quarter Chinese blood is, likewise, cause for concern despite the cultural diversity of San Francisco. Called by her Chinese name, Lai Ming, and dressed like a little Asian princess, Aurora is still sent to a school outside Chinatown in the "world of whites, where undoubtedly she would have more opportunities than among Chinese" (291). Her Hispanic features are welcomed as they hide her Asian background and aid her transition into Chilean society.

While the hierarchy of race clearly placed Hispanic cultures above Asian ones in the nineteenth-century West, white settlers were still the dominating influence, as Paulina del Valle painfully discovers when even her tremendous financial success cannot remove the stigma of her heavy Spanish accent. That obstacle, coupled with her diminishing fortune, prompts Paulina to move back to her homeland and raise Aurora as a "Chilean señorita" (133). In Chilean society, the del Valle name is prized for its Spanish origins and the family for their white skin and enormous wealth. The insurmountable class divisions practiced in Chile make Aurora uncomfortable even after her experiences in Chinatown. She feels self-conscious accompanying her grandmother on their charity missions as they drive into impoverished neighborhoods to offer handouts to the resentful poor. Surrounded by modern women who encourage Aurora's independence, the girl notices how these same women depart from those beliefs when issues of race or class emerge. While Paulina displays a liberal attitude in allowing female artists to participate in her salon, she does not extend the same tolerance to those outside her station or ethnicity.

At various points in the novel, Allende includes an understated critique of the Chilean attitude toward native Indians. As in many South American countries, Chilean society divides along questions of origin. The uppermost class, in particular the rich landowners like the del Valles, count the Spanish *conquistadores* (conquerors who came from Europe to claim South American land) as their ancestors. They point to their white skin as proof of their European roots. In truth, nearly all Chileans have *mestiza* or mixed blood, with ancestors from native Indians as well as conquering Spaniards. However, the people labeled *mestizas* are those with darker skin and Indian features. Also called *campesinos,* they work the farms for wealthy landowners called *patrones,* and make up the massive peasant class of Chile. The people with the least power within the society are the vestiges of Indian tribes left over from the conquest. A variety of episodes in the novel communicate the racism they suffer. For example, the del Valle uncles terrorize Aurora and her cousins with stories of how "Indians stole newborn babies to turn them into *imbunches*" (165), evil creatures with grotesque bodies and supernatural powers. Later, Aurora worries that the *meica,* the Mapuche Indian woman sent to help Nívea give birth in the country, will steal the infant to make an *imbunche* out of it (167). While she is living on the Domínguez estate, Aurora witnesses a strange scene with a group of Pehuenche Indians who arrive for the Christmas festivities. The quiet men arrive with an offering of unwashed apples and a rabbit that has begun to spoil. Diego's father warns the others to keep a close eye on these Indians because they will steal at any opportunity. Though Aurora has traveled hundreds of miles from her home in Chinatown, attitudes toward those from minority cultures have changed very little, as Allende's pointed references emphasize.

Since its inception, multicultural criticism has maintained the important goal of bringing writers outside the canon into the mainstream, thereby introducing readers to cultures and people different from their own. With *Portrait in Sepia* and her earlier novels available in translation to readers the world over, Isabel Allende has succeeded in bridging the enormous gulf that separated Western readers for many decades from the rich literature of Hispanic writers. Bringing South American history alive, and with it the concerns of subjugated groups, including women and minorities, Allende has made an invaluable contribution to the efforts of multicultural criticism and to contemporary literature as a whole.

Bibliography

WORKS BY ISABEL ALLENDE

Books by Isabel Allende

Novels

The House of the Spirits. Trans. Magda Bogin. New York: Alfred A. Knopf, 1985.
Of Love and Shadows. Trans. Margaret Sayers Peden. New York: Alfred A. Knopf,
   1987.
Eva Luna. Trans. Margaret Sayers Peden. New York: Alfred A. Knopf, 1988.
The Infinite Plan. Trans. Margaret Sayers Peden. New York: HarperCollins,
   1993.
Daughter of Fortune. Trans. Margaret Sayers Peden. New York: HarperCollins,
   1999.
Portrait in Sepia. Trans. Margaret Sayers Peden. New York: HarperCollins, 2001.

Short Story Collection

The Stories of Eva Luna. Trans. Margaret Sayers Peden. New York: Atheneum,
   1991.

Memoir

Paula. Trans. Margaret Sayers Peden. New York: HarperCollins, 1995.

Nonfiction

Aphrodite: A Memoir of the Senses. Trans. Margaret Sayers Peden. New York: HarperCollins, 1998.

Young Adult Fiction

City of the Beasts. Trans. Margaret Sayers Peden. New York: HarperCollins, 2002.

Children's Book

La Gorda de Porcelana. Madrid: Alfaguara, 1983.

Other Works By Isabel Allende

Contributed Short Stories

"An Act of Vengeance." In *Short Stories by Latin American Women: The Magic and the Real.* Ed. Celia Correas de Zapata, 11–17. Houston, TX: Arte Publico Press, 1990.

"Tosca." *Latin American Literary Review* 19.37 (January–June 1991): 34–42.

"Toad's Mouth." Trans. Margaret Sayers Peden. In *A Hammock Beneath the Mangoes: Stories from Latin America.* Ed. Thomas Colchie, 83–88. New York: Plume, 1992.

Sound Recording

Giving Birth, Finding Form: Three Writers Explore Their Lives, Their Loves, Their Art. Performed by Alice Walker, Isabel Allende, Jean Shinoda Bolen. Boulder, CO: Sounds True, 1993.

Theater Plays

"El Embajador" (1971).
"La Balada del Medio Pelo" (1973).
"Los Siete Espejos" (1974).

Articles and Reviews by the Author

"The Amazon Queen." *Las Mujeres.* Web site. <www.lasmujeres.com/isabelallende/amazon.shtml.>

"Breath of Hope: On the Writings of Eduardo Galeano." *Monthly Review* 48.11 (April 1997): 1–6.

"Foreword." In *Conversations with Isabel Allende.* Ed. John Rodden, ix–xi. Trans. Virginia Invernizzi. Austin, TX: University of Texas Press, 1999.

"Foreword." In *Tapestries of Hope, Threads of Love: The Arpillera Movement in Chile* by Marjorie Agosín. xi–xiii. Trans. Celeste Kostopulos-Cooperman. Albuquerque, NM: University of New Mexico Press, 1996.

"Gourmet Love: Aphrodisiacs are the Bridge Between Gluttony and Lust." *Utne Reader* 88 (July/August 1998): 80–84.

"A Mule on a Piano, Cezanne Hung Upside Down, the Lost Generation Wobbles." With David Rockefeller and Fanny Brennan. *Newsweek International,* 19 July 1999, 57.

"My House is Full of People." *American Libraries* 27.4 (April 1996): 42–43.

"Pinochet Without Hatred." *New York Times Magazine,* 17 January 1999, 24.

"Pinochet's Ghost." *New Perspectives Quarterly* 16.3 (Spring 1999): 22.

"Questions and Answers." *Isabel Allende.* Web site. <www.isabelallende.com/curiousframe.htm.>

"The Short Story: A Writer's Comments on Her Work and Techniques." (Special Issue on the Multicultural Short Story in the Americas and the Third World.) *Journal of Modern Literature* 20.1 (Summer 1996): 21–28.

"Writing as an Act of Hope." In *Paths of Resistance: The Art and Craft of the Political Novel.* Ed. William Zinsser, 41–63. Boston: Houghton Mifflin, 1989.

WORKS ABOUT ISABEL ALLENDE

General Information and Personal Interviews

Agosín, Marjorie. "Entrevista a Isabel Allende/Interview with Isabel Allende." Trans. Cola Franzen. *Imagine: International Chicano Poetry Journal* 1.2 (Winter 1984): 42–56. Reprinted as "Pirate, Conjurer, Feminist" in *Conversations with Isabel Allende.* Ed. John Rodden, 35–42. Trans. Virginia Invernizzi and John Rodden. Austin: University of Texas Press, 1999.

Boland, Roy C. "A Special Number in Honour of Sally Harvey: Rebelling in the Garden: Critical Perspectives on Isabel Allende, Cristina Peri Rossi, Luisa Valenzuela." *Antipodas: Journal of Hispanic Studies of the University of Auckland & La Trobe University* 6/7 (1994–1995): 229–237.

Brosnahan, John. "Transforming Stories, Writing Reality." *Booklist* 87.20 (June 1991): 1930–1931. Reprinted in *Conversation with Isabel Allende.* Ed. John Rodden, 159–165. Trans. Virginia Ivernizzi and John Rodden. Austin: University of Texas Press, 1999.

Butler, Katy. "The Sixth Sense: Isabel Allende on California's Mythic Past." *Los Angeles Times,* 10 October 1999, 1.

Cruz, Jacqueline, Jacqueline Mitchell, Silvia Pellarolo, and Javier Rangel. "A Sniper Between Cultures." *Mester* 20.2 (1991): 127–143. Reprinted in *Conversations with Isabel Allende.* Ed. John Rodden, 203–222. Trans. Virginia Invernizzi and John Rodden. Austin: University of Texas Press, 1999.

Crystall, Elyse, Jill Kuhnheim, and Mary Layoun. "An Interview with Isabel Allende." *Contemporary Literature* 33.4 (Winter 1992): 585–600.

Dölz-Blackburn, Inés, George McMurray, Paul Rea, and Alfonso Rodríguez. "Of Love and Truth." *Confluencia: Revista Hispánica de Cultura y Literatura* 6.1 (Fall 1990): 93–103. Reprinted in *Conversations with Isabel Allende*. Ed. John Rodden, 141–158. Trans. Virginia Invernizzi and John Rodden. Austin: University of Texas Press, 1999.

Foster, Douglas. "Isabel Allende Unveiled." *Mother Jones* 13.10 (December 1988): 42–46.

Gautier, Marie-Lise Gazarian. "'If I Didn't Write, I Would Die.'" *Interviews with Latin American Writers*, 5–24. Elmwood Park, IL: Dalkey Archive Press, 1989. Reprinted in *Conversations with Isabel Allende*. Ed. John Rodden, 125–140. Trans. Virginia Invernizzi and John Rodden. Austin: University of Texas Press, 1999.

Iftekharuddin, Farhat. "An Interview with Isabel Allende." In *Speaking of the Short Story: Interviews with Contemporary Writers*. Eds. Farhat Iftekharuddin, Mary Rohrberger, and Maurice Lee, 4–14. Jackson, MS: University Press of Mississippi, 1997.

Invernizzi, Virginia and Melissa Pope. "An Interview with Isabel Allende." *Letras Femeninas* 15.1–2 (Spring–Fall 1989): 119.

Levine, Linda and Jo Anne Engelbert. "'The World is Full of Stories.'" *Review: Latin American Literature and Arts* 34 (January–June 1985): 18–20. Reprinted in *Conversations with Isabel Allende*. Ed. John Rodden, 43–47. Trans. Virginia Invernizzi and John Rodden. Austin: University of Texas Press, 1999.

Manguel, Alberto. "A Sacred Journey Inward." *Queen's Quarterly* 99.3 (Fall 1992): 621–626. Reprinted in *Conversations with Isabel Allende*. Ed. John Rodden, 269–275. Trans. Virginia Invernizzi and John Rodden. Austin: University of Texas Press, 1999.

Montenegro, David. Interview with Isabel Allende. *Points of Departure: International Writers on Writing and Politics*. Ann Arbor, MI: University of Michigan Press, 1991.

Moody, Michael. "On Shadows and Love." *Discurso Literario: Revista de Temas Hispánicos* (Paraguay) 4.1 (Autumn 1986): 127–143. Reprinted in *Conversations with Isabel Allende*. Ed. John Rodden, 49–62. Trans. Virginia Invernizzi. Austin: University of Texas Press, 1999.

Mujica, Barbara. "The Life Force of Language." *Americas* (English Edition) 47.6 (November/December 1995): 36–43.

Munro-Clar, Margaret. "An Interview with Isabel Allende: Love, Life and Art in a Time of Turmoil." *Antipodas: Journal of Hispanic Studies of the University of Auckland & La Trobe University* 6/7 (1994–1995): 15–27.

"Photographic Memory—An Interview with Isabel Allende." *Fireandwater.com.* HarperCollins, 2001. Web site. <http://www.fireandwater.com/authors/interview.asp?interviewid=386.>

Piña, Juan Andrés. "The 'Uncontrollable' Rebel." *Conversaciones con la narrative chilena.* Santiago, Chile: Editorial Los Andes, 1991. Reprinted in *Conversations with Isabel Allende.* Ed. John Rodden, 167–200. Trans. Virginia Invernizzi and John Rodden. Austin: University of Texas Press, 1999.

Pinto, Magdalena García. "Chile's Troubadour." *Women Writers of Latin America: Intimate Histories.* Trans. Trudy Balch and Magdalena García Pinto, 21–42. Austin: University of Texas Press, 1991. Reprinted in *Conversations with Isabel Allende.* Ed. John Rodden, 71–94. Trans. Virginia Invernizzi. Austin: University of Texas Press, 1999.

"Questions and Answers." *Isabel Allende.* 2002. Web site. <www.isabelallende.com.>

Richards, Linda. "January Interview: Isabel Allende." *January Magazine* (November 1999). Web site. <http://www.januarymagazine.com/profiles/allende.html.>

Rodden, John, ed. *Conversations with Isabel Allende.* Trans. Virginia Invernizzi and John Rodden. Austin: University of Texas Press, 1999.

Ross, Jean W. "Speaking Up." *Contemporary Authors,* vol. 130. Farmington Hills, MI: Gale Research, 1990. Reprinted in *Conversations with Isabel Allende.* Ed. John Rodden, 95–102. Trans. Virginia Invernizzi and John Rodden. Austin: University of Texas Press, 1999.

Sanoff, Alvin. "Modern Politics, Modern Fables." *U.S. News and World Report,* 21 November 1988, 67.

Snell, Marilyn Berlin. "The Shaman and the Infidel." *New Perspectives Quarterly* 8 (Winter 1991): 54–58. Reprinted in *Conversations with Isabel Allende.* Ed. John Rodden, 237–246. Trans. Virginia Invernizzi and John Rodden. Austin: University of Texas Press, 1999.

Zapata, Celia Correas de. *Isabel Allende: Life and Spirits.* Trans. Margaret Sayers Peden. Houston, TX: Arte Publico Press, 2002.

Literary Criticism

Carullo, Sylvia G. "Fetishism, Love-Magic and Erotic Love in Two Stories by Isabel Allende." Trans. James A. Dunlop. *Readerly/Writerly Texts: Essays on Literature, Literary/Textual Criticism, & Pedagogy* 3.1 (Fall–Winter 1995): 193–200.

Foreman, P. Gabrielle. "Past-on Stories: History and the Magically Real, Morrison and Allende On Call." *Feminist Studies* 18.2 (Summer 1992): 369–389.

Frenk, Susan. "The Wandering Text: Situating the Narratives of Isabel Allende." *Latin American Women's Writing: Feminist Readings in Theory and Crisis.* Eds. Anny Brooksbank Jones and Catherine Davies, 66–84. New York: Oxford University Press, 1996.

Friedman, Mary Lusky. "Isabel Allende and the More than Reliable Narrator." *Explicacíon de Textos Literarios* 24.1/2 (1995–1996): 57–63.

Hart, Patricia. *Narrative Magic in the Fiction of Isabel Allende.* Rutherford, NJ: Fairleigh Dickinson University Press, 1989.

Laurila, Marketta. "Isabel Allende and the Discourse of Exile." In *International Women's Writing: New Landscapes of Identity.* Eds. Anne E. Brown and Marjanne E. Gooze, 177–186. Westport, CT: Greenwood Press, 1995.

Rojas, Sonia Riquelme and Edna Aguirre Rehbein, eds. *Critical Approaches to Isabel Allende's Novels.* New York: Peter Lang, 1991.

Roof, Maria. "W.E.B. DuBois, Isabel Allende, and the Empowerment of Third World Women." *CLA Journal* 39.4 (June 1996): 401–416.

Shea, Maureen E. "Love, Eroticism, and Pornography in the Works of Isabel Allende." *Women's Studies* 18.2/3 (September 1990): 223–232.

Zamora, Lois Parkinson and Wendy B. Faris, eds. *Magic Realism: Theory, History, Community.* Durham, NC: Duke University Press, 1995.

REVIEWS AND ARTICLES ON INDIVIDUAL NOVELS

The House of the Spirits

Antoni, Robert. "Paradox or Piracy: The Relationship of *The House of the Spirits* to *One Hundred Years of Solitude.*" *Latin American Literary Review* 16.32 (July–December 1988): 16–28.

Carvalho, Susan de. "*Escrituras y Escritoras:* The Artist-Protagonist of Isabel Allende." *Discurso: Revista de Estudios Iberoamericanos* 10.1 (1992): 59–67.

Cohn, Deborah. "To See or Not to See: Invisibility, Clairvoyance, and Re-visions of History in *Invisible Man* and *La casa de los espíritus.*" *Comparative Literature Studies* 33.4 (Fall 1996): 372–395.

Coleman, Alexander. "Reconciliation among the Ruins." *New York Times Book Review,* 12 May 1985, 1, 22–23.

Earle, Peter G. "Literature as Survival: Allende's *The House of the Spirits.*" *Contemporary Literature* 28.4 (1987): 543–554.

Fernández, Enrique. "Send in the Clone." *Village Voice,* 4 June 1985, 51.

Jenkins, Ruth Y. "Authorizing Female Voice and Experience: Ghosts and Spirits in Kingston's *The Woman Warrior* and Allende's *The House of the Spirits.*" *MELUS* 19.3 (Fall 1994): 61–74.

Levine, Linda Gould. "A Passage to Androgyny: Isabel Allende's *La casa de los espíritus.*" In *In the Feminine Mode: Essays on Hispanic Women Writers.* Eds. Noel Valis and Carol Maier, 164–173. Cranbury, NJ: Associated University Presses, 1990.

Meyer, Doris. "'Parenting the Text': Female Creativity and Dialogic Relationships in Isabel Allende's *La casa de los espíritus.*" *Hispania* 73 (May 1990): 360–365.

Roof, Maria. "Maryse Conde and Isabel Allende: Family Saga Novels." *World Literature Today* 70.2 (Spring 1996): 283–289.

Shapiro, Harriet. "Isabel Allende, Salvador's Niece, Builds a *House of the Spirits* from the Ashes of Exile." *People Weekly,* vol. 23, 10 June 1985, 145+.

Zamora, Lois Parkinson. "The Magical Tables of Isabel Allende and Remedios Varo." *Comparative Literature* 44.2 (Spring 1992): 113–143.

Of Love and Shadows

Bell-Villada, Gene H. "Eros Makes War." *New York Times Book Review,* 12 July 1987, 23.

Gordon, Ambrose. "Isabel Allende on Love and Shadows." *Contemporary Literature* 28.4 (Winter 1987): 530–542.

Kakutani, Michiko. "Of Love and Shadows." *New York Times,* 20 May 1987, C27.

Lefevere, Patricia. "Telling Tales of Love and Shadows." *National Catholic Reporter* 24.34 (1 July 1988): 9.

Meyer, Doris. "Exile and the Female Condition in Isabel Allende's *De amor y de sombra.*" *International Fiction Review* 15.2 (Summer 1988): 151–157.

Moody, Michael. "Isabel Allende and the Testimonial Novel." *Confluencia-Revista Hispanica de Cultura y Literatura* 2.1 (Fall 1986): 39–43.

Updike, John. "Resisting the Big Guys." *New Yorker,* 24 August 1987, 83–86.

Eva Luna

Craig, Herbert E. "The Search for an Equal Mate in Two Novels about Venezuela: *Ifigenia* (1924) by Teresa de la Parra and *Eva Luna* (1987) by Isabel Allende." *Platte Valley Review* 20.1 (Winter 1992): 66–74.

Diamond-Nigh, Lynne. "*Eva Luna:* Writing as History." *Studies in Twentieth Century Literature* 19.11 (Winter 1995): 29–42.

Krich, John. "Rich Little Poor Girl." *New York Times Book Review,* 23 October 1988, 13.

Williams, Claudette. "Isabel Allende's *Eva Luna:* In Search of an Affirmative Feminist Discourse." *Revista Interamericana de Bibliografía* 48.2 (1998): 437–441.

The Stories of Eva Luna

Amago, Samuel. "Isabel Allende and the Postmodern Literary Tradition: A Reconsideration of *Cuentos de Eva Luna.*" *Latin American Literary Review* 28.56 (July–December 2000): 43–61.

Hart, Patricia. "Review of *The Stories of Eva Luna.*" *Nation* 252.9 (11 March 1991): 314–316.

———. "Magic Feminism in Isabel Allende's *The Stories of Eva Luna.*" In *Multicultural Literatures through Feminist/Poststructuralist Lenses.* Ed. Barbara Frey Waxman, 103–136. Knoxville, TN: The University of Tennessee Press, 1993.

Kingsolver, Barbara. "Fish Fall from the Sky for a Reason." *New York Times Book Review,* 20 January 1991, 13.

Urquhart, Jane. "Tales from Isabel Allende's Passionate, Magical World." *Quill and Quire* 56.11 (November 1990): 25.

The Infinite Plan

Bly, Robert. "Westward to the New Age Covered Wagon." *New York Times Book Review,* 16 May 1993, 13.

Rubin, Merle. "Unusual Characters Pursue Their Dreams." *Christian Science Monitor,* 10 June 1993, 14.

Simon, Linda. "The Odyssey of an Evangelist's Son." *The Wall Street Journal,* 24 May 1993, A8.

Daughter of Fortune

Bradberry, Grace. "A Woman of Spirit." *The London Times,* 8 January 2000, 16.

Donaldson, Peter. "Novel of the Week." *New Statesman* 128.4466 (December 1999): 57

Lopez, Ruth. "Left on a Genteel Doorstep: Isabel Allende's Novel Follows Its Foundling Heroine from an English Colony in Chile to the California Gold Rush." *New York Times Book Review,* 24 October 1999, 17.

Novella, Cecilia. "*Daughter of Fortune* (Review)." *Americas* (English Edition) 51.5 (September 1999): 61.

Rodden, John. "Isabel Allende, Fortune's Daughter." *Hopscotch: A Cultural Review* 2.4 (2001): 32–39.

Portrait in Sepia

Ervin, Andrew. "A Woman's Reconstruction." *New York Times Book Review,* 4 November 2001, Sec. 7, 32.

Graham, Philip. "Portrait in Sepia (A Less Magical Realism)." *New Leader* 84.6 (November–December 2001): 38–39.

Stavans, Ilan. "Portrait in Sepia: Review." *Times Literary Supplement,* 5 October 2001, 26.

Wood, Michael. "Girls with Green Hair." *New York Review of Books* 49.4 (March 14, 2002): 40–42.

OTHER SECONDARY SOURCES

Critical Theory

Anaya, Rudolfo. "'I'm the King': The Macho Image." In *Muy Macho: Latino Men Confront Their Manhood.* Ed. Ray González, 57–74. New York: Anchor, 1996.

Anzaldúa, Gloria. *Borderlands/La Frontera.* San Francisco: Aunt Lute Press, 1987.

Ashcroft, Bill, Gareth Griffiths, and Helen Tiffin. *The Empire Writes Back: Theory and Practice in Post-Colonial Literature.* New York: Routledge, 1989.

Bhabha, Homi K. "Representation and the Colonial Text: A Critical Exploration of Some Forms of Mimeticism." In *The Theory of Reading.* Ed. Frank Gloversmith, 92–122. Brighton, Sussex, United Kingdom: Harvester Press, 1984.

———. *The Location of Culture.* London: Routledge, 1994.

De Salvo, Louise. *Writing as a Way of Healing: How Telling Our Stories Transforms Our Lives.* San Francisco: HarperSanFrancisco, 1999.

Eagleton, Terry. *Literary Theory: An Introduction.* Minneapolis: Minnesota Press, 1983.

Gilbert, Sandra M. "What Do Feminist Critics Want? A Postcard from the Volcano." In *The New Feminist Criticism: Essays on Women, Literature, and Theory.* Ed. Elaine Showalter, 29–45. New York: Pantheon Books, 1985.

Grobman, Laurie. "Toward a Multicultural Pedagogy: Literary and Nonliterary Traditions." *MELUS* (Spring 2001): 221–240.

Jameson, Fredric. *The Political Unconscious: Narrative as a Socially Symbolic Act.* Ithaca, NY: Cornell University Press, 1981.

Kaplan, Amy and Donald E. Pease, eds. *Cultures of United States Imperialism.* Durham, NC: Duke University Press, 1993.

Montenegro, David. *Points of Departure: International Writers on Writing and Politics.* Ann Arbor: University of Michigan Press, 1991.

Morrison, Toni. *Playing in the Dark: Whiteness and the Literary Imagination.* New York: Vintage, 1992.

Nunn, Frederick M. *Collisions with History: Latin American Fiction and Social Science from El Boom to the New World Order.* Athens, OH: Ohio University Press, 2001.

Roh, Franz. "Magical Realism: Post-Expressionism." 1925. Reprinted in *Magical Realism: Theory, History, Community.* Eds. Lois Parkinson Zamora and Wendy B. Faris.

Said, Edward. *Orientalism.* New York: Pantheon, 1978.

———. *Culture and Imperialism.* London: Chatto and Windus, 1993.

Shaw, Donald L. *The Post-Boom in Spanish-American Fiction.* SUNY Series in Latin American and Iberian Thought and Culture. Ithaca, NY: SUNY Press, 1998.

Spivak, Gayatri. *In Other Worlds.* New York: Methuen, 1987.

———. "Can the Subaltern Speak?" In *Marxism and the Interpretation of Culture.* Eds. Cary Nelson and Larry Grossberg, 271–313. Chicago: University of Illinois Press, 1988.

Swanson, Philip. *The New Novel in Latin America: Politics and Popular Cultures After the Boom.* New York: St. Martin's Press, 1995.

Historical Reference

Boorstein, Edward. *An Inside View . . . Allende's Chile.* 1977. New York: International Publishers, 1987.

Collier, Simon and William F. Sater. *A History of Chile, 1808–1994.* Cambridge: Cambridge University Press, 1996.

Spooner, Mary Helen. *Soldiers in a Narrow Land: The Pinochet Regime in Chile.* Berkeley: University of California Press, 1994.

Other Writers

Selected Latin American Boom Writers

Borges, Jorge Luis. *Collected Fictions.* 1951. New York: Viking, 1998.

Carpentier, Alejo. *The Lost Steps.* 1953. New York: Alfred A. Knopf, 1956.

Cortázar, Julio. *Hopscotch.* New York: Pantheon Books, 1966.

Donoso, José. *The Obscene Bird of Night.* 1970. New York: Alfred A. Knopf, 1973.

Fuentes, Carlos. *Where the Air is Clear.* 1958. New York: Farrar, Straus, & Giroux, 1960.

———. *The Death of Artemio Cruz.* 1962. London: Collins, 1964.

García Márquez, Gabriel. *One Hundred Years of Solitude.* 1967. New York: Harper & Row, 1970.

Llosa, Mario Vargas. *The Time of the Hero.* 1963. New York: Grove Press, 1966.

Selected Contemporary Writers

Alvarez, Julia. *How the García Girls Lost Their Accents.* Chapel Hill, NC: Algonquin Books, 1991.

Benítez, Sandra. *A Place Where the Sea Remembers.* Minneapolis: Coffee House Press, 1993.

Castillo, Ana. *So Far from God.* New York: W.W. Norton, 1993.

Cisneros, Sandra. *House on Mango Street.* Houston, TX: Arte Publico Press, 1984.

Escandón, María Amparo. *Esperanza's Box of Saints.* New York: Scribner, 1999.

Esquivel, Laura. *Like Water for Chocolate.* New York: Doubleday, 1992.

Hijuelos, Oscar. *The Mambo Kings Play Songs of Love.* New York: Farrar, Straus, & Giroux, 1989.

Valenzuela, Luisa. *The Lizard's Tail.* New York: Farrar, Straus, & Giroux, 1983.

Veciana-Suarez, Ana. *The Chin Kiss King.* New York: Farrar, Straus, & Giroux, 1997.

Index

Allende, Isabel: awards, 8; background in her work, 9–12; childhood and adolescence, 1–3, 24; children of, 4; early success, 5; education, 3; exile as literary motivation, 12; feminism in her work, 9, 11, 13–14, 20–24, 26–27, 44–47; grandfather's role in first novel, 5, 30; historical elements in her writing, 19–20, 24–27; influences of Latin American and other authors, 14–15, 24; journalistic style in her writing, 4, 10–11, 19, 93–94; life in California, 6–7; life in Venezuela, 4–6, 20; magical realism in her writing, 14–18; marriage to Miguel Frías, 3–6; marriage to William Gordon, 6; memory as an element in her writing, 24–27; Paula's illness, 6–7; political influences in her writing, 18–19, 40–41; theater and screen adaptations of her work, 7; writer's block, 7–8, 115, 139; writing habits, 4–7, 11, 50, 93–94

Allende, Salvador, 2; overthrow of, 4, 44, 64
Allende, Tomás, 1–2
Anaya, Rudolfo, 21
Andieta, Joaquín (*Daughter of Fortune*), 118, 122, 123, 127; as gold seeker, 119, 122; love affair with Eliza Sommers, 118–119, 132. *See also* Murieta, Joaquín
Aphrodite: A Memoir of the Senses, 7–8, 11, 115
Ashcroft, Bill, 133

Bhabha, Homi K., 133
Balcells, Carmen, 5, 7
Barros, Francisca (Panchita) Llona, 1–3, 5, 8, 11
Beltrán, Beatriz (*Of Love and Shadows*), 51, 53, 55, 57; as representative of bourgeoisie, 68; as social climber, 61, 63
Beltrán, Irene (*Of Love and Shadows*), 18, 50–59, 62–63, 64, 87; awakening,

19; characterization of, 58–59; flight into exile, 58; as Francisco's love interest, 62–63; as journalist, 50; murder attempt on, 56; taping of Sergeant Rivera, 54, 56

Benedict, King (*The Infinite Plan*), 94–95, 101, 102; characterization of, 107

Berkeley, California, in *The Infinite Plan*, 94, 96, 99

Bildungsroman, in *The Infinite Plan*, 108–109; in *Portrait in Sepia*, 150

Bonecrusher, Joe (*Eva Luna*), 24, 123–125

Boom, the (Latin American literary renaissance), 14–15, 20, 35

Borges, Jorge Luis, 14, 17, 18

Carlé, Lukas (*Eva Luna*), 23, 86, 91; murder of, 74

Carlé, Rolfe (*Eva Luna*), 19, 81–82, 88, 89; characterization, 86–87; as documentary filmmaker, 79; Eva Luna's story for, 82–83; interview of Comandante Rogelio, 81; life in La Colonia, 75, 78; relationship with Eva Luna, 83, 84–85

Carpentier, Alejo, 14

Chi'en, Tao (*Daughter of Fortune, Portrait in Sepia*), 19, 23, 142, 143; Americanization of, 130; in California, 122–123, 125–127; characterization of, 129–130; crusade against prostitution, 125–126, 130, 132, 149; death of, 149; marriage to Lin, 121; as physician's apprentice, 120; relationship with Eliza Sommers, 137, 139, 141, 150–151, 155, 158; smuggles Eliza onto ship, 119–120; visited by Lin's ghost, 19, 121, 126, 132; as *zhong yi*, 120, 125

Chile: background of, 43–44; class divisions in, 158–159; in *Daughter of Fortune*, 115–117, 129, 131, 134; in

Portrait in Sepia, 139, 142, 143, 144–145; war in, 156–157

City of Beasts, 9

Cortázar, Julio, 14

Daughter of Fortune, 8–9, 10, 11, 19, 23, 24–26, 115–137, 139, 150; characters in, 127–130; Oprah's Book Club selection, 8, 116; plot of, 116–127; postcolonial criticism in, 132–137; setting of, 115–116; themes in, 130–132

del Valle, Aurora (*Portrait in Sepia*), 26, 140–149, 152, 158; birth of, 142; characterization of, 150; early childhood, 142–143; importance of memory, 153–154; life with Paulina, 143–147; marriage to Diego Domínguez, 147–148, 150; as narrator, 140, 150; as photographer, 140, 143, 146, 147, 153, 154; recurring nightmare, 143, 146, 149; relationship with Iván Radovic, 149, 150

del Valle, Matías (*Portrait in Sepia*), 141–142, 144, 153; characterization of, 152; death of, 145–146

del Valle, Paulina (*Daughter of Fortune, Portrait in Sepia*), 117, 140–141, 146, 153, 158–159; as Aurora's guardian, 143; characterization of, 151; as entrepreneur, 131, 154–155; escape with Feliciano Rodríguez de Santa Cruz, 117–118; established in San Francisco, 125, 131; illness and death, 147–148; marriage to Frederick Williams, 144, 155–156

del Valle, Severo (*Portrait in Sepia*), 141, 144, 153; adolescence of, 141; characterization of, 151–152; love for Lynn Sommers, 141–142, 152; injured in Chilean war, 143

desaparecidos, 56, 61, 65–66

About the Author

KAREN CASTELLUCCI COX is a professor in the English Department at City College of San Francisco, where she teaches courses in composition and literature. She has published in *College English* and in *Healing Cultures*.

Critical Companions to Popular Contemporary Writers
Second Series

Julia Alvarez *by Silvio Sirias*
Rudolfo A. Anaya *by Margarite Fernandez Olmos*
Maya Angelou *by Mary Jane Lupton*
Ray Bradbury *by Robin Anne Reid*
Louise Erdrich *by Lorena L. Stookey*
Ernest J. Gaines *by Karen Carmean*
Gabriel García Márquez *by Rubén Pelayo*
John Irving *by Josie P. Campbell*
Garrison Keillor *by Marcia Songer*
Jamaica Kincaid *by Lizabeth Paravisini-Gebert*
Revisiting Stephen King *by Sharon A. Russell*
Barbara Kingsolver *by Mary Jean DeMarr*
Maxine Hong Kingston *by E. D. Huntley*
Terry McMillan *by Paulette Richards*
Larry McMurtry *by John M. Reilly*
Toni Morrison *by Missy Dehn Kubitschek*
Gloria Naylor *by Charles E. Wilson, Jr.*
Chaim Potok *by Sanford Sternlicht*
Amy Tan *by E. D. Huntley*
Anne Tyler *by Paul Bail*
Leon Uris *by Kathleen Shine Cain*
Kurt Vonnegut *by Thomas F. Marvin*
Tom Wolfe *by Brian Abel Ragen*

Critical Companions to Popular Contemporary Writers
First Series—*also available on CD-ROM*

V. C. Andrews
  by E. D. Huntley

Tom Clancy
  by Helen S. Garson

Mary Higgins Clark
  by Linda C. Pelzer

Arthur C. Clarke
  by Robin Anne Reid

James Clavell
  by Gina Macdonald

Pat Conroy
  by Landon C. Burns

Robin Cook
  by Lorena Laura Stookey

Michael Crichton
  by Elizabeth A. Trembley

Howard Fast
  by Andrew Macdonald

Ken Follett
  by Richard C. Turner

John Grisham
  by Mary Beth Pringle

James Herriot
  by Michael J. Rossi

Tony Hillerman
  by John M. Reilly

John Jakes
  by Mary Ellen Jones

Stephen King
  by Sharon A. Russell

Dean Koontz
  by Joan G. Kotker

Robert Ludlum
  by Gina Macdonald

Anne McCaffrey
  by Robin Roberts

Colleen McCullough
  by Mary Jean DeMarr

James A. Michener
  by Marilyn S. Severson

Anne Rice
  by Jennifer Smith

Tom Robbins
  by Catherine E. Hoyser
  and Lorena Laura Stookey

John Saul
  by Paul Bail

Erich Segal
  by Linda C. Pelzer

Gore Vidal
  by Susan Baker and
  Curtis S. Gibson